From Constantine the Great to Kandinsky

Studies in Byzantine and post-Byzantine art and architecture

Elisabeth Piltz

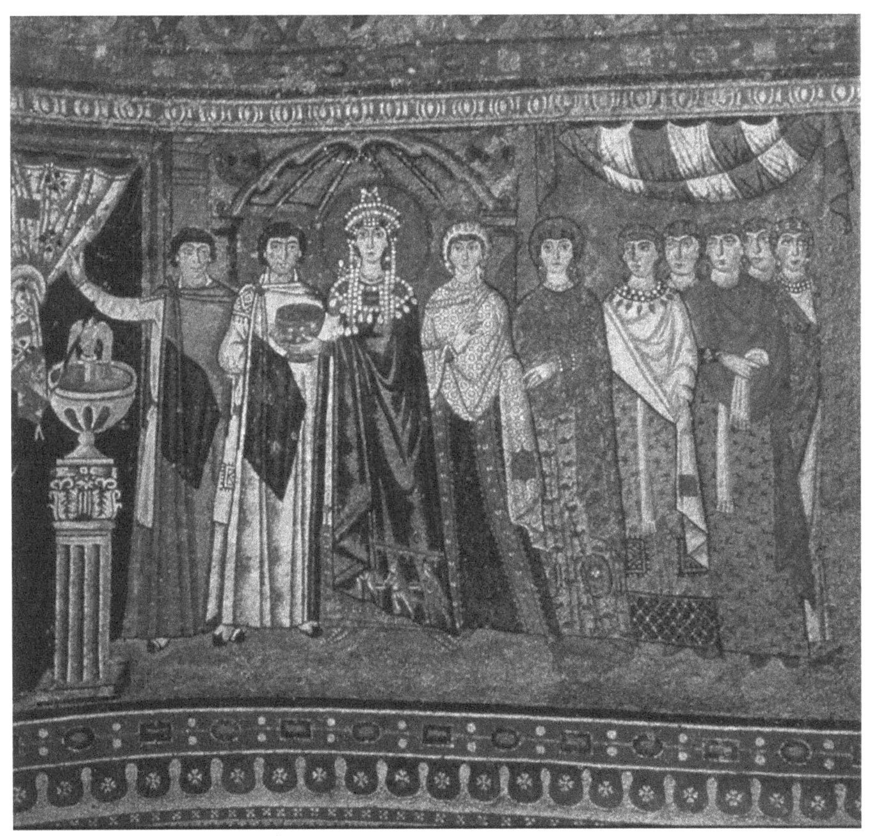

BAR International Series 1669
2007

Published in 2016 by
BAR Publishing, Oxford

BAR International Series 1669

From Constantine the Great to Kandinsky

ISBN 978 1 4073 0104 4

BAR Publishing is the trading name of British Archaeological Reports (Oxford) Ltd. British Archaeological Reports was first incorporated in 1974 to publish the BAR Series, International and British. In 1992 Hadrian Books Ltd became part of the BAR group. This volume was originally published by Archaeopress in conjunction with British Archaeological Reports (Oxford) Ltd / Hadrian Books Ltd, the Series principal publisher, in 2007. This present volume is published by BAR Publishing, 2016.

Printed in England

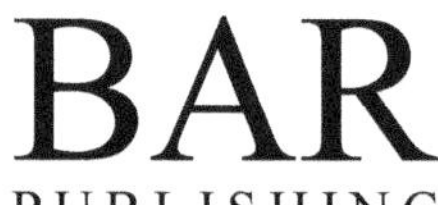

BAR titles are available from:

BAR Publishing
122 Banbury Rd, Oxford, OX2 7BP, UK
EMAIL info@barpublishing.com
PHONE +44 (0)1865 310431
FAX +44 (0)1865 316916
www.barpublishing.com

CONTENTS

List of illustrations iii

Chapter 1 The *raison d'être* of research on Byzantium 1
The abstract image in Late Antiquity and Byzantium – the New Rome – the renaissances

Chapter 2 Byzantine architecture I 4
A synthesis of Late Antique and Oriental influences – the transformation of the Christian basilica – House churches and Martyria – Imperial basilicas – Constantinople, the Queen of Cities – the Sacred palace

Chapter 3 Byzantine architecture II 16
The Exarchate of Ravenna – development in Sicily, Bulgaria, Serbia, Cappadocia, Armenia and Georgia

Chapter 4 Byzantine sculpture 28
Statues reliefs ivory plates steatites

Chapter 5 Mosaics and mural painting 35
Pearl hosiery and artistic handicraft

Chapter 6 Manuscript illuminations 49
From rotulus to codex – magnificent manuscripts as gifts and liturgical mass production

Chapter 7 Painting in the Balkans and in Scandinavia 55

Chapter 8 Rus′ 60
Kiev a new Constantinople – Moscow the Third Rome – the New Jerusalem

Chapter 9 Iconology – the world as icon 63
The Iconoclasm and the attitude of the Popes

Chapter 10 Byzantium and the Periphery 67
Post-Byzantine art – Greece, Bulgaria, Serbia, Romania, Russia – the manuals of painting – Abstract art and the 20th century

Bibliography 75

List of Illustrations

1. Constantine the Great (324-337), Palazzo dei Conservatori, Rome
2. The arch of Constantine *ca* 330 Rome
3. Christ in the Deesis in Hagia Sophia, mosaic, 12th or 13th century
4. Gold medallion of Justinian I (527-565)
5. The Ecumenical Patriarch Athenagoras I (1948-1972)
6. Maxentius basilica, Rome, 4th century
7. The Holy Sepulchre on Golgotha, Jerusalem, 335
8. Apostoleion, the Holy Apostles in Constantinople, built in the 4th century, Ms Grec 1208, fol 3 v, first half of the 12th century, Homilies to the Virgin by the monk Jacob of Kokkinobaphos, Bibliothèque nationale, Paris
9. San Pietro, Rome, 4th century
10. Kalat Siman, 470
11. SS Sergius and Bacchus, Constantinople, 537
12. a, b Hagia Sophia, Constantinople, 537
13. Hagia Eirene, Constantinople, 6th century
14. St Demetrius, Thessaloniki, 7th century
15. Nea Moni, Chios, 1042
16. Hosios Loukas, Stiris, Phokis, 1040
17. Myrelaion, Budrum Camii, Constantinople, 930
18. Kariye Camii, Constantinople, 12th century
19. Holy Apostles, Thessaloniki, 1312-1315
20. Tekfur Serai, Constantinople, late 13th century
21. The Lavra, Mount Athos, 960
22. The Great Palace, Constantinople
23. The Barletta Colossus, the cathedral of Barletta, *ca* 450
24. Justinian I's statue drawn by Mordmann, The Seraglio, Istanbul
25. The Baptistery of the Orthodox, Ravenna, *ca* 450
26. The mausoleum of Galla Placidia, Ravenna *ca* 425
27. Christ as the Good Shepherd, mosaic, the mausoleum of Galla Placidia
28. San Vitale, Ravenna, 547
29. Justinian I with suite, mosaic, San Vitale, 548
30. Theodora with suite, mosaic, San Vitale, 548
31. San Apollinarie in Classe, The Transfiguration of Christ, 549, mosaic, Ravenna
32. San Apollinare Nuovo, martyrs, from 554, mosaic, Ravenna
33. Roger II (1101-1154) crowned by Christ, La Martorana, Palermo
34. Christ Pantocrator, Endre church, Gotland, *ca* 1250
35. Christ Pantocrator, Monreale, Palermo, mosaic, *ca* 1150
36. The icon of Saint Theodore, 9th century, Sofia
37. The Ossuary of Batchkovo, fresco in the apse, Theotokos with archangels, 11th century
38. Tsar Ivan Alexander (1331-1371), Ossuary of Batchkovo, second floor
39. Sebastocrator Kalojan and Desislava, Boiana, outside Sofia, 1259
40. Gracanica, Serbia, 1310
41. Toqali Kilisse, Göreme, Cappadocia, middle of the 10th century
42. Zwarthsnotz, Armenia, 641-661
43. Achtamar, Armenia, 915-921
44. Djivari, Georgia, 7th century
45. The Khakuli triptych, Tiflis, enamel, 10th-11th century Michael VII Doukas (1071-1078) and Mary of Alany
46. MS Coislin 79, fol 2 v, Nicephoros III Botaneiates (1078-1081) and Mary of Alany, Bibliothèque nationale, Paris
47. The Tetrarchs, San Marco, Venice, porphyry, beginning of the 4th century
48. The coachman Porphyrios from the Hippodrome in Constantinople, The archaeological museum. Istanbul, 6th century
49. Bronze horses, San Marco, Venice, 4th century BC

50. Junius Bassus sarcophagus, marble, 359, The Vatican, Rome
51. The Lipsanothek in Brescia, ivory, 360-370, Museo Civico, Brescia
52. Maximianus (545-553) throne, Ravenna, ivory, The Archiepiscopal museum, Ravenna
53. Theodosius missorium, silver plate, 388, Real Academia, Madrid
54. The Riha plate in silver, found in Syria, The Communion of the apostles, end of 6th century, Dumbarton Oaks collection, Washington DC
55. Pala d'oro, enamel and gold, Treasury of San Marco, Venice, 11th to 13th century
56. Empress Ariadne, Museo Bargello, Florence, ivory, *ca* 500
57. The Barberini diptych, ivory, Louvre, Paris, *ca* 530
58. Constantine VII Porphyrogennetos (913-959) crowned by Christ, ivory, State Historical Museum, Moscow
59. Romanos IV (1069-1071) and Eudokia, ivory, Cabinet des médailles, Bibliothèque nationale, Paris
60. Otto II (955-983) and Theophano, ivory, Musée Cluny, Paris
61. The Veroli Cascet, ivory 10th-11th century, Victoria and Albert museum, London
62. Stavrosis, The Crucifixion, steatite, Källunge, Gotland, 12th century
63. Santa Pudenziana, mosaic, Rome, beginning of 5th century
64. Santa Maria Maggiore, mosaic, 432-440, Abraham and Lot, Rome
65. The rotunda of Saint George, mosaic, second half of the 5th century, Thessaloniki
66. Saint Demetrius, mosaic, Thessaloniki, *ca* 635
67. Aquileia, mosaic, the cathedral of Aquileia, 5th century
68. The Great palace mosaic, Constantinople, 6th century
69. The Virgin in the apse mosaic in Hagia Sophia, Constantinople, 867
70. Justinian I and Constantine the Great in the entrance vestibule in Hagia Sophia, Constantinople, mosaic, 10th century
71. Constantine IX Monomachos and Zoe, mosaic, Hagia Sophia, Constantinople, *ca* 1030
72. John II Comnenos (1118-1143) and Irene, mosaic, Hagia Sophia, Constantinople *ca* 1120
73. Fethiye Camii, mosaic, Christ Pantocrator, 11th century
74. Hosios Loukas, mosaic, 11th century
75. Daphni, Christ Pantocrator, mosaic, end of the 11th century
76. Nea Moni, Chios, mosaic, 1042-1055
77. Torcello, mosaic, 11th century
78. Hagios Nicolaos tis Stegis, Cyprus, beginning of 11th century, the Forty Martyrs
79. Peribleptos, Mistra, fresco painting, The Birth of Christ, middle of 14th century
80. Kariye Camii, The Anastasis, fresco painting, Constantinople, 14th century
81. The icon of the Virgin and Child, Saint Catherine monastery, Mount Sinai, 6th century
82. The icon of Saint Peter, Saint Catherine monastery, Mount Sinai, 6th century
83. The Virgin of Santa Maria in Trastevere, Rome, 7th century, icon
84. "La dalmatique de Charlemagne", saccos, Sancta Sanctorum, The Vatican, Rome, end of 14th century, the Chosen in paradise
85. Metropolitan Photios Big sakkos, Orushejnaja palata, the Kremlin, Moscow, 1415, front
86. The tapestry of Bamberg, cathedral treasury, Bamberg, *ca* 1064
87. The Joshua roll, Biblioteca Vaticana, Rome, Vat Pal Gr 431, Joshua and the angel, first half of the 10th century, illumination
88. The Menologion of Basil II (976-1025), Biblioteca Vaticana, Rome, Vat Gr 1613, The translation of the relics of Saint John Chrysostome to the church of the Holy Apostles in Constantinople, illumination
89. The Codex Rossanensis, cathedral of Rossano, illumination, 6th century, Christ's entrance into Jerusalem
90. Juliana Anicia, frontispiece of the Dioscurides manuscript, Nationalbibliothek, Vienna, Med Gr 1, fol 6 v, 512, illumination
91. Par Gr 139, David in the desert, illumination, Manuscript department, Bibliothèque nationale, Paris, early 10th century
92. The Sinope fragment, Codex Sinopensis, Ms suppl. grec 1286, fol. 29, 6th century, illumination, Bibliothèque nationale, Paris
93. The Rabbula evangeliary, 586, Biblioteca Laurentiana, Florence, illumination, Pentecost
94. Basil II (976-1025) in Marc Gr 17, San Marco library, Venice, illumination
95. Ms Gr 9, the evangelist Luke, illumination, Uppsala university library Carolina rediviva, 1300
96. Kral Milutin and kralaina Simonis, Studenica, fresco painting, Serbia, 1314
97. The angel announcing Christ's resurrection, Mileseva, fresco painting, Serbia, *ca* 1228
98. Thomas and Christ, Sopocani, 1265, fresco painting, Serbia
99. Gracanica, kral Milutin crowned by Christ through an angel, fresco painting, 1318-1321
100. Saint Boris, Garda church, fresco painting, Gotland, third quarter of the 12th century

101. Last Judgment fragment, Källunge, fresco painting, Gotland, third quarter of the 12th century
102. An angel of the Last Judgment fragments, Sundre, Gotland, painting on wood, first half of the 12th century
103. Icon of the Pantocrator, Nationalmuseum, Stockholm, 14th century
104. Saint Sophia, Novgorod, 1034
105. Saint Sophia, Kiev, *ca* 1050
106. Saint Dmitrij Vladimir, 12th century
107. Vassilij Blachennij, The Moscow Kremlin, 1555-1560
108. Bogomater Vladimirskaja, icon, Tretjakov gallery, Moscow, 11th century
109. The Trinity by Andrej Rublev, Tretjakov gallery, Moscow, 1425
110. Voronetz, Romania, 1488-1547
111. The Uspenskij cathedral, The Kremlin, Moscow, 1475-1479
112. The fishnet in the scene Christ walking on the sea of Tiberias, Garda church, fresco painting, Gotland, third quarter of the 12th century

(Thanks to Mr Olle Lavemark and Mr Owe Wennman, Carolina rediviva)

CHAPTER 1

THE *RAISON D'ÊTRE* OF RESEARCH ON BYZANTIUM

The abstract image in Late Antiquity and Byzantium – the New Rome – the Renaissances

When can we speak about research, in the proper sense of the word, concerning Byzantium, the Eastern Roman Empire, whose existence depended on the decision of Constantine the Great to move the centre of the Roman Empire away from its ancient central point in Italy – *translatio imperii* – to the seat of Byzantion, an ancient Greek colony founded by emigrants from Megara about 650 BC? What really provoked this decision, which was carried through with much zeal and consequence, and which contributed to the preservation of the Byzantine culture for more than a thousand years, is not known. The new city, named Constantine's city, *Konstantinoupolis*, and New Rome, was adorned with lots of ancient statues that had been brought from Rome and important provincial towns. It was situated close to the Hellespont, the passage to Asia, at a strategic strait not far from Nicomedia, the residence of the East Roman Emperor. The senators were moved there and the state apparatus was established as in Imperial Rome, but developed in the direction of a strictly hierarchic and bureaucratic society with a strong administrative and military division in dioceses and with a well-developed system of taxes, that later on was replaced by the military division into themata. Perhaps Constantine the Great had great intuition and envisioned what was going to happen with the Western Roman Empire. Already by the end of the 3rd century the essential part of the Empire had been transferred to the east, when the frontiers at the Euphrates and the Donau were attacked by Persians, Goths and Bactrians and in the west the Germans advanced over the *limes* and Rhine. In any case the Roman and the Greek traditions that here were cultivated side by side became fused with Oriental impulses from Persia, Syria, Armenia, Egypt, Palestine and Anatolia.

The Empire lasted until 1453, but had been reduced to a minor state during the period 1204-1261, the so-called Latin interregnum, when Frankish emperors had taken possession of Constantinople. During this time in particular the capital was sacked of its treasures and many of these valuable goods were shipped to Venice and Genoa.

When the Empire had finally fallen to the Turks it did not last long, until scholars in the west started to deal with the Greek collections of manuscripts, coins and artefacts. The first attempt at Byzantine research was carried out in Venice in the 16th century. In the 17th century the first text editions started to be printed in France called *Byzantines du Louvre.* At the same time the erudite Charles du Fresne sire du Cange published his two *Glossaria* of medieval Latin and medieval Greek and thereby the fundament was laid for research that today is carried out in all parts of the world.

What is then the *raison d'être* of the research on Byzantium? The past lived on in Byzantium, and Western Europe came into direct contact with this Empire during the Crusades, while the Scandinavian and English Varangians were involved in commerce with Byzantium and served as bodyguards and mercenaries in the Imperial army. The Byzantine Empire is a Christian version of antiquity and its culture spread over vast peripheral areas, to Syria, Egypt, the Balkans, Italy, Sicily, Russia, Georgia and Armenia. If we limit ourselves to art history, the Byzantine legacy lies hidden in Romanesque and Gothic art and influenced Scandinavian baptismal fonts and glass windows, particularly on Gotland. There are different varieties of Byzantine crosses on the Runic stones and early tombs in Scandinavia and it is now acceptable to speak of a Byzantine mission in Scandinavia during the first half of the 11th century. It is not an exotic and foreign culture, but as a matter of fact a part of our own European past.

Byzantium can be approached in many different ways, for instance by reading the Old Norse Sagas and their descriptions of Miklagardr, the imposing great city of Constantinople, called by the patriarch Photios the Queen of Cities. One can take into account the travel narratives written by pilgrims on their way to the Holy Land, so-called *itineraria*, including that of Saint Bridget, who in the seventh chapter of her *Revelaciones coelestes*, Divine revelations, warns the Greeks in Cyprus about the consequences of not subordinating themselves to the Pope of Rome and the Latin rites, and predicts the fall of Byzantium. This happened during a pilgrimage to the Holy Land in 1372 via Cyprus, the year before her death.

Another way is to confront oneself with the visual record, the artefacts in all their various forms. If we turn to Late Antique portraits, mummy portraits, and not least the picture of Constantine the Great (Fig. 1) with the pneumatic form of expression, or to the arch of Constantine (Fig. 2) in Rome that forms a line of demarcation between antiquity and Byzantine art, we notice that something has happened that was not possible since archaic times in the arts of antiquity – the image has become abstract, and this is even stranger considering that there were many well-

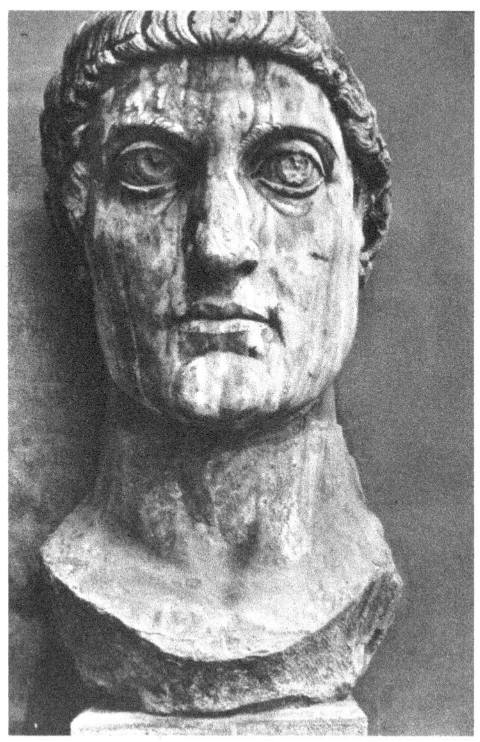

FIGURE 1. CONSTANTINE THE GREAT (324-337), PALAZZO DEI CONSERVATORI, ROME

trained artists very familiar with three dimensional art. In fact it is a visual revolution that is difficult to explain, but the Norwegian archaeologist and art historian Henrik L'Orange has made this the object of his brilliant studies in ancient and Late Antique art and he believed that the answer is to be found in the transformation of societal development to a stricter hierarchical and well-organized system with strong military aspects.

How the arts depend on the social structure is a big mystery and the explanation may partly lie in the ascetic ideals that were spread from the Neoplatonic philosophers to Christianity. But it would be a mistake to call Byzantine art ascetic. On the contrary it is a splendid feast for the eye. It uses specific formulas and schemes that are abstract, but the colours are very substantial and receive special brilliance from the rich amount of gold. Oriental luxury is combined with and reduces the ascetic tendency. Another trait is the strongly emphasized geometrical character of both form and space. The endlessness that already is expressed in the elevated and hieratic supermundane character of the imperial image is expressed with the help of circles and arc forms in exquisite combinations and proportions, both in the interior of Hagia Sophia and in the figure of Christ between the Virgin and John the Baptist (Fig. 3) on the wall of the southern vestibule in the same cathedral. The degree of abstraction varies and leads unfailingly to an overwhelming conscience of the antique legacy that characterizes the Byzantine Renaissance.

If the Justinian era was called a golden age by André Grabar (Fig. 4) – the Empire reached at this time approximately the same size as the earlier Roman Empire at its largest extent and fairly dominated the Mediterranean area – the first real renaissance in the arts originated at the court of the Macedonians about 867, where there was a new concentration of strength after a period of decline in the 8th century. It expressed itself in the arts in conscious pastiches of Late Hellenistic painting. How it expressed itself in the literature is explained by Paul Speck, who has written about and stated this concept with most emphasis in the literature (*Scandinavie et Byzance*, Acta universitatis Upsaliensis, series Figura, nova series 19, 1981, p. 237-242, and in *XIX International Congress of Byzantine*

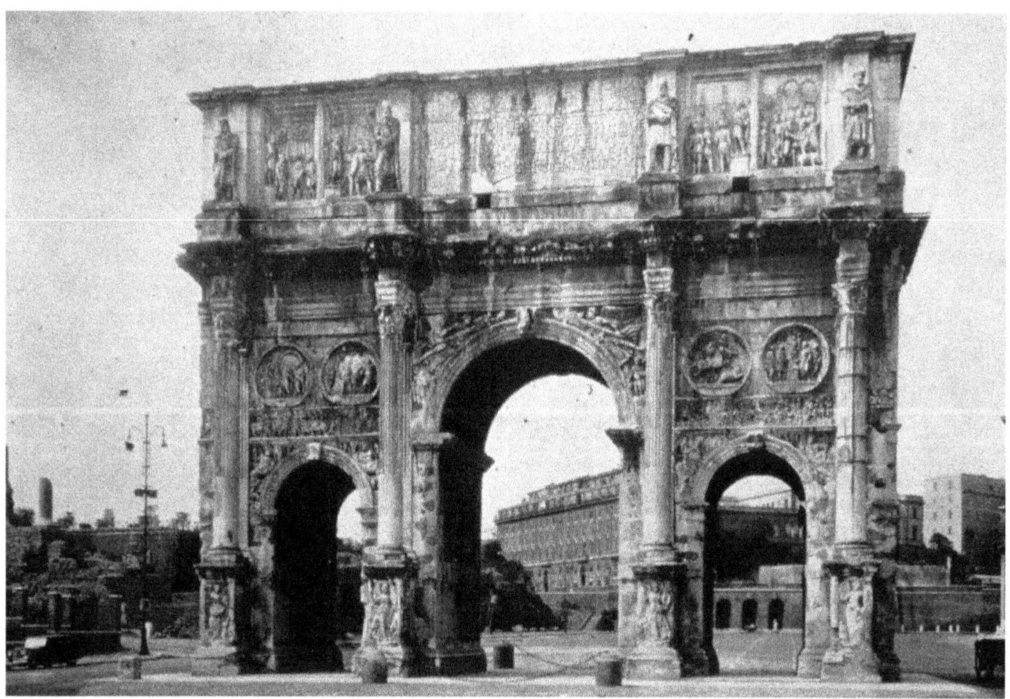

FIGURE 2. THE ARCH OF CONSTANTINE, *CA* 330, ROME

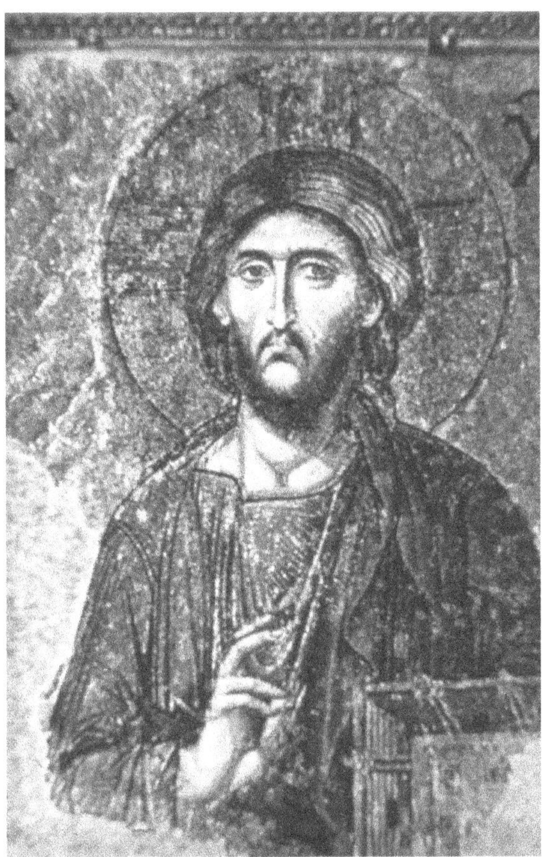

FIGURE 3. CHRIST IN THE DEESIS IN HAGIA SOPHIA, MOSAIC, 12TH OR 13TH CENTURY

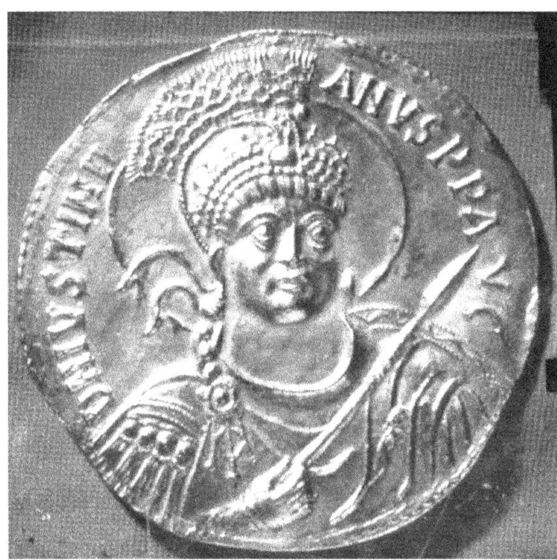

FIGURE 4. GOLD MEDALLION OF JUSTINIAN I (527-565)

studies, Copenhagen 1996, Major papers, pp. 17-25). This Macedonian renaissance is also considered to include the time of the Comnenes and that seems quite in order when reading the historians Psellos and Anna Comnena, but in the arts it is above all during the Paleologian era, when the Empire is threatened on all sides by the Seldjucs and Ottomans that an admirable final floruit takes place after the re-establishment of the Empire in the middle of the 13th century. At this time there is a contemporary development, noticable particularly in the Balkans, toward greater plasticity in the forms, in particular in the frescoes in Saint Clemens in Ochrid, in Sopocani and on certain icons of the 14th century. This is the legacy that Giotto builds on when he creates the preparatory studies of central perspective.

The new capital still plays a crucial part in the life of the Greek Orthodox church and its head, the Ecumenical patriarch, bears the title Archbishop of Constantinople and New Rome. A collection of letters from the Ecumenical Patriarch Athenagoras I (Fig. 5) to the author are documented in the manuscript department of the university library in Lund.

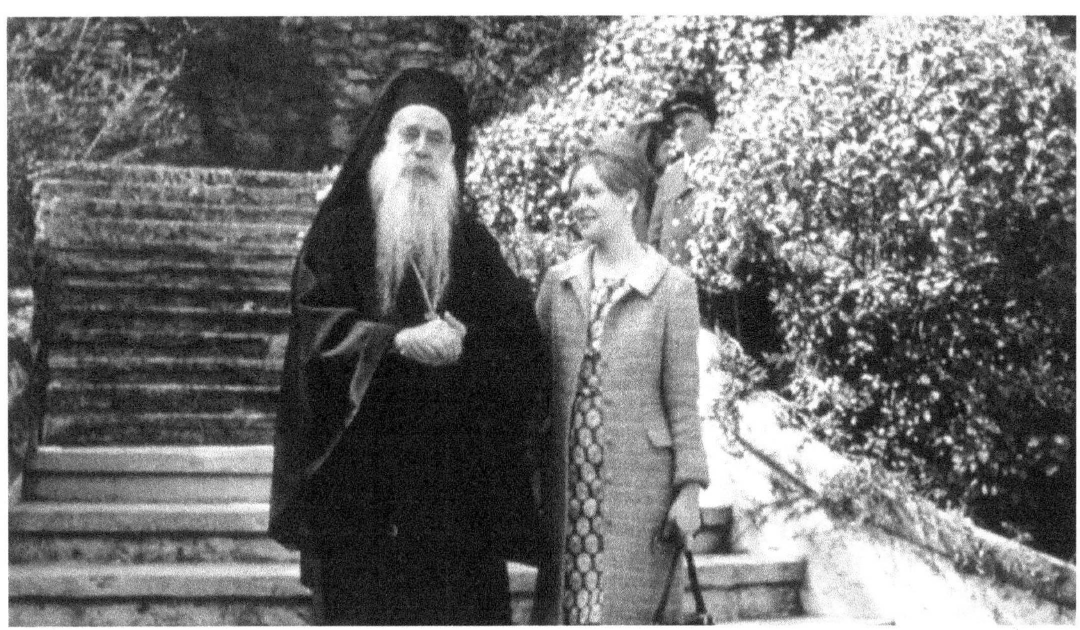

FIGURE 5. THE ECUMENICAL PATRIARCH ATHENAGORAS I (1948-1972)

Chapter 2

Byzantine architecture I

A synthesis of Late Antique and Oriental influences – the transformation of the Christian basilica – House churches and Martyria – Imperial basilicas – Constantinople, the Queen of cities – the Sacred palace

The Christian faith developed in conflict with the official imperial cult, ending in blood and martyrdom, in the Roman Empire. The official cult included gods who guaranteed the existence of the Empire, Jupiter, Sol invictus or the divine majesty of the emperor (*dominus et deus*). The places for the cult of Mithras, Kybele and Isis were small. Saint Paul spread the gospel to Jews and pagans in the Hellenistic cities of Greece. The Christian congregation gathered on Sundays on the topmost floor of private dwellings with an open view, in the *amageion* or the *hyperoon*, where the Eucharist was celebrated and sermons were held. In the evening a meal was given with blessed bread, the *agape* meal.

At the middle of the 3rd century the Christian church had already developed a stronghold in the Roman Empire and some prominent Church Fathers educated in the art of the ancient rhetoric made themselves known. Persecutions arose however during the reigns of the Emperors Nero in the sixties AD, Hadrian in Smyrna in 117, Marcus Aurelius in Lyon in 177, the Thracian Emperor Maximinus in 250, Gallienus in Rome, Carthage and Alexandria in 257-260, and Decius in Rome in 302-303.

House churches and Martyria

The Christian congregations were at that time led by an ecclesiastical hierarchy that made use of gardens and congregational places, house churches called *domus ecclesiae* or *oikos ekklesias*. These were often confiscated, but were completely returned to the Christian owners by Constantine the Great's edict of tolerance issued in Milan in 313. Only when religious liberty was established could specific basilicas be built for the celebration of the Christian liturgy. Masses had been celebrated at the graves of the martyrs above ground and in the catacombs. Now the martyrion was included in the eastern part of the basilica and according to the demands of the liturgy the church was provided with several naves. The bishop was throned in the apse as the Roman magistrate had earlier been. In Dura Europos in Mesopotamia a building for a Christian congregation has been found with a differentiated room formation beside the synagogue that is dated to 257 AD.

Imperial basilicas

San Clemente in Rome was transformed in about 380 to a cult room from having been a profane commercial hall. Santa Pudenziana is a building that earlier was an antique Roman bath. The empty martyr shrine of Saint Peter is preserved from the early 2nd century, another early covered basilica with three naves and clerestory is Maxentius' basilica (Fig. 6) from the 4th century, which served as a model for future development.

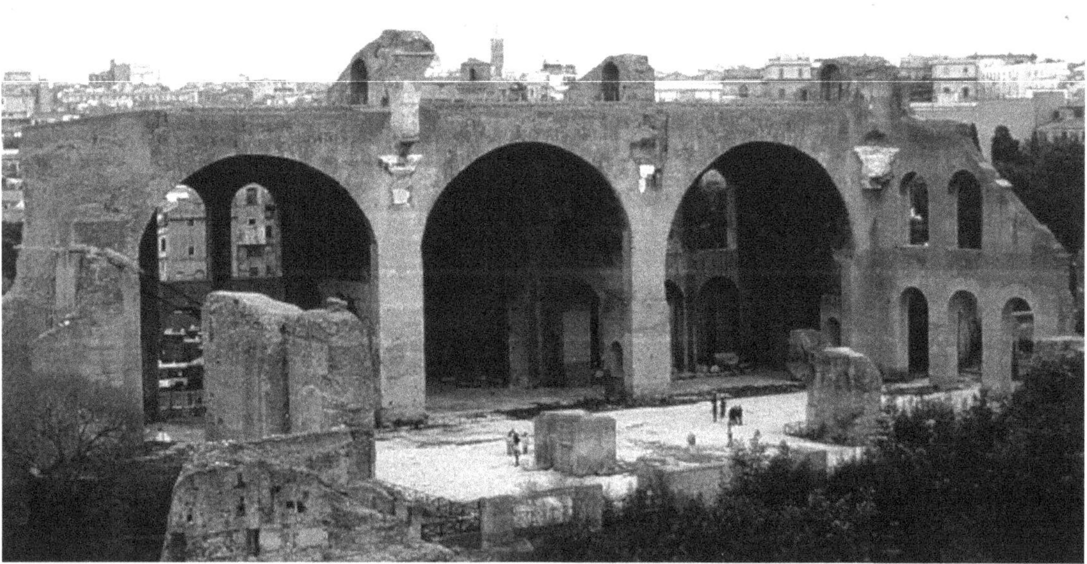

Figure 6. Maxentius' basilica, Rome, 4th century

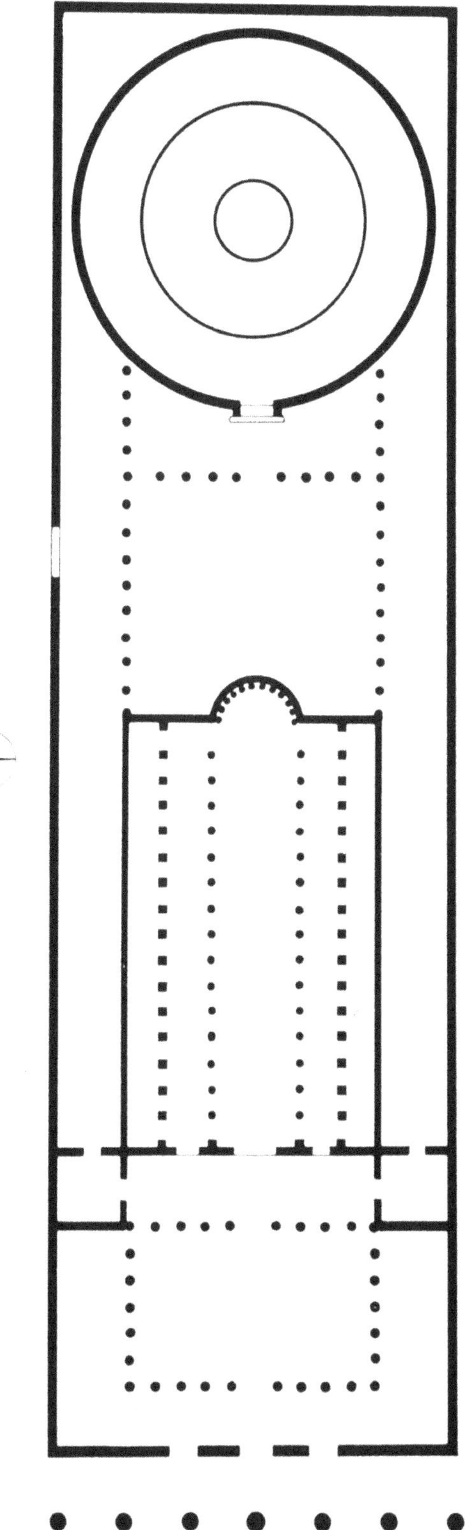

FIGURE 7. THE HOLY SEPULCHRE ON GOLGOTHA, JERUSALEM, 335

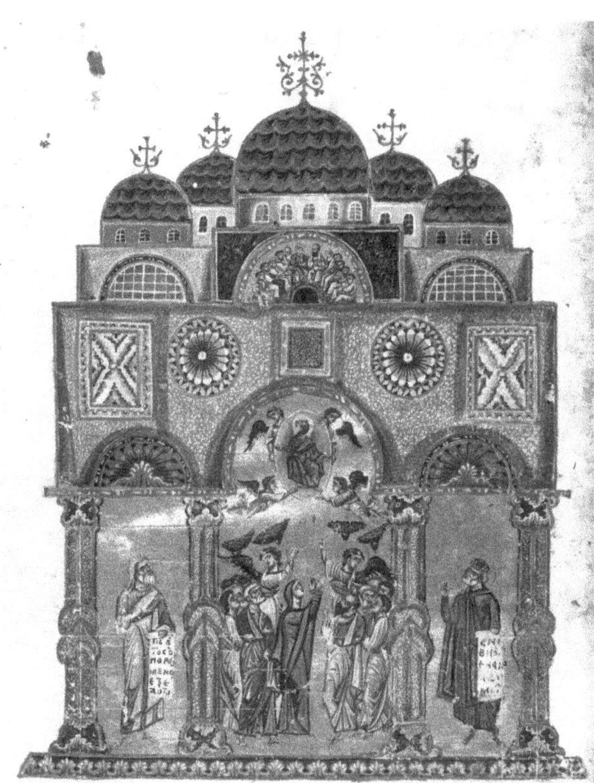

FIGURE 8. APOSTOLEION, THE HOLY APOSTLES IN CONSTANTINOPLE, BUILT IN THE 4TH CENTURY, MS GREC 1208, FOL 3 V, FIRST HALF OF THE 12TH CENTURY, HOMILIES TO THE VIRGIN BY THE MONK JACOB OF KOKKINOBAPHOS, BIBLIOTHÈQUE NATIONALE, PARIS

The Constantinian buildings are all the result of the spread of the imperial basilica. In Carthage, Trier, Aquileia, Antioch, Caesarea in Cappadocia, Milan, Alexandria, Rome and Constantinople magnificent imperial basilicas were erected. Near Constantine's palace in the Lateran in Rome a covered basilica was built in 320 with a column-adorned entrance hall, propyleum, and monumental colonnades facing the street. In 330 San Lorenzo fuori le mura was built in Rome and in 337 Santa Croce in Jerusalem. The Constantinian complexes of buildings in Palestine were spacious magnificent basilicas that were exceptionally luxurious, with rich decorations of gold and silver. The Birth cathedral in Bethlehem was erected in 333, an octagon over the birth cave with a forecourt, atrium, and a basilica with three naves. To it was added in the 6th century a part shaped as a trefoil, the trifolium. The basilica on Golgotha, the church of the Holy Sepulchre (Fig. 7), was inaugurated in 335. San Lorenzo in Milan was built in 370, the church of the Holy Apostles in the same city in 382 and Saint Gereon in Cologne in 380.

In the 4th century the church of the Holy Apostles (Fig. 8), Apostoleion, was erected in Constantinople, as a cross-cupola church, that has since inspired the architecture of San Marco in Venice and St Front in Périgeux and the first basilica of Hagia Sophia and the church of Hagia Eirene. In San Pietro in Rome (Fig. 9) about 400 martyria were united over the saint's grave with a basilica with five naves and an atrium. In Ephesus Saint Mary's was built about 400 and Saint John's basilica in 450. At the end of the 5th century the basilica of Saint Demetrius was built in Thessaloniki.

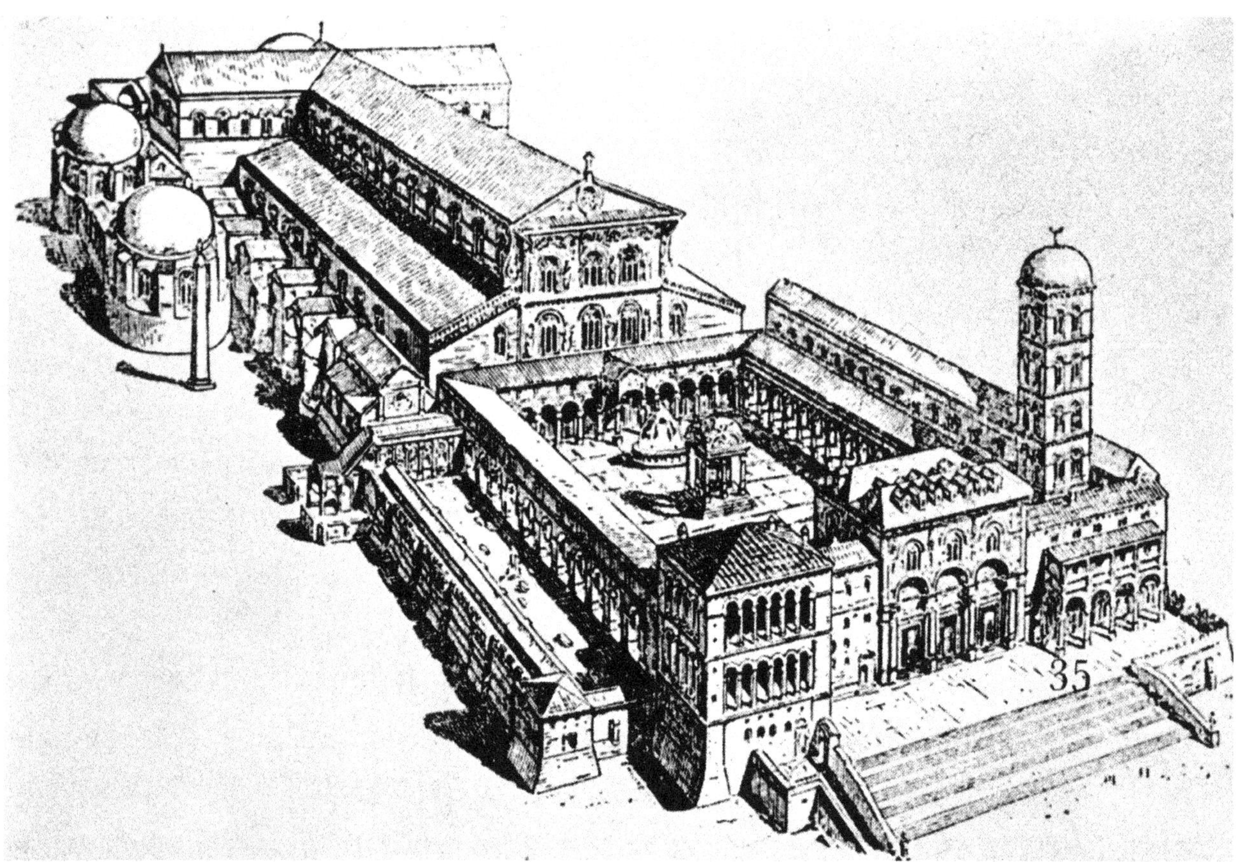

FIGURE 9. SAN PIETRO, ROME, 4TH CENTURY

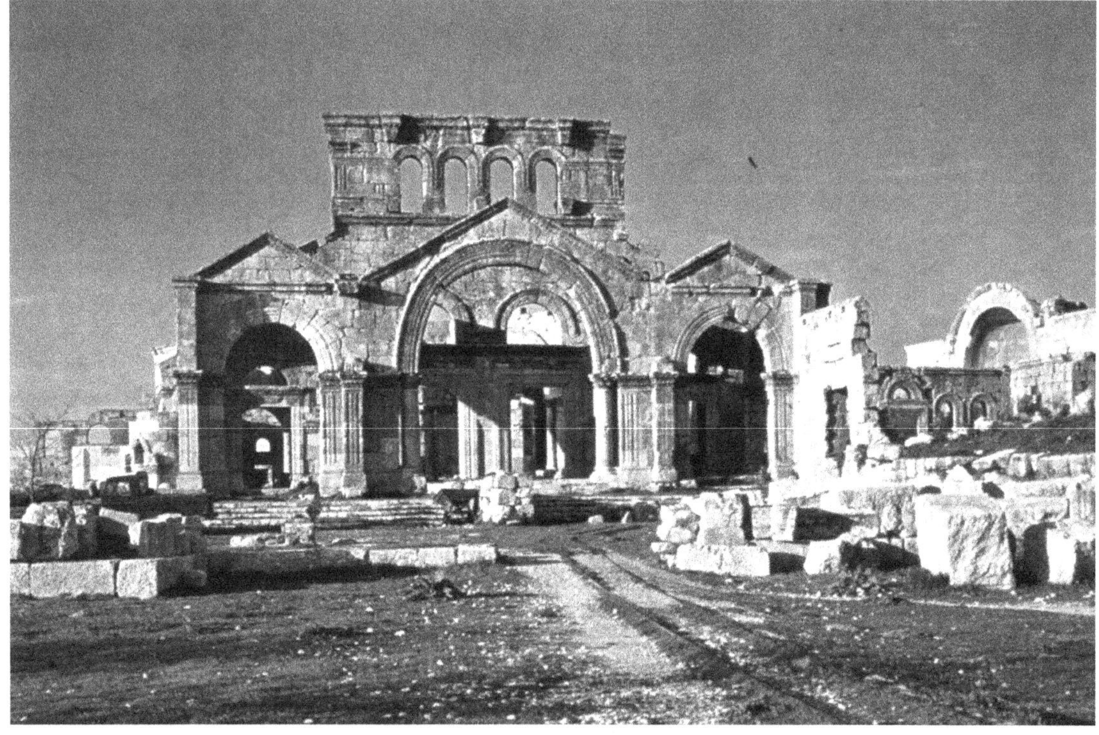

FIGURE 10. KALAT SIMAN, 470

In Syria a four-armed cross-building with three naves was created in 470 with a monastery block, Kalat Siman (Fig. 10), around Simeon the Stylite's central pillar, as a cross-shaped martyrium with an octagon in the middle where hosts of pilgrims gathered. The central octagon originally had a timber roof that rose over the pillar where Simeon spent his lifetime. The four cross-arms are basilicas with three naves, the western and southern have

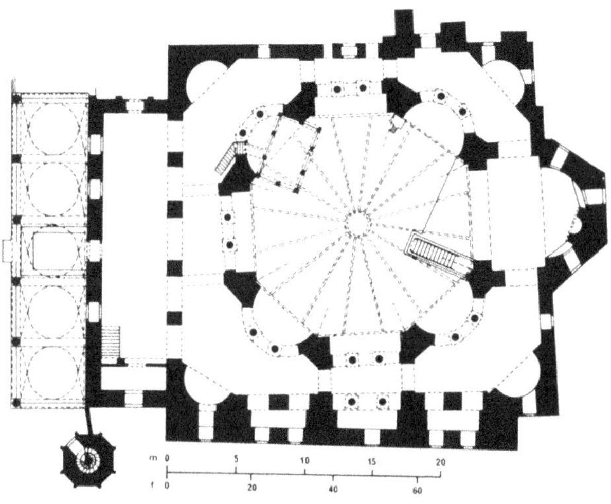

Figure 11. SS Sergius and Bacchus, Constantinople, 537

narthices and the eastern three apses. This foundation was realized through imperial donations. There are two basilicas in R'safa Sergiopolis where Saint Sergius is worshipped, of which one, his martyr shrine, was built in 520. Other cathedrals follow the local building tradition. The apses are framed by lateral rooms, the entrances are placed both on the façade and on the two flanks. The supports vary. According to north Syrian custom there are columns that support the central nave in Tourmanin, while the central nave in Qalb Luzeh, Ruweha and the Sergius church in R'safa are supported by pillars.

Between 524 and 527 the church of Saint Polyeuktos in Constantinople was rebuilt by the daughter of the West Roman Emperor Flavius Anicius Olybrius, the female patrician Juliana Anicia (Fig. 90) in the quarter Constantiniana (nowadays Sarachane) with an atrium in the west and an associated baptistery. The plan, which is difficult to reconstruct, included a dome with several exedras and galleries. In the same city SS Sergius and Bacchus' (Fig. 11) octagonal plan inscribed in a square is a forerunner of the gigantic volume of Hagia Sophia (Fig. 12 a, b), a domed basilica inscribed in a rectangle, inaugurated in 537. SS Sergius and Bacchus was built by Emperor Justinian I and Empress Theodora in the Hormisdas palace and was united with the SS Peter and Paul basilica with a common atrium. Cyril Mango argues that the church was built by Empress Theodora for Syrian monophysite monks. It consists of an octagonal nave inscribed into an irregular rectangle. The dome is 17 metres in diameter put on squinches with alternating flat and concave segments. It is decorated with green antique columns and a sculptured horizontal entablature with epigrams in honour of the imperial couple. The ambulatory of the bottom floor is repeated by the galleries in the upper floor.

The first Hagia Sophia basilica was built by Constantios in 360 and was called *He megale ekklesia*, the great church. It was burnt down by the adherents of patriarch John Chrysostom in 404 in protest to his deposition and was rebuilt as a basilica by Theodosius II in 415. Of this building only a column-adorned portico remains in one of the façades of the atrium. It was destroyed in the fatal Nika revolt in 532 that shook the reign of Justinian I. A new domed basilica was inaugurated on 27 December 537, created by the architects Anthemios from Tralles and Isidoros from Miletos. It combines a longitudinal plan

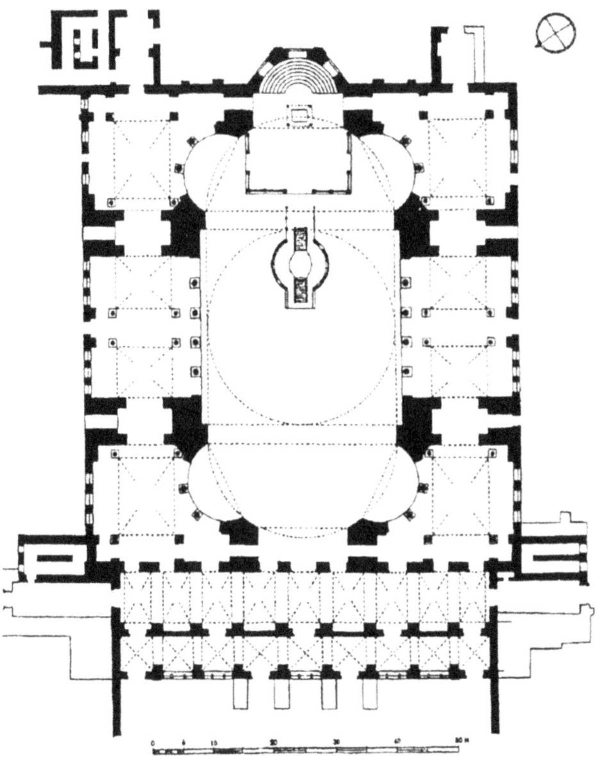

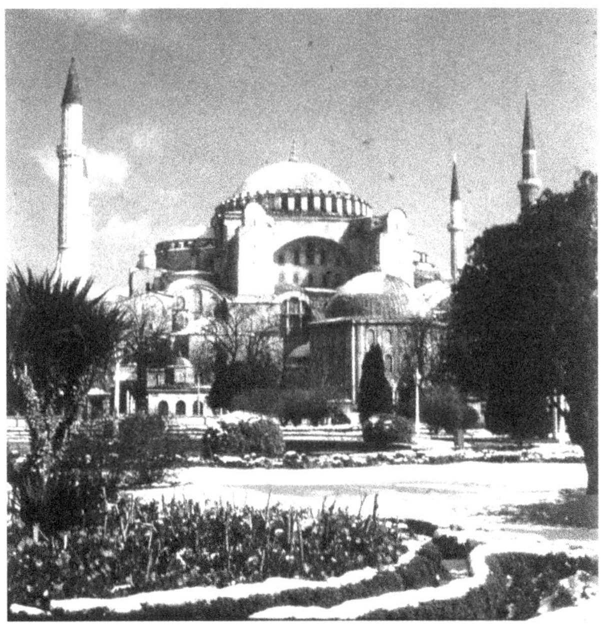

Figure 12a & b. Hagia Sophia, Constantinople, 537

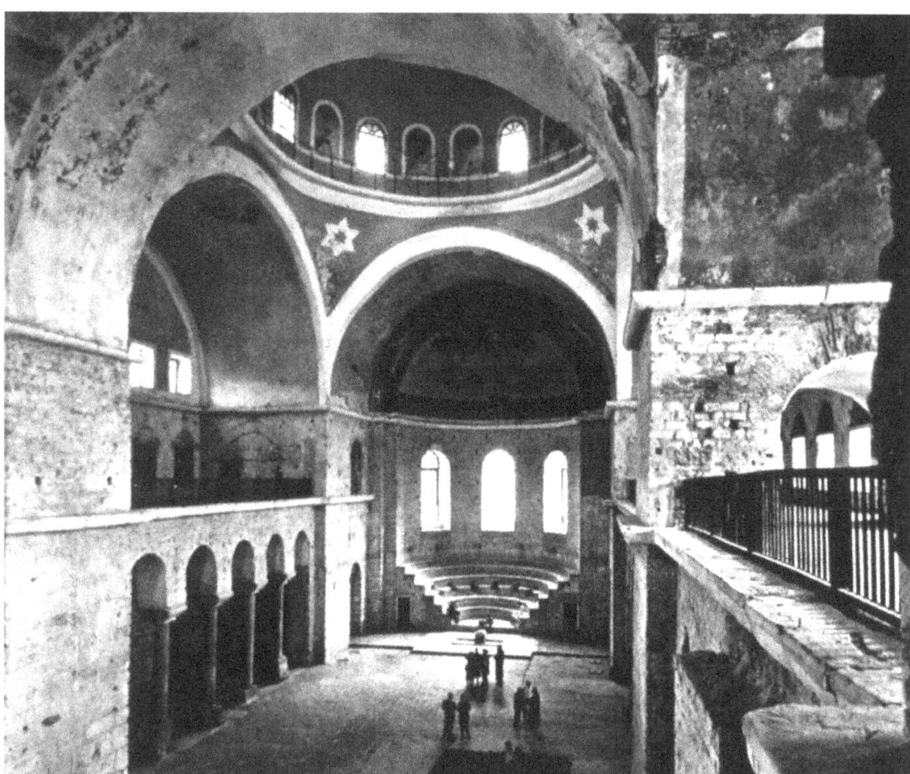

FIGURE 13. HAGIA EIRENE, CONSTANTINOPLE, 6TH CENTURY

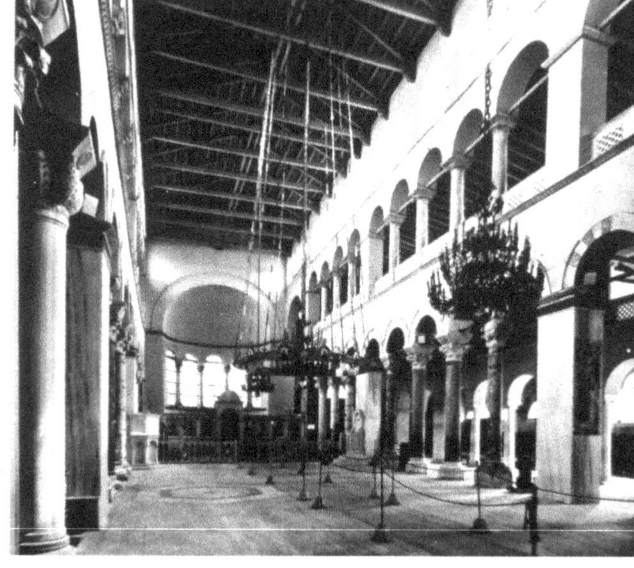

FIGURE 14. ST DEMETRIUS, THESSALONIKI, 7TH CENTURY

with a central plan inscribed in a rectangle. The central nave that is covered by the dome is 100 Byzantine feet at the sides. The dome now rises 56 metres above the ground. Two semi-cupolas surround the central dome. The cathedral is divided into three naves with galleries over the aisles and an inner narthex. Double narthices, exonarthex and endonarthex, form the entrance from the atrium that is surrounded by porticos. The original dome collapsed in 558 and was rebuilt by Isidoros the younger 7 metres higher. In the year 989 a part of the dome collapsed again and was reconstructed by an Armenian architect Trdat, who imitated the same dome in the cathedral of Ani in Armenia. In 1346 the eastern arch collapsed and was repaired in 1353. In the interior the walls are covered with richly coloured sorts of marble and *opus sectile*, marble slabs in geometrical patterns and mosaics.

The basilica of Saint John the Baptist in the Studios monastery in Constantinople was built in 463 by the patrician Studios, who had been Roman consul in the year 454 during the reign of Emperor Markianos. The church was repaired during the reigns of the Emperor Isaac Comnenos (1057-1058) and the Emperor Andronikos II Palaiologos about 1290. The basilica with atrium is surrounded on three sides by monastic passages in the middle of which there was a phiale, a marble fountain. Five doors led from the narthex into the church that had one central nave and two aisles that were isolated by

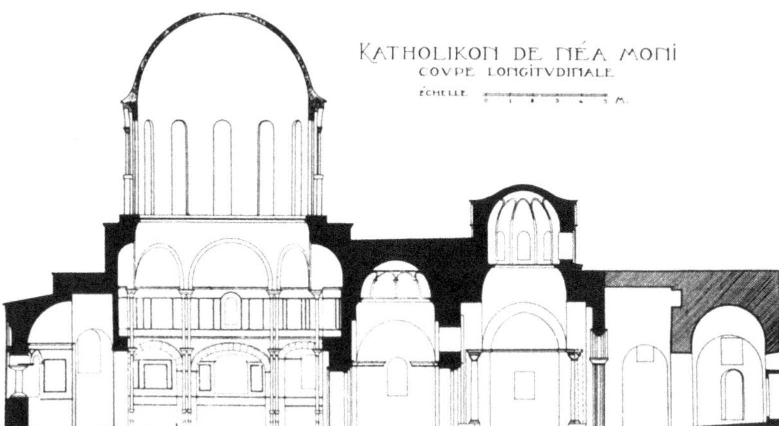

FIGURE 15. NEA MONI, CHIOS, 1042

colonnades with seven columns in green antique marble carrying a Corinthian entablature. Galleries of wood surrounded the northern, southern and western side of the church. The central nave ended in a big apse, semicircular in the interior and triangular on the exterior.

The Saint Eirene church (Fig. 13) in Constantinople was extended in the 6th and 7th centuries. Saint Demetrius (Fig. 14) in Thessaloniki was rebuilt as a basilica with five naves in the 7th century. In the 8th century the Koimesis cathedral to the Dormition of the Virgin was built in Nicea, as was Hagia Sophia in Thessaloniki and in the middle of the 9th century Kalender Camii in Constantinople was built as a cross cupola church with influence from the Armenian architectural tradition.

Concerning the regenerating principal Byzantine monuments, SS Sergius and Bacchus and Hagia Sophia, a vivid discussion has been carried on about the spread of these architectural elements. Josef Strzygowski maintained that the central plan had been transmitted from Persia via Armenia. Other scholars like Richard Krautheimer pointed to the origin of the vault technique in Mesopotamia, and argued that dome and cross-vaults had been carried over from buildings of the Roman Imperial period, but confessed that the dematerialized wall decoration was inspired by Parthian and Sassanian architecture and that the central plan was either Armenian or Roman, where Maxentius' basilica was united with the dome of the Pantheon. This discussion will certainly continue.

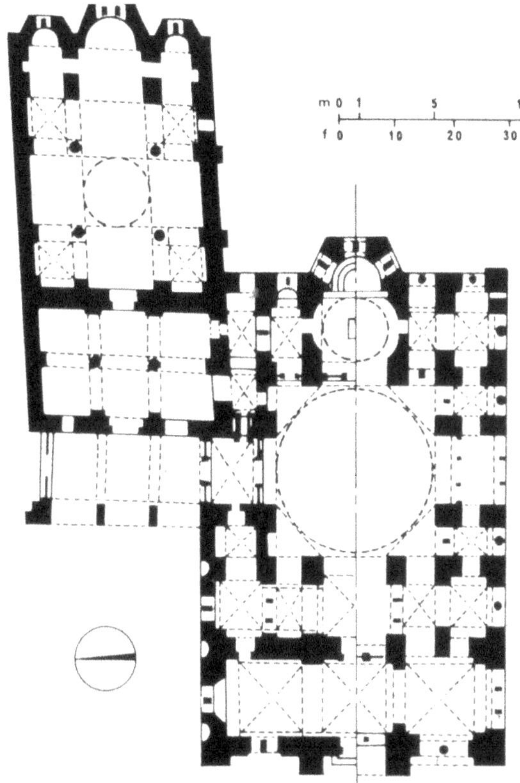

FIGURE 16. HOSIOS LOUKAS, STIRIS, PHOKIS, 1040

Middle Byzantine architecture was characterized by a certain closeness in the exterior with lesenes and recesses and several domes of somewhat smaller size. The monastery Nea Moni on Chios got a katholikon (Fig. 15), the church of the monks, as a cross-cupola church, built by Emperor Constantine IX Monomachos in 1042-1056 just like the Hosios Loukas katholikon in Stiris in Phokis that was built in 1020. The Theotokos church, the church of the Mother of God, in the same ensemble was added in 1040 (Fig. 16), a so-called *quincunx* with nine cupolas on and outside the cross-arms. The church in Constantinople built by Basil I (867-886), the *Nea Ekklesia*, is the original model for these church structures, as well as for the Myrelaion (Fig. 17), Budrum Camii about 930, the contemporary Constantine Lip's church Fener Isa Camii and for the Pantocrator monastery in Constantinople.

Late Byzantine architecture added to the body of the building an independent particular chapel, the parecclesion, for instance in the Kariye Camii (Fig. 18), the Chora church in Constantinople, that originally was built in the 12th century and was decorated with mosaics and frescoes by a high dignitary in the ministry of finances, the Grand Logothete Theodore Metochites in the 14th century. Other important monuments from this era are the Paragoritissa church in Arta built in 1282-1289 and the church of the Holy Apostles in Thessaloniki (Fig. 19) from 1312-1315.

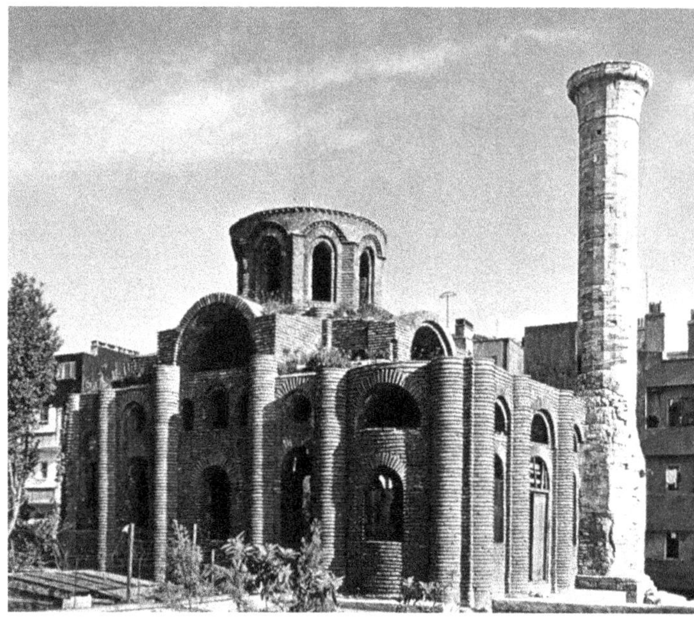

FIGURE 17. MYRELAION, BUDRUM CAMII, CONSTANTINOPLE, 930

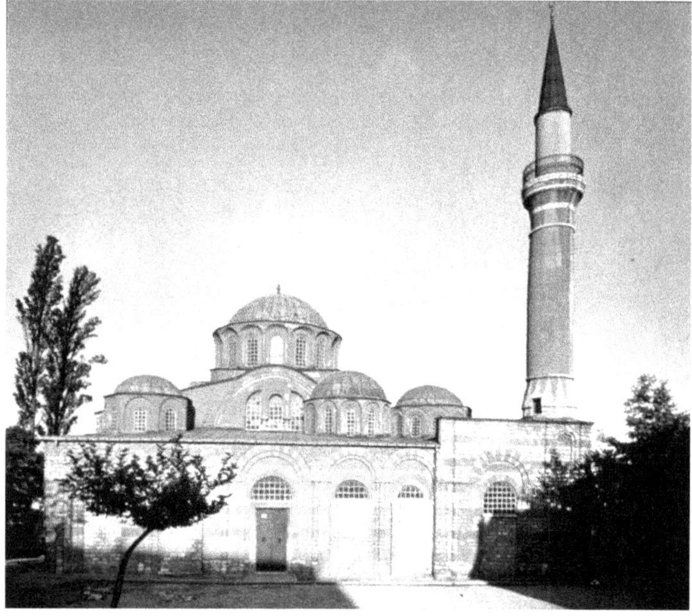

FIGURE 18. KARIYE CAMII, CONSTANTINOPLE, 12TH CENTURY

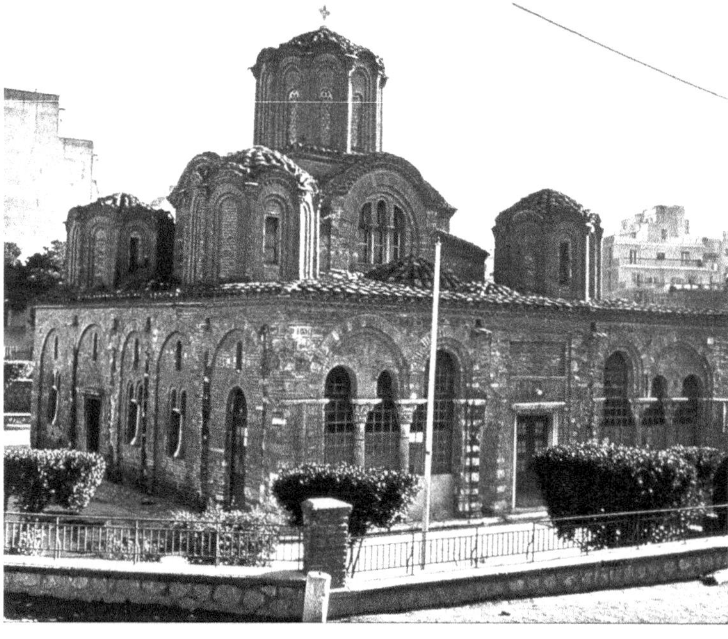

FIGURE 19. HOLY APOSTLES, THESSALONIKI, 1312-1315

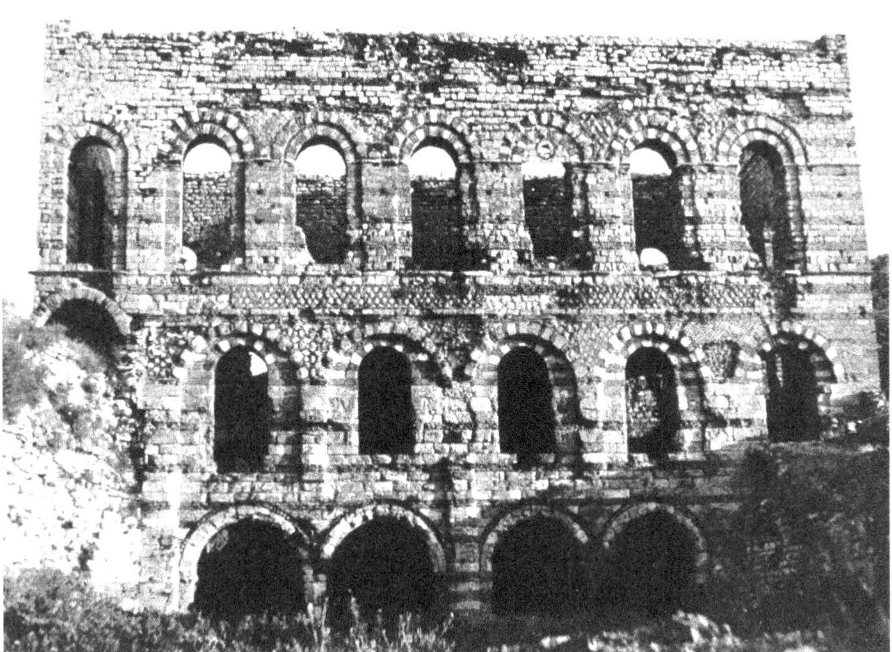

Figure 20. Tekfur Serai, Constantinople, late 13th century

The Emperors Michael VIII Palaiologos (1259-1282) and Andronikos II Palaiologos (1282-1328) built the palace Tekfur Serai (Fig. 20), the southern church of the Lips monastery, the monastery Pammakaristos and the nunnery The Virgin of Certain Hope, Bebaios Elpis.

The Greek monastic republic on Athos, *To Hagion Oros*, was already populated by hermits in the 9th century. The Lavra was founded in 963 by the Athonite Athanasios, an orphan from Trebizond who was raised by relatives in Constantinople. He was the confessor of Emperor Nicephoros II Phocas (963-969). The model for the typikon, the monastery rule, was taken from the Studios monastery in Constantinople. The convent was a caenobium, a community convent, that only allowed five hermits in the vicinity. Emperor Nicephoros II Phocas and John I Tzimisces (969-976) favoured the monastery, which became a great proprietor of the entire territory around the peninsula of Chalkidike. Iveron was founded in 976, Vatopedi after 972, Xeropotamou around 1030, Esphigmenou during the early 11th century, Docheiariou before 1046 and Chilandar in 1197 by the Serbian prince Stefan Nemanja. Beside the coenobitic system there was also a so-called idiorhythmic, more free, system where the asceticism was less pronounced.

Two kinds of founders, monastic and laymen, both imperial and princely, donated funds and contributed influence. The monastic founders were either single hermits or groups of three cell inhabitants, whose most important monk gave the monastery its name in genitive. In general the rule of Basil the Great from the 4th century was practised. The Protos or the governor of Athos resided in Karyes. Its Protaton church is one of the oldest preserved on Mount Athos, a Greek cross inscribed into a rectangle. The roof is made of timber. The four corners are treated as separate rooms for among others things the prothesis and the diakonikon, the preparation room for the Eucharistic gifts and the vestiary. The eastern apses form an outer semicircle, the transepts lack apses and the narthex is a narrow passage from the west side. The interior is dignified and has frescoes from the 14th century attributed to Panselenos, a series of icons representing the founder saints for twenty autonomous convents and the Life of Christ and his miracles and the Life of the Virgin with the Koimesis, the Dormition.

The Lavra (Fig. 21), the oldest monastery, includes a chapel devoted to the founder, where the relics of Athanasios are also on view. From the outside the monastery resembles a fortified city with numerous towers. Among the independent buildings the katholikon is noticable, devoted to the Koimesis. It consists of a central nave, the inner narthex and the exonarthex with two flanking chapels, the one on the left devoted to the Forty martyrs and the other on the right to Saint Nicholas. The transepts are provided with apses. The central dome, the largest on Mount Athos in diameter is rather flat and is supported by pillars in mortar. The inner narthex is narrow and covered by a dome with two semi-cupolas. It is connected to the aisles, the central nave and the outer narthex. The two aisles have cupolas on four columns. The central nave has a mosaic floor and the apses of the transepts have a frieze of Persian slabs. The chapel of Saint Nicholas is adorned with frescoes. The refectory that was built by Archbishop Gennadios of Serres in 1512 is the most magnificent on Mount Athos, a cross-shaped hall with an apse in the west with an entrance through a portico along the eastern side. It is decorated with paintings from the 16th century and has a wooden roof. The tables are Sigma-shaped in marble. In the katholikon there are frescoes from 1635 that represent the donator Emperor Nicephoros II Phocas and the ktitor, the founder, Emperor John I Tzimisces with donations to the monastery. The Acathistos hymn, a homage to the Virgin,

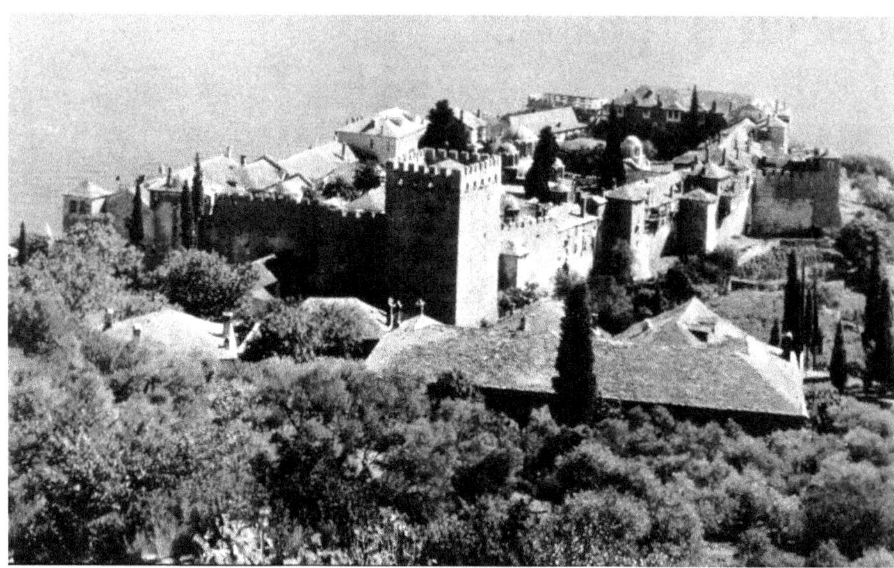

FIGURE 21. THE LAVRA, MOUNT ATHOS, 960

the Last Judgment and the Root of Jesse are represented in pictures.

Vatopedi has sumptuous mosaics from the 11th and 12th centuries that represent the Annunciation and a Deesis, an image of intercession with Christ surrounded by the Virgin and John the Baptist. Chilandar is attributed to the Serbian Prince Stefan Nemanja and his son Saint Sava, who gave their monastic vows in Vatopedi in 1186. The original katholikon was rebuilt by Kral Stefan Uros II Milutin in 1293 and the exonarthex by Kral Lazar I in 1374. The most important chrysobulls were Russian and Byzantine, the latter almost all issued by Emperor Andronikos II Palaiologos (1282-1328), whose daughter the Kralaina Simonis was married to Kral Milutin. The church is devoted to the Exposition of the Virgin in the temple. The interior is divided into a central nave and two narthices. In the central nave lies the most magnificent mosaic floor on Mount Athos. There is found the tomb of Stefan Nemanja with the portrait of the Prince together with Kral Milutin and Saint Sava in full figure and the famous icon the Virgin with the three hands, *Tricheirousa*. In the dome is pictured Christ Pantocrator and on the walls the Life of Christ and his miracles. In the trapeza of Chilandar, the refectory, there are frescoes from 1621 devoted to the Acathistos hymn.

The palaces

Constantinople was founded by Constantine the Great in 324 on the seat of the ancient Greek city Byzantion and was inaugurated on 11 May 330. It was the policy of the tetrarchs to found imperial governmental residences in the provinces. Diocletian had already established Nicomedia as imperial residence, but Byzantion seems to be more strategically important. It dominated the inflow to the Black Sea and was situated in the crossing of two main military roads, the Via Egnatia from Europe and the road from Chalcedon via Nicomedia to the Orient. But its weak point was that the town was completely unprotected from the countryside. The Great Palace and the Hippodrome block was placed within the ancient city. From there ran a colonnaded street founded by Septimius Severus to the old city gate. Constantine created a circle-shaped forum outside this city gate and he let the main boulevard, the Mese, continue straight to the west. 1.2 kms to the west of Constantine's forum the Capitolium was situated. There the main boulevard divided itself into one arm to the south towards the Golden Gate and another to northwest towards a new wall that formed an arc from the Propontis, i.e. the Marmara Lake, to the Golden Horn.

Constantine counted on an increasing population and ordered crops from Egypt for 80,000 people. It has been calculated that the population in the 5th century amounted to between 250,000 and a million. The city was completely dependent on the imports from Egypt to provide food for the population of the city. Aside from the low prices on bread and oil, luxurious baths, the theatres and the circus, various entertainments attracted people to move there.

The ancient temples were left intact. Constantine built three churches, the cathedral Hagia Eirene and two martyria, Saint Mokios and Saint Akakios. Apostoleion, the church of the Holy Apostles, was built by Constantios (337-361) and was Constantine's mausoleum.

The Gothic invasion and Emperor Valens' defeat at Hadrianopolis in 378 necessitated new defensive measures. A network of aqueducts reached from Thrace and covered 100 kms. In 413 the land wall reached 1.5 kms to the west of Constantine's wall and the new area became a cemetery. Three immense open cisterns were situated within the city area. With the capacity of one million cubic metres of water, these were Aetios' cistern built in 421, Aspars' cistern built in 459 and Saint Mokios' cistern which was attributed to Anastasios I (491-518). Later on a defensive line was built from Selembrya at the Black Sea, 65 kms from the city, the so-called Anastasian or the Long Wall that was 45 kms long. It was abandoned in the 7th century.

The Theodosian emperors provided the city with granaries and a large harbour at the Propontis. One single statistical source preserved from the year 425, *Notitia urbis Constantinopolitanae*, describes 14 town regions of which 12 were situated within the city walls. The 13th was Sykai or Galata and the 14th was situated at the opposite side of the Golden Horn. There were 5 palaces, 14 churches, 8 public Roman baths and 153 private baths, 4 forum squares, 4 harbours, 52 grand columns decorating the streets, 322 smaller streets, 4,388 domus, privately owned houses of the patricians. The apartment houses with several floors were also situated within such intervals that gave a view to the sea. A fire in the year 465 destroyed half of the city. The Nika revolt in 532 laid the centre of the city in ashes, prompting the Emperors Justinian I and Justin I to build new quarters. The town population was reduced to its half by the "Justinian pestilence" in 542.

Building activity ceased around the year 600. The crop import from Egypt became irregular. In 626 Constantinople was besieged by the Arabs and in 674-678 the city was blockaded by the Arabic fleet. In 740 an earthquake demolished great parts of the city wall and was followed by a pestilence seven years later. During this time only defensive works were built. In the 9th century, however, the population increased again, and commerce and handicrafts flourished. Russian attacks on the capital were launched in 860, 911, 941 and 1043. The 11th and 12th centuries brought expansion. Bronze doors were exported. Foreign commercial colonies were established. While the Russians were kept at bay, in Saint Mamas' quarter at the lower flow of the Bosphorus, Amalfitans, Venetians, Pisans, Genovesians, Anconitans and Germans were permitted to settle down along the Golden Horn opposite Galata with their own storehouses and commercial churches. The size of the colony of the Latins at the end of 12th century was estimated to be at least 7,000 people. The emperors and the aristocrats founded in the 11th and 12th centuries great urban foundations for education, welfare and financial purposes, the Virgin Peribleptos, the Admired, Cosmas and Damianos, Mangana, Christos Pantocrator and Saint Paul's foundation for orphans, so extended by Alexios I Comnenos that it took a whole day to walk through the complex.

The great fire of 1203 and the Latin occupation 1204-1261 destroyed the Comnenian city which became the object of a systematic sack. After the re-establishment of the Empire, the Paleologian emperors founded new imperial and aristocratic foundations, Saint Andreas in Krisei, the Virgin Pammakaristos, the Blessed, and Christ in the Chora. However, by the middle of 13th century a strong decline set in. Large parts of the city were abandoned. At the assault in 1453 the city had perhaps only about 50,000 inhabitants.

The Great Palace in Constantinople, *to mega palation,* (Fig. 22) was built during the reign of Constantine the Great (324-337). Other later palaces in the capital were

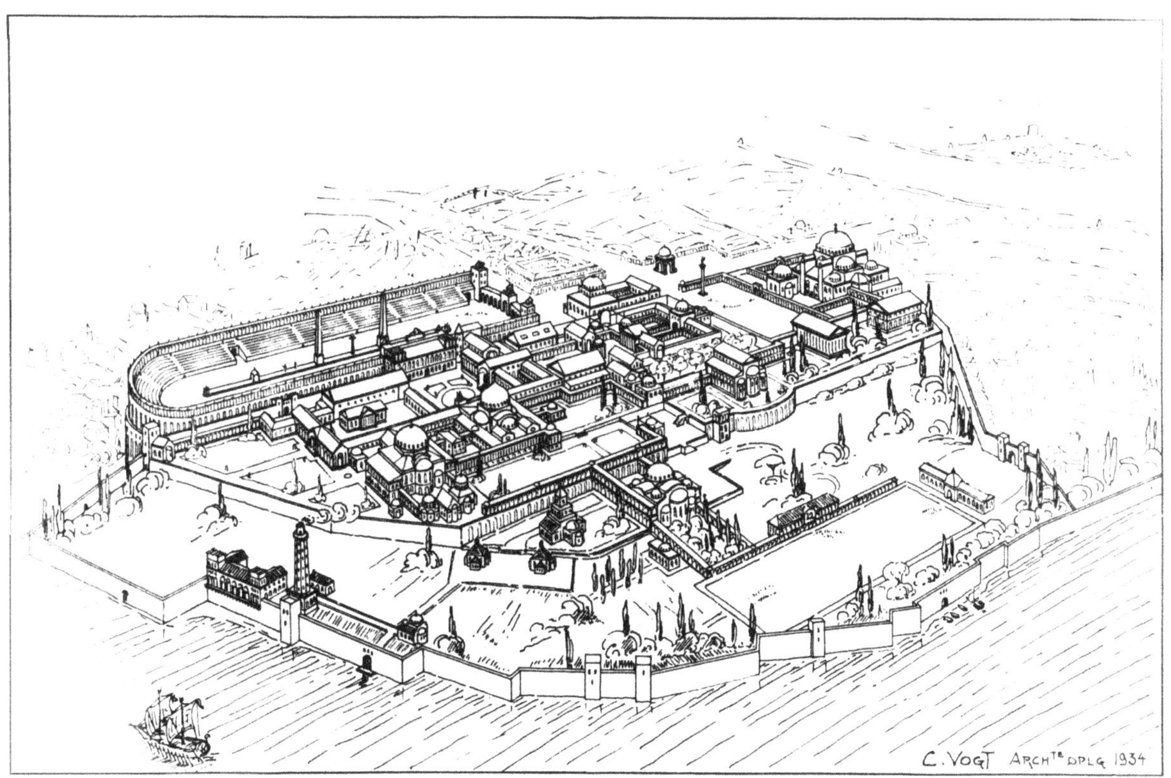

FIGURE 22. THE GREAT PALACE, CONSTANTINOPLE

Bukoleon and the Hormisdas palace from the 5th century, Myrelaion from the 10th century, the Mangana palace from the 11th century, the Blachernae palace from the 12th century and the palace of the late 13th century, in Turkish called Tekfur Serai.

From the beginning of the 4th century to the 7th century the Great Palace was open towards the city according to Roman tradition. When the city experienced a decline in the 7th and 8th centuries it became fortified. In the 13th and 14th centuries an urban palace block detached from the rest of the city arose, perhaps under western influence. To the residence belonged a palace church and it has been discussed whether SS. Sergius and Bacchus originally had this function. From the time of Justinian I (527-565) churches were integrated parts of the palace architecture. There are few traces of them left. We only find them mentioned in the literature. Between the early 9th century and the middle of the 11th century there were in the Great Palace the Christ chapel, the chapel of the Virgin and of the Archangel Michael, built by Theophilos (829-842) and Saint Anne's palace church, built by Leon VI (886-912). The church of the Saviour, the church of the Prophet Elia, Saint Peter, Saint Paul, Saint John the Evangelist, Saint Barbara and the regenerating Nea Ekklesia were built by Basil I the Macedonian. Budrum Camii has been identified with the palace chapel of Romanos I Lecapenos (920-944) near the monastery Myrelaion. Saint George's church near the monastery and palace Mangana was built by Constantine IX Monomachos (1042-1053). Its remains have been found.

The Great Palace on a slope between the Hippodrome and the sea wall was originated by Constantine the Great and remained an imperial residence until the time of Alexios I Comnenos (1081-1118). He moved the court to the Blachernae palace that was a residence also for the Latin emperors. His palace is mentioned in the Old Norse Sagas under the name of Laktjarner. The only remaining part of the Great Palace is a sea wall towards Bukoleon, a piece of the defensive wall built by Nicephoros II Phocas to the north towards the sea and the remnants of a hall with an apse and a peristyle of 66 x 55 metres with floor mosaics from the Justinian era (Fig. 68). The palace is best known from the 9th and 10th century and was an irregular composition of buildings from different times, separated by gardens and sport buildings. All efforts at reconstruction suffer from uncertainty.

The early Great Palace had a monumental domed vestibule called *Chalke*, the Bronze Gate, that opened towards the main boulevard Mese to the southwest of Hagia Sophia. An area was inhabited by the palace guards, the *scholarii*, the *excubitores* and the *candidati*, and a public part surrounded a large courtyard, the Tribunal or Delphax, with the meeting room the Consistorium and the Augusteus and a festival hall, the Triclinium of the 19 Couches. The dwelling pavilion Daphne was connected to the imperial loge *Kathisma* on the Hippodrome by a spiral-formed staircase, *kochlias*. The Empress Pulcheria added a chapel to Saint Stefanos in 428 and another to Saint Michael some years later. The palace had its own harbour and landing area and was protected by a wall. A private sports arena called "The Covered Hippodrome" presumably stems from the same period. A ceremonial hall in the periphery to the west of the Augusteion was called the Magnaura, *magna aula*. It was used for receptions of foreign ambassadors and envoys and was famous for its automata, silk strings on pillars, bronze lions that surrounded the throne baldaquin and gilted trees with birds. When the ambassadors were introduced the emperor was lifted up into the ceiling sitting in the throne baldaquin, the curtain was drawn and they had to make proskynesis, i.e. to fall to the ground on their faces. At the same time the lions roared, showing their tongues and slapping the floor with their tails and the birds twittered in different tones. These installations were Persian Arabic.

Chalke and the courtyard quarters were burnt down in the Nika revolt in 532 and were rebuilt by Justinian I. The magnificent Golden Hall in the *Chrysotriclinos,* attributed to Justin II (565-578) was a domed octagon that was a throne hall and centre for ceremonies in the palace. Tiberius I renewed the northern part of the palace as a dwelling after 578 and Justinian II (685-696) further enlarged it by strengthening the palace walls and building a large reception hall called the Justinianos or the Triclinium of Justinian. The next building phase was inaugurated by Theophilos who created the two storey complexes the Triconchos and the Sigma, and several pavilions. Basil I added the Kainourgion and the Pentakobouclion, and a polo arena called Tzykanisterion for ball-games on horseback.

Nicephoros II Phocas surrounded the central part that had views towards the palace harbour, the Bukolion, with a strong wall. In the middle of the 12th century Manuel I Comnenos (1143-1180) built a hall called the Manouelites with mosaics that honoured his victories and another called the Mouchrotas to the west of the Chrysotriclinium. During the Paleologian period the Great palace decayed. The Blachernae palace was built about 500 and contained a hall called the Anastasiakos, another the Okeanos and a third the Danoubios. The Palace was the residence of the Comnenes and was fortified with a citadel. Alexios I and Manuel I built magnificent halls. The Paleologian emperors also resided there.

To the south of the Great palace towards the Marmara Lake was situated the Bukoleon, a quarter with two palaces, the Leon Makellos palace and the House of Justinian. These buildings survived the fall of Constantinople and are described in the 16th century by visitors from the west. Bukoleon means bull and lion and the building takes its name from an ancient statue with these two animals.

Constantinople was built with all the elements of an ancient great city, with an avenue framed by colonnades, *emboloi,* called Mese, that ran from the Milion arch on the

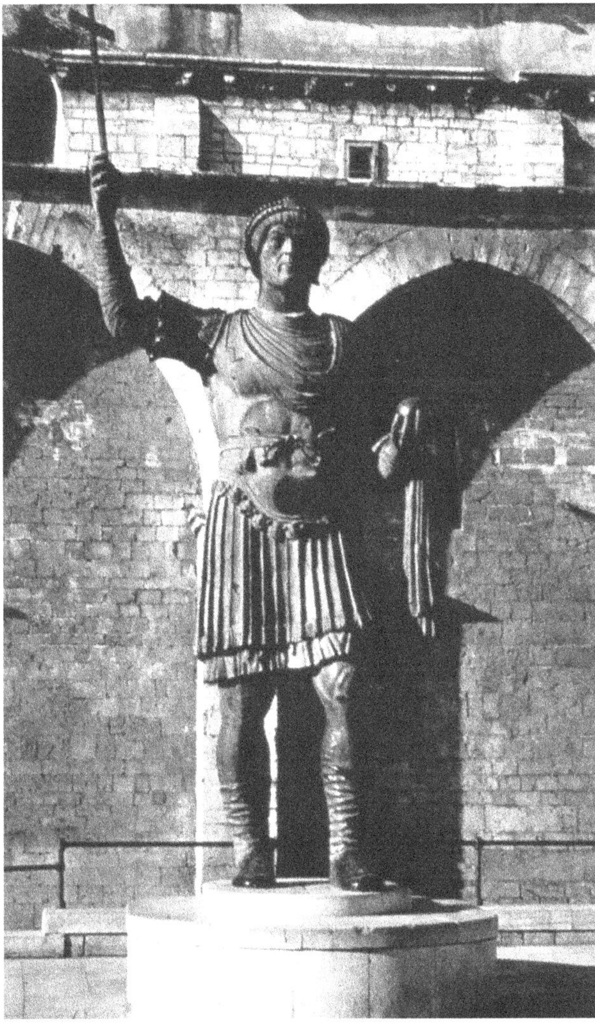

FIGURE 23. THE BARLETTA COLOSSUS, THE CATHEDRAL OF BARLETTA, *CA* 450

Hippodrome to the Capitolium, a distance of 1.7 kms and further to the Constantinian Golden Gate. This avenue was crossed by another avenue with a tetrapylon, a four-sided portal, at the crossing. Within certain intervals along the avenue there were squares, fora, of which two were inherited from Byzantion, the Strategion that was reshaped by Theodosius I (379-395) and the Tetrastoon that became the Augusteion square. The focal point in Constantine's city was a circular forum, the Phoros, with porticos. In its centre there was a statue of Constantine as Apollo with a crown of rays on his head. On the north side was situated the Senatorial Palace with a portico of porphyry columns. To the south there was a monumental fountain, the Nymphaeum. The next forum to the west, the Forum Tauri, was built by Theodosius I in imitation of Trajan's forum in Rome with a triumphal arch, a

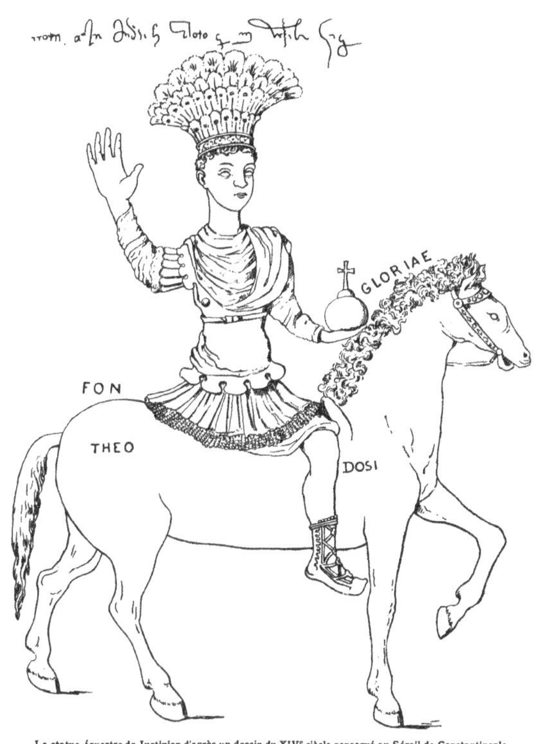

FIGURE 24. JUSTINIAN I'S STATUE DRAWN BY MORDMANN, THE SERAGLIO, ISTANBUL

basilica and a gigantic column with spiral-formed reliefs that recorded the Emperor's military victories. It was destroyed in 1500.

Further foundations of fora to the west were the Forum Bovis, the Ox Square, and the Forum Amastrianos, and on the seventh hill of the city Arkadios' Forum with another column with spiral-shaped decorations. The western frontier of the wall surrounded the city and the Golden Gate (both Constantine's original and Theodosius II's (408-450) later gate) had the form of a triumphal arch. Most emperors raised columns, the column of the Goths, Constantine's and Markianos' (450-457) columns. An immense Corinthian capital has been connected with either Leon I's (457-474) column or the Barletta Colossus (Fig. 23) that is identified as Markianos'. Justinian I was honoured with a column with an equestrian statue on the Augusteion (Fig. 24). Justin I put up a column in the Deuteron quarter and another close to Zeuxippos' bath, and Phokas (602-610) raised a column near the Tetrapylon. Aside from that there were many of ancient gods and heroes, representations from mythology, statues of philosophers and coachmen. The Senatorial Palaces, the baths and the theatres were richly adorned.

Chapter 3

Byzantine architecture II

The Exarchate Ravenna – development in Sicily, Bulgaria, Serbia, Cappadocia, Armenia and Georgia

Ravenna

Honorius moved the imperial court from Milan to Ravenna in 402. As capital for the Western Roman Empire and seat of the praetorian prefect in Italy, it was expanded in the 5th century during the reign of Valentinian III (425-455) with palaces and churches. The cathedral was built at the end of the 4th century by Bishop Ursus. Ravenna continued to be the capital of Italy during the rule of Odovacar and the Ostrogothic kings. Theoderic's palace was built along with several Arian churches.

Justinian's general Belisarios took control over Ravenna in 540 during the Gothic war. Archbishop Maximianus' ivory throne and the mosaic portraits in San Vitale indicate that Ravenna was a centre for luxury production and exquisite handicrafts. In 568 the Byzantine Exarchate was installed in Ravenna, building a close connection between the Byzantine administration and the church of Ravenna. The town fell to the Lombards in 751.

Among Late Roman buildings are found the baptistery of the Orthodox church or of Bishop Neon (451-471) of Ravenna. In the middle of the dome there is a large medallion with the Baptism of Christ surrounded by apostles among vegetative candelabras (Fig. 25). Below there are eight small fields of column-decorated exedras with empty thrones and open gospels.

Galla Placidia's mausoleum was built in 421. Galla was the daughter of Theodosius the Great. She was captured by the West Goths and married to Ataulf. After his murder she was given as wife to this general Constantius by her brother Honorius. She ruled the West Roman empire during the minority of her son Valentinian III and died in 450. The mausoleum (Fig. 26) is a cross-formed oratory that nowadays is called San Nazaro e San Celso. The building might have been a martyrium for San Lorenzo as this saint is represented in a mosaic. In the barrel-vaults of the transept there are wine creepers and acanthus loops against a background of dark shining blue. In the tympanon areas Saint Laurentius is represented with the grill and the young Christ as the Good Shepherd with his lambs (Fig. 27), a mosaic inspired both from Antioch and Alexandria (and by Persian *hwarena* landscapes, descriptions of paradise, according to Josef Strzygowski). In the dome on the cross middle there is depicted a cross against a blue starred background and the four beings in the vision of Ezechiel.

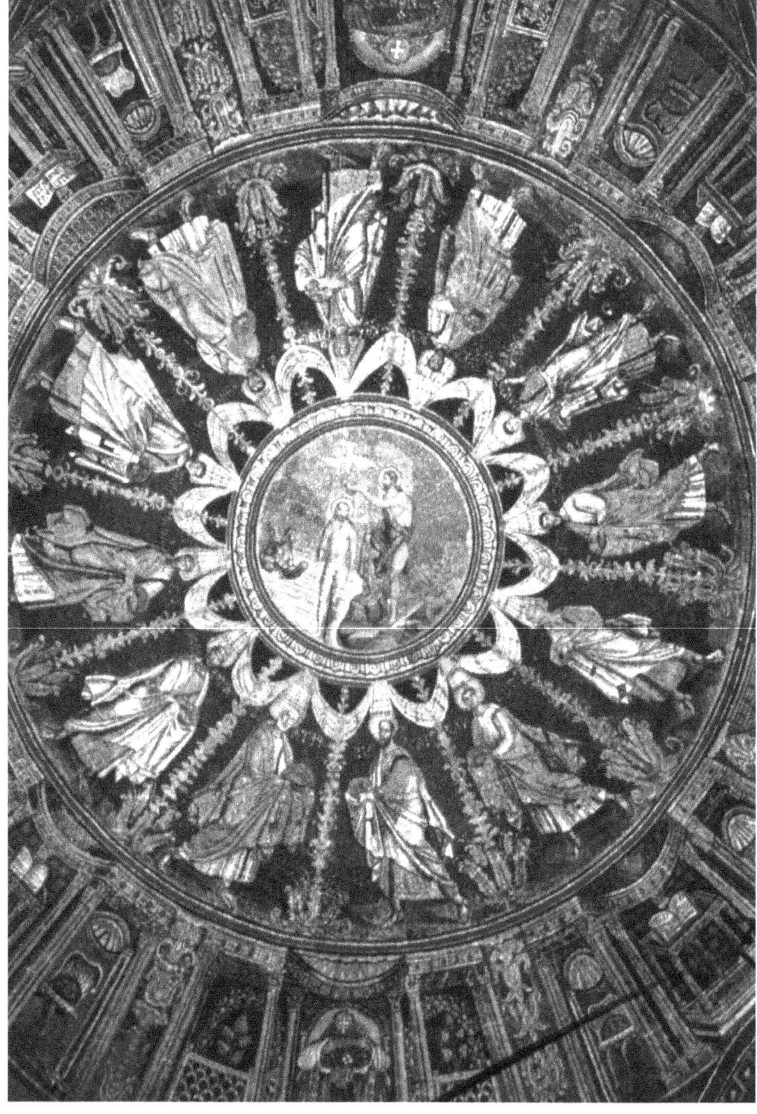

Figure 25. The Baptistry of the Orthodox, Ravenna, *ca* 450

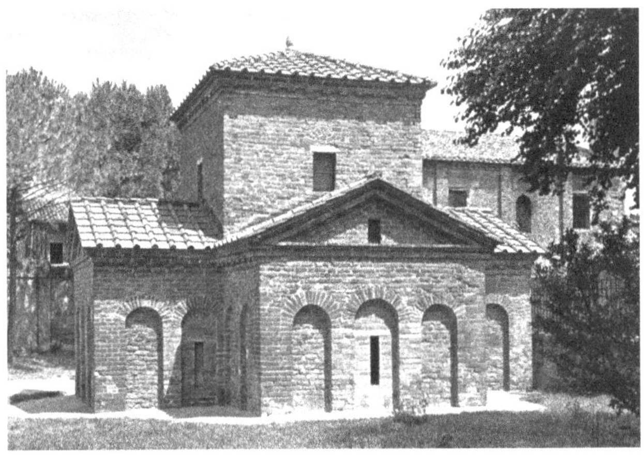

FIGURE 26. THE MAUSOLEUM OF GALLA PLACIDIA, RAVENNA *CA* 425

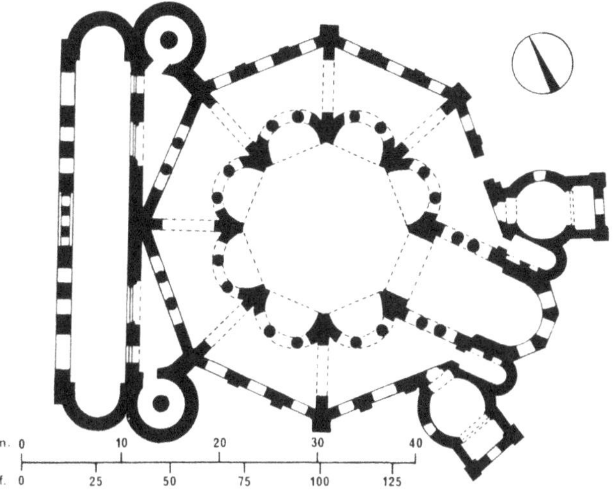

FIGURE 28. SAN VITALE, RAVENNA, 547

The baptistery of the Arians was inaugurated in 520. Also represented there is Christ's baptism and among the surrounding details also Hetoimasia, the empty throne is noticed. San Vitale (Fig. 28) that imitates the plan of SS Sergius and Bacchus in Constantinople, forms an octagonal central room with ambulatories and a dome on eight stone pillars connected to arc-shaped colonnades in two floors and a narthex arranged crosswise. The apse is surrounded by two aisles. Richard Krautheimer and Friedrich Deichmann suppose that the master builder was an Italian, who worked according to a Byzantine model. The founder was bishop Ecclesius. The church was inaugurated in 547 by Archbishop Maximinian. He is represented together with Emperor Justinian I on one of the ktitor mosaics in the bema that shows the imperial couple with their suite (Fig. 29, 30). The Empress Theodora is dying of an incurable disease. It is dated to the year 548, the year of her death.

San Giovanni in Fonte is a domed octagon from 525. San Apollinare in Classe situated close to the grave of the first bishop of Ravenna, Apollinaris, was inaugurated by Maximinian in 549. It is a longitudinal basilica with colonnades of imported Greek and Proconnesian marble. A symbolic Metamorphosis scene, the Transfiguration of Christ (Fig. 31), is represented in the apse. On the wall below there are two plates from the 7th century that show a privilege given by Emperor Constantine IV (668-695).

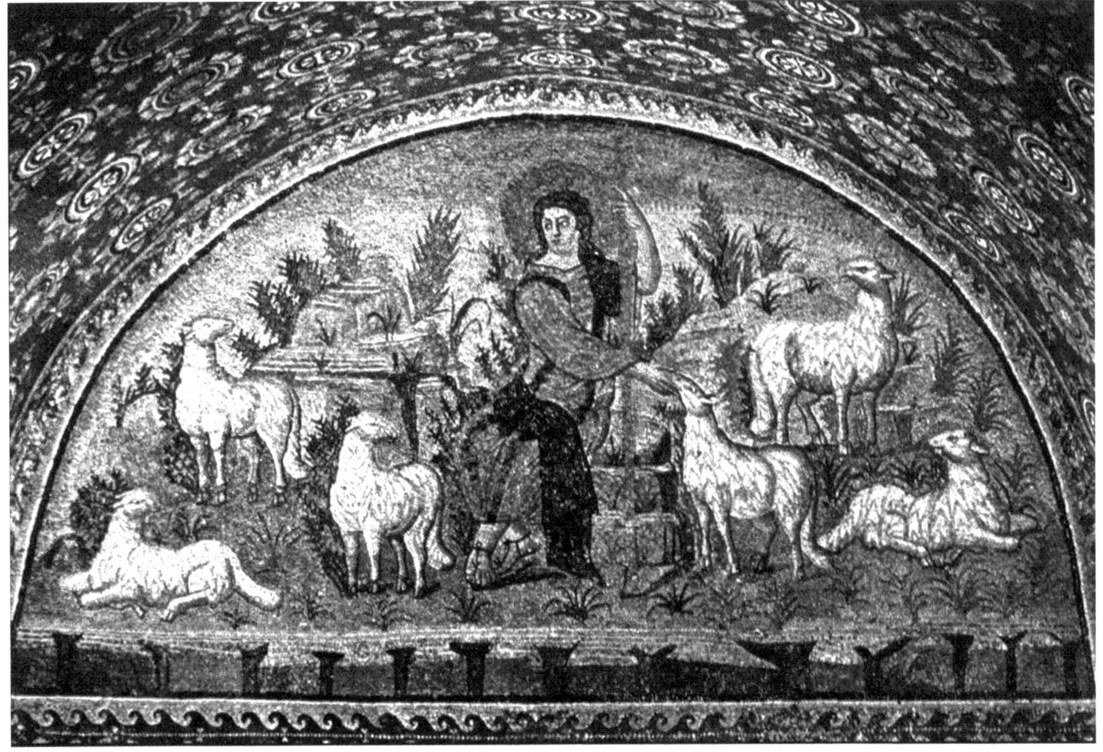

FIGURE 27. CHRIST AS THE GOOD SHEPHERD, MOSAIC, THE MAUSOLEUM OF GALLA PLACIDIA

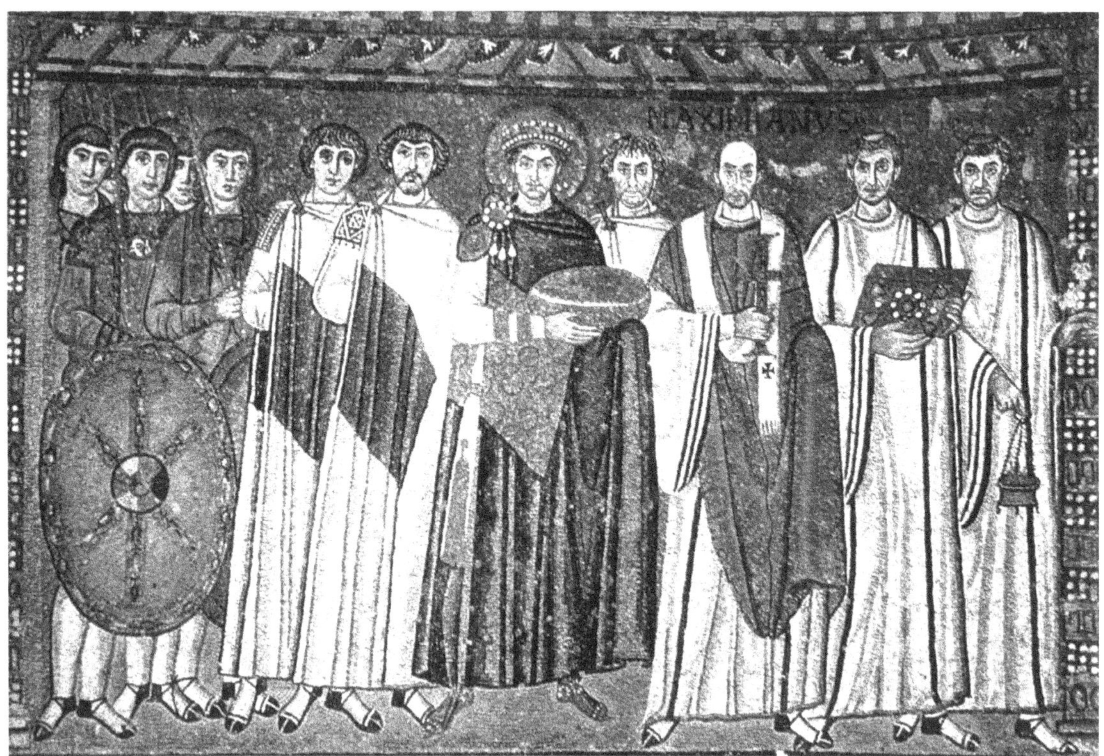

Figure 29. Justinian I with suite, mosaic, San Vitale, 548

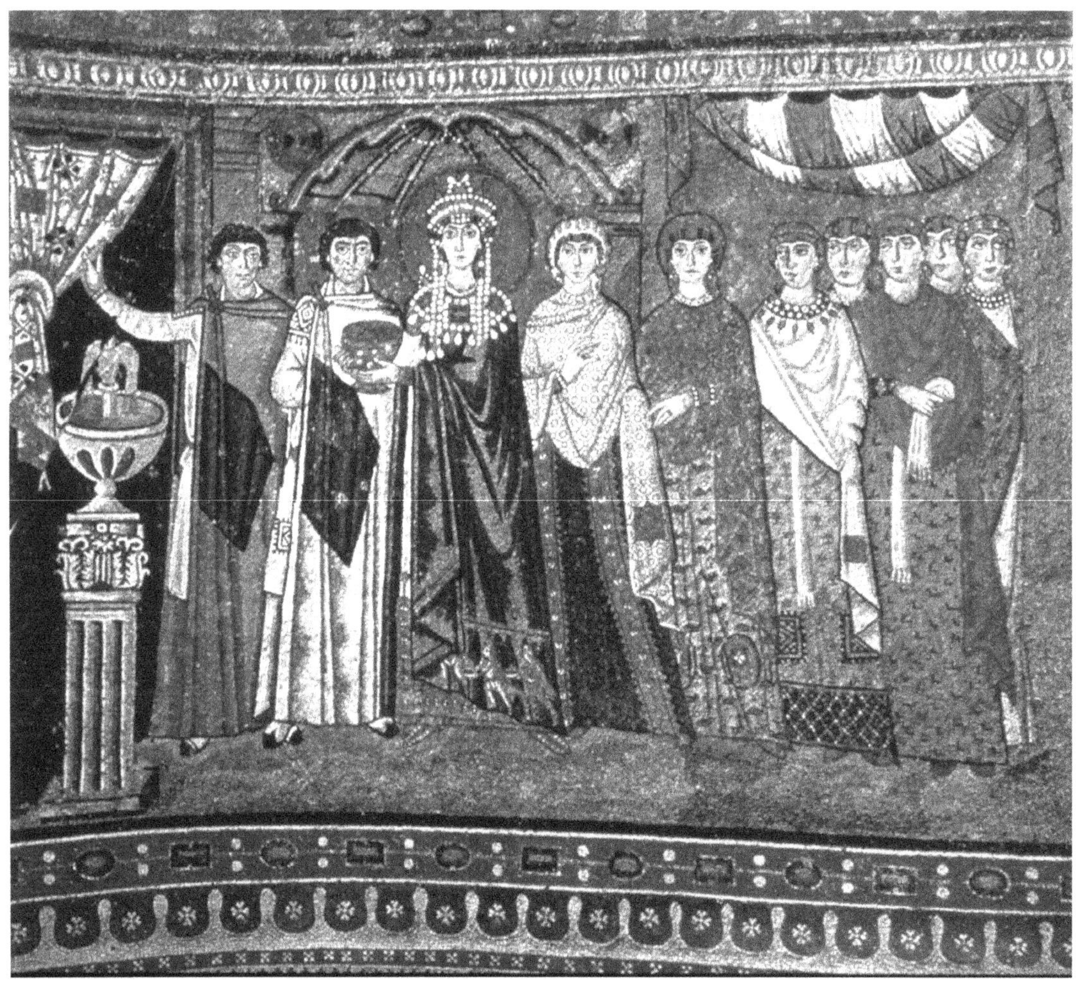

Figure 30. Theodora with suite, mosaic, San Vitale, 548

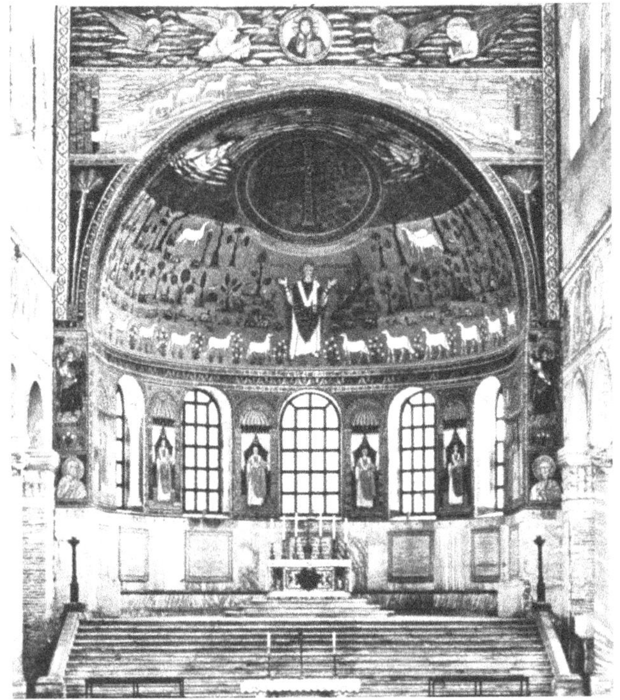

FIGURE 31. SAN APOLLINARIE IN CLASSE, THE TRANSFIGURATION OF CHRIST, 549, MOSAIC, RAVENNA

From the beginning San Apollinare Nuovo was an Arian church built by Theoderic in 520 as a column basilica with Byzantine impost capitals, decorated with mosaics with long processions of saints (Fig. 32) and partly reshaped in 550 when it was taken over by the Orthodox church. The chapel of the Archbishop's palace was finished about 500. The mosaics in Ravenna are attributed to masters from Constantinople by Ernst Kitzinger as a paradigm for Justinianic style. The inscriptions indicate that San Vitale and San Apollinare in Classe were paid for by Julian Argentiarius, a Byzantine treasurer. In 1112 the apse of the Basilica Ursiana was decorated by a master who also worked in San Marco in Venice. It was destroyed in 1733.

Sicily

Palermo (Panormos) fell to the Vandals in 440 and to the Ostrogoths in 491. The Byzantine general Belisarios reconquered Sicily in 535-536 and the island remained in Byzantine hands until the 9th century. In 831 Sicily was conquered by the Arabs, flourished under the Moslems and then was conquered by the Normans in 1072.

The ambivalent relationship of the Sicilian Norman court with the court in Constantinople, devoted admiration mixed with a wish to compete, resulted in the Cappella Palatina that was built by Roger II, and the cathedral of Santa Maria, which was founded by the Admiral George of Antioch. It was called Martorana because of a nearby nunnery founded by Gaufredus de Marturanu. Byzantine masters from Constantinople decorated it with mosaics.

Cappella Palatina has a south Italian architectural plan and is a basilica with three apses and a dome on a high drum with squinches that recede in three steps in front of the central apse with an Islamic *muquarnas* ceiling, stalactites, in the central nave, and columns in the corner niches, also an Islamic influence. The barrel-vaults are slightly pointed. This basilica combines a longitudinal plan with a central plan. The central nave, the two aisles, the two transepts and the central square are barrel-vaulted, while the apse and the presbytery have semi-cupolas. A mixed Arabic, Greek and south Italian tradition is found together here in the mosaics. The semi-cupola represents Christ Pantocrator with rows of angels below and is dated to 1143 according to a Greek inscription. A chronicle attributed to the Archbishop of Salerno Romauld II mentions mosaics that had been made during the reign of Wilhelm I (1154-1166). These are perhaps the scenes from the Old and New Testament that we find in the central nave and the aisles that Otto Demus and other scholars have attributed to Sicilian pupils of the Byzantine masters that worked for Roger II.

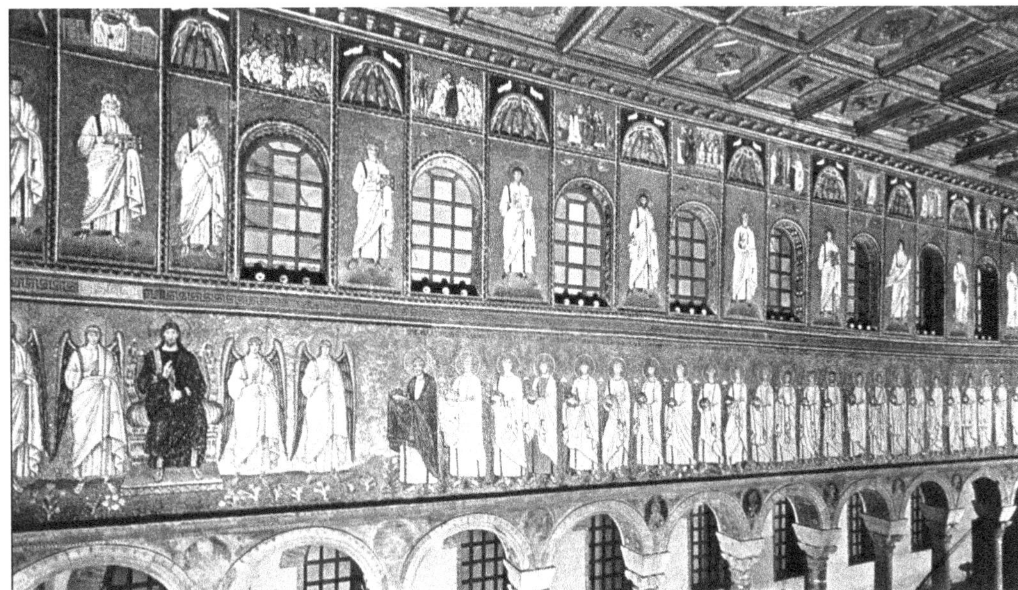

FIGURE 32. SAN APOLLINARE NUOVO, MARTYRS, FROM 554, MOSAIC, RAVENNA

La Martorana is completely Byzantine in plan with a typical Sicilian silhouette. It forms a cross plan with four columns inscribed into a square with a dome on squinches over the cross centre and the ambulatory. The cross arms are barrel-vaulted and higher than the cupola-vaulted corners. The decoration was influenced by the Cappella Palatina and Cefalù and is dated to 1143 and 1151, the year when George of Antioch died. A Pantocrator image in semi-figure in the dome with four angels in proskynesis, the Birth of Christ and the Dormition of the Virgin, a lower vault with the ktitor image of George of Antioch in proskynesis in front of the Theotokos and Roger II crowned by Christ (Fig. 33) are classical Byzantine compositions.

Cefalù was founded by Roger II in 1125, 1128 or 1129. The architecture is western and combines a longitudinal plan with a central plan. The presbytery and the southern transept are vaulted. The wooden roof is flat and on the façade there are two towers. In the apse Christ Pantocrator is enthroned in semi-figure, the prototype for the glass paintings with the same image at Gotland (Fig. 34) in the 1250s.

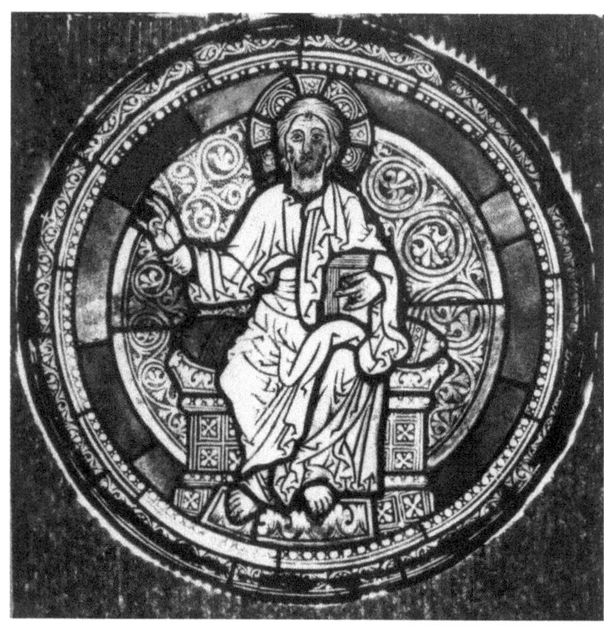

FIGURE 34. CHRIST PANTOCRATOR, ENDRE CHURCH, GOTLAND, *CA* 1250

Monreale stems from the 1150s. It was founded by Roger II, extended by Wilhelm II and lies enclosed in a monastery complex. The church unites the Latin basilica with a Greek cross inscribed in a square. The Pantocrator image in the vault of the apse substitutes for the cupola (Fig. 35).

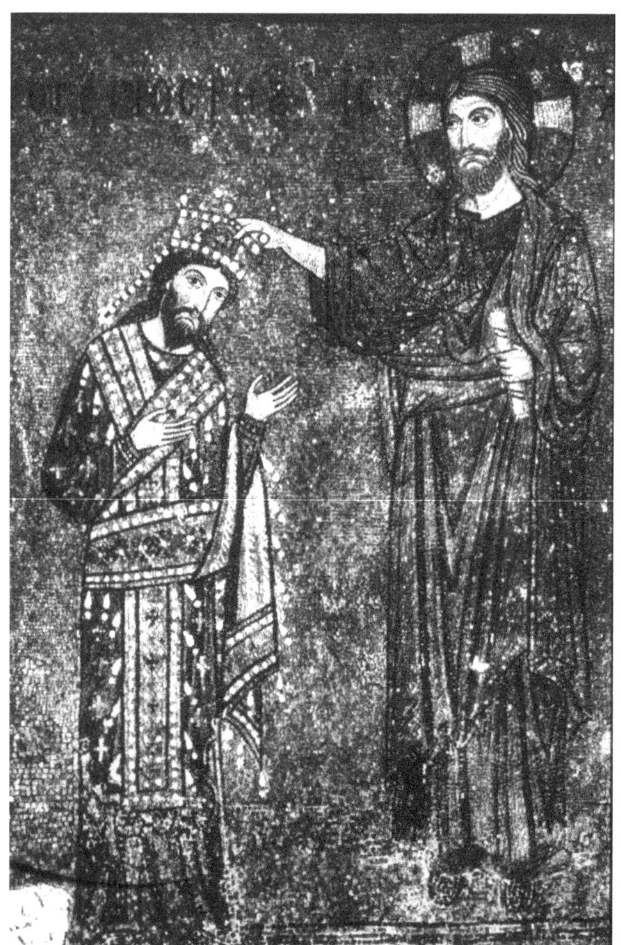

FIGURE 33. ROGER II (1101-1154) CROWNED BY CHRIST, LA MARTORANA, PALERMO

Norman Sicilian architecture can be divided into three periods:

1. Roger II (1101-1154) built the apse in Cefalù and the first plan to Cappella Palatina and created the decoration in Martorana. This art is eclectic.
2. Wilhelm I created the mosaics of the presbytery in Cefalù, the eastern part of Capella Palatina according to a new plan and the mosaics in the naves.
3. Wilhelm II (1166-1189) introduced the late Comnenian style in Monreale.

Henry Maquire has shown that the choice of and the place of the mosaics in these churches are influenced by Byzantine rhetorical conventions well known from homilies.

Bulgaria

The first Bulgarian empire was founded on a territory that was rich in Roman and Byzantine spoils. These and other sources were used to create an art that served the national needs of the new state. Pliska was the earliest administrative centre and was founded as a double fortress like the succeeding capital Great Preslav. The large relief in the rock at Madara from about 705 shows a horseman who raises a bowl with a lion below and a dog who runs behind, presumably representing Khan Tergel. The relief has Sassanian models from the rock reliefs in Persia.

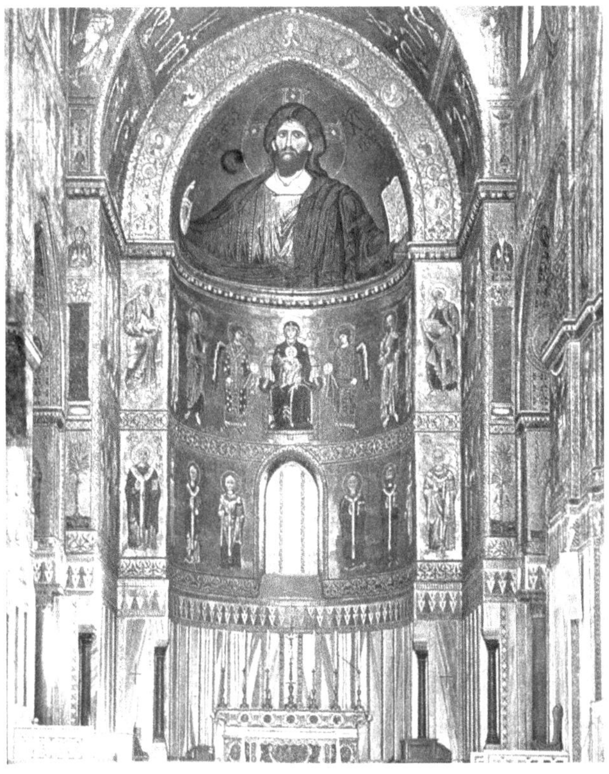

Figure 35. Christ Pantocrator, Monreale, Palermo, mosaic, *ca* 1150

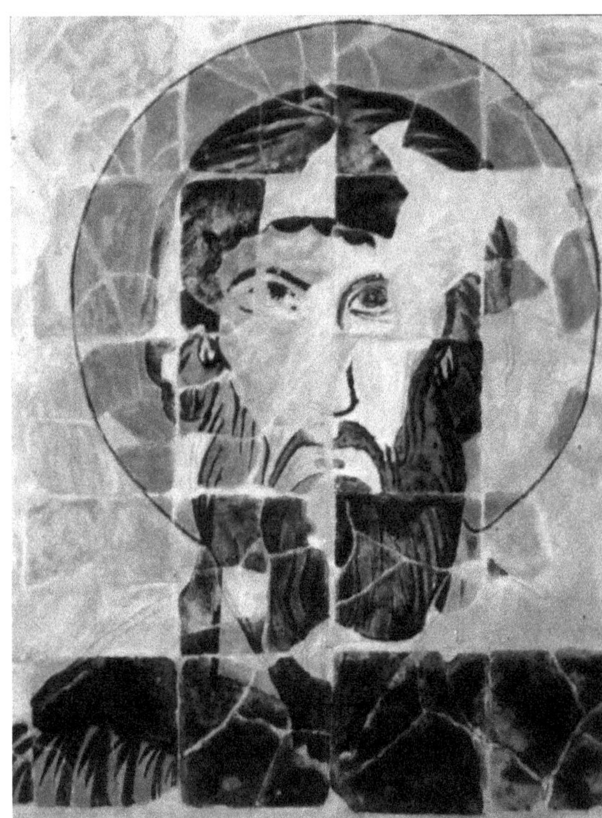

Figure 36. The icon of Saint Theodore, 9th century, Sofia

Bulgarian ceramic plates have Oriental inspiration. Most famous is the icon of twenty tiles of Saint Theodore (Fig. 36) from Sofia and a group of small icons in a plate with saints from Tuzlaluk, most of them with flowers and geometrical motives. They are found in the monastery churches around Preslav, the oldest in the Round church in Preslav from about 907. Similar plates are found in Constantinople, of Arabic inspiration.

The Round church in Preslav is eclectic. The form of the church is a domed rotunda with an inner colonnade in two rows preceded by an atrium enclosed by walls with niches and columns that recall Armenian architecture, while the mosaics show Byzantine influence, recalling Late Roman baptisteries.

Byzantine art dominated Bulgaria during the 11th and 12th centuries, when the territory was included in the Byzantine empire, for instance the frescoes in the Ossuary of the monastery Petritzos, a sanctuary where the skeletons of dead holy monks were preserved. The Second Bulgarian Empire brought prosperity in architecture and painting. The foundations of the noblemen, the churches on the Trapezitsa hill in Trnovo and the Hreljo convent in the Rila monastery are such examples. The churches have two floors for graves that level uneven ground inspired by Byzantine or Caucasian prototypes. Other churches are elaborate variants of Paleologian models from the 14th century, for instance the churches of Mesembria with stone, brick or ceramic slabs that create a rich textile pattern on the exterior totally without connection to the inner disposition. The St George cathedral in Sofia from the 12th century is built with Mesopotamian barrel-vaults.

The painting indicates two tendencies. Many monuments return to Byzantine prototypes from the 11th and 12th centuries like the Ossuary, the lower church at Bachkovo where the Mother of God surrounded by archangels (Fig. 37) is represented in the apse. Others are more influenced by contemporary tendencies in Constantinople, in particular the foundations of Ivan Alexander (1331-1371) (Fig. 38), like the upper church on the 11th century structure in Bachkovo with the portrait of the Tsar. Bojana has an uncommon fresco of the image of a Christ Emmanuel and a portrait of the princely couple Kalojan and Desislava (Fig. 39) from the 1250s. The rock church in Cûrkvata in Ivanovo with figures in crossed positions in front of elaborated architectural façades is a hesychast church with flat roof and small scenes in squared frames.

Serbia

The first Byzantine dominance in the arts was developed during the reign of Stefan Nemanja in the later part of the 12th century. His foundations, Saint Nicholas in Kursumlja and the dome on the church of the Virgin in Studenica, show works of Comnenian masters, presumably from Constantinople. The second more pronounced phase

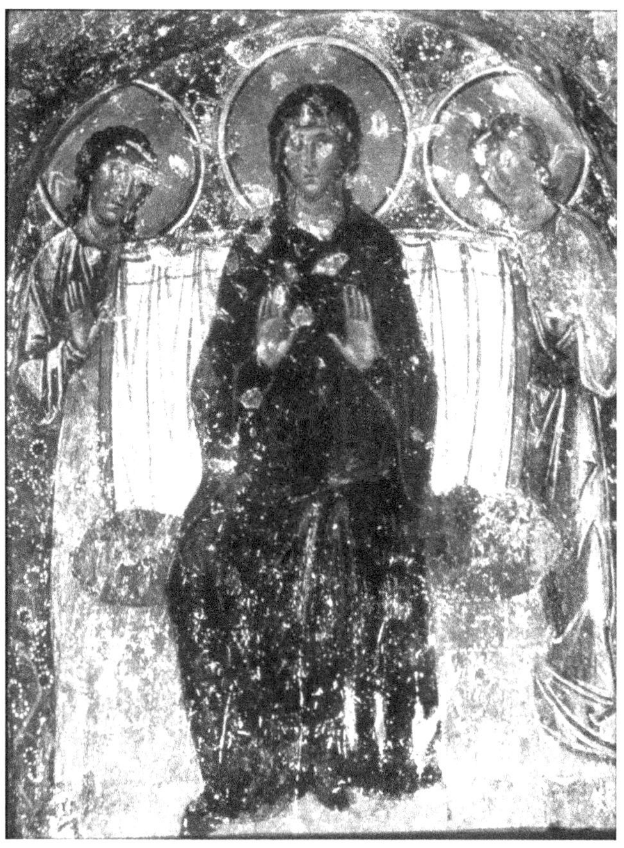

Figure 37. The Ossuary of Batchkovo, fresco in the apse, Theotokos with archangels, 11th century

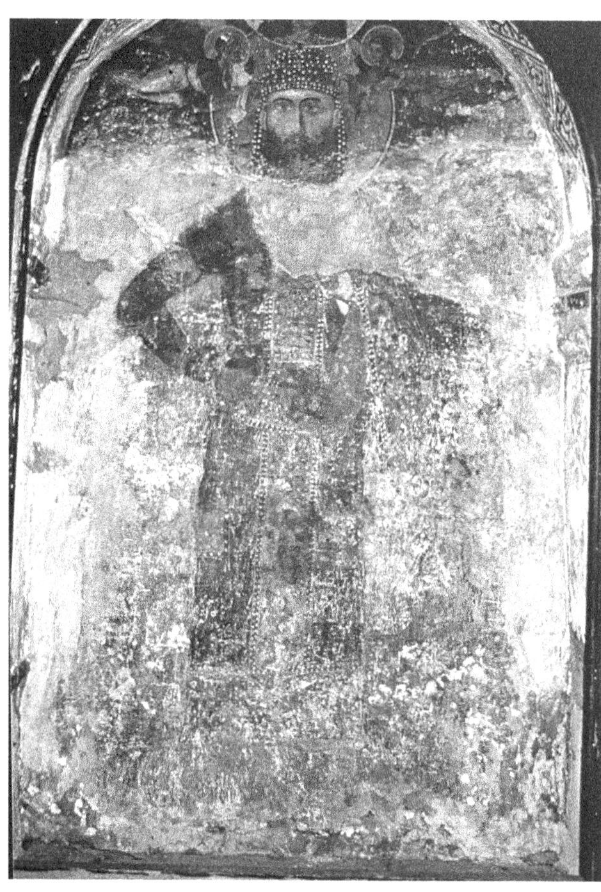

Figure 38. Tsar Ivan Alexander (1331-1371), Ossuary of Batchkovo, second floor

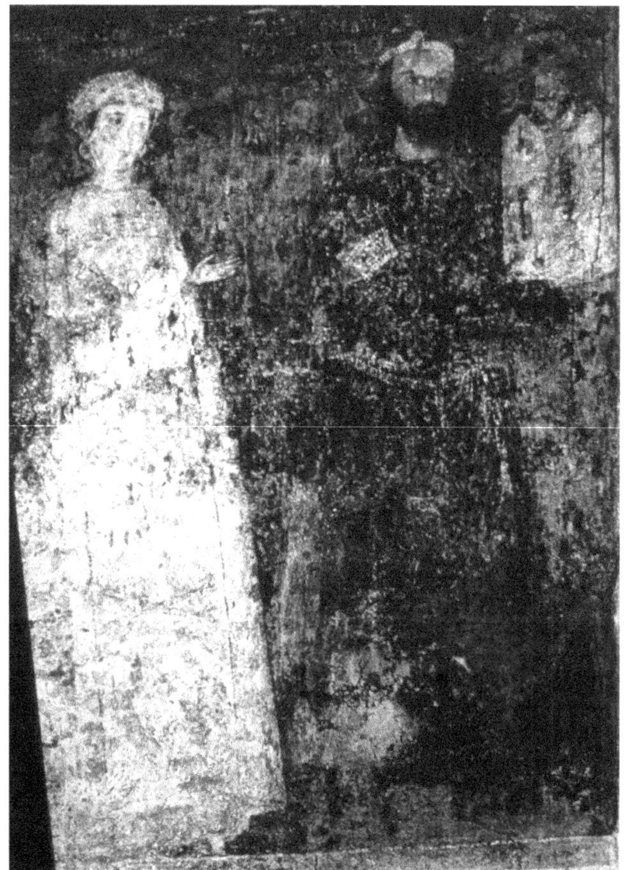

Figure 39. Sebastocrator Kalojan and Desislava, Boiana, outside Sofia, 1259

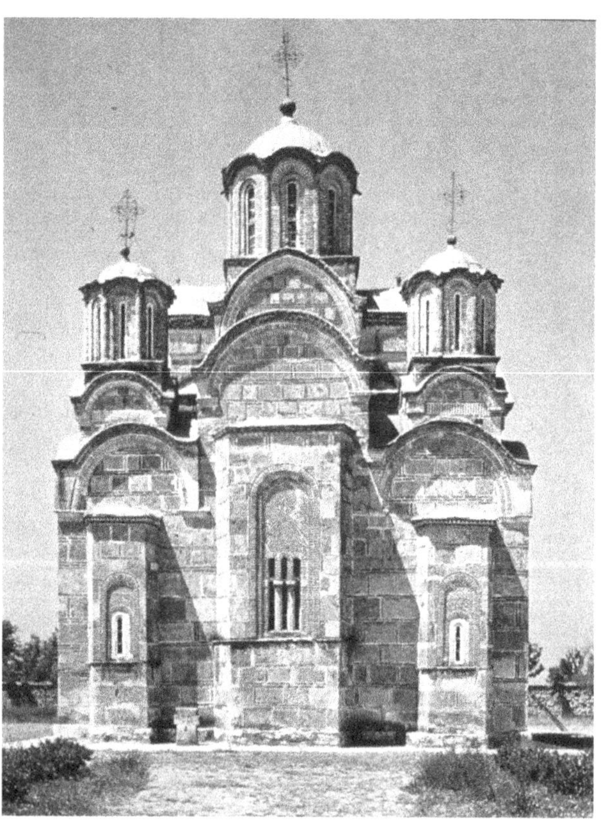

Figure 40. Gracanica, Serbia, 1314

of active Byzantinization in Serbia occurred during the reign of Kral Stefan Uros II Milutin (1300-1321). The churches of Saint Nikita in Cucer, Bogoroditsa Ljeviska in Prizren, Saint George in Staro Nagoricino and the Koimesis cathedral in Gracanica (Fig. 40) show influence from Thessaloniki and perhaps Epiros.

The last phase of direct Byzantine import occurred during the reign of Tsar Stefan Uros IV Dusan (1331-1355). Church buildings and noblemen's foundations have strong links to Constantinople and Thessaloniki. The church of the Archangels in the monastery with the same name in Prizren, the church of the Virgin in Mateic, Saint Demetrios in Markov monastir show dependence on Constantinople, while the church of the Archangel Michael in Lesnovo was influenced from Thessaloniki.

Cappadocia

Cappadocia is a mountainous region in central Asia Minor that reached from the Pontic mountains to Taurus and from the Salt Lake to the Euphrates. With the exception of some areas of plain, Cappadocia was barely fertile and had never had any great population numbers. In antiquity there were three towns: Caesarea, Melitene and Tyana. The emperor owned the main part of the country and the inhabitants were his tenants. Cappadocia is rich in minerals and was famous for its herds of cattle, sheep and horses. It dominated the main road across Anatolia and was situated close to the frontier. The wars in the 3rd century AD diminished the population. The Emperor Diocletian reduced the extent of the area by founding the province Armenia from its eastern regions. To the remaining part with the capital Caesarea was added the diocese of Pontos. Hannibalianus, the nephew of Constantine the Great, was grand king, *rex regum*, over Cappadocia, Pontos and Armenia 335-337. When the Emperor Constantine the Great confiscated the temple treasures the imperial properties increased. They became *domus divina per Cappadociam* and their treasures supported the Imperial Treasury. In 371 the Emperor Valens detached the southern part and created a new province called Cappadocia Secunda with the capital in Tyana.

The writings of the Cappadocian Fathers – Basil the Great, Gregory of Nazianz and Gregory of Nyssa – offer much information about Cappadocia in the 4th century, a time of prosperity. After 363, when the area to the east of Euphrates was ceded to Persia, the strategical importance of Cappadocia increased and it also became more exposed. The Tzannoi, the Isaurians and the Huns devastated it in the 5th century and brought about a programme of fortification that was supported by the Emperor Justinian I. He rebuilt Caesarea and created a new fortified centre in Mokissos. The Persians destroyed Sebasteia in 575 and Caesarea in 611. The Arabic attacks started with a temporary conquest of Caesarea and were intensified after they took control of the Cilician gates and Tyana in 708. The wars led to the construction of strong fortifications at great distances from each other for the protection of the country. As the eastern part of the country was depopulated, Slavs from the Balkans were transferred there to strengthen the fortifications.

After the military division into themata was introduced Cappadocia was divided between thema Anatolikon and thema Armeniakon. When the military districts then were reduced at the beginning of the 9th century the old Cappadocia was divided into thema Charsianon and thema Cappadocia. In Byzantine bureaucratic language Cappadocia was a smaller southern part of the Empire that became a separate thema about 830. It then reached from Tauros to Halys and had its stronghold in Korone in the mountains above the principal invasion road of the Arabs. The governor of the province, who was also a military strategos, earned 20 gold pounds and commanded more than 4,000 men and a considerable number of fortifications. Emperor Leon VI extended Cappadocia by adding an area in the northwest at the Salt Lake.

In the middle of the 9th century the Paulicians, a religious sect, attacked Cappadocia from their base Theochrike east of the frontier. The threat was averted in 878 but the Arabic raids continued until Melitene was conquered by the Byzantines in 934. New security in the region was established by moving the border some distance to the east. The depopulation and the continuous expansion of the military land gave rise to political tensions. The Syrian and Armenian settlers helped to repopulate the country. The increasing power of the magnates resulted in a series of revolts led by Bardas Phokas and Bardas Skleros spreading from Cappadocia to Anatolia from 963 to 989. After Basil II won control with the help of the Russian Varangians, he marched against the Cappadocian aristocrats and confiscated the riches of such families as the Maleinoi. He won victories in the east and absorbed Armenia into his empire. As a compensation Armenian princes and their subjects were given land and offices in Cappadocia. A great part of the country became Armenian which led to hostility with the indigenous population. In 1057 the general over Cappadocia, Bryennios, revolted as a result of the constant Turkish attacks. The same year the Turks destroyed Melitene and in 1059 Sebasteia. After the devastation of Caesarea in 1067 Romanos IV tried to reestablish the military order in the country. He marched through Cappadocia in 1071 on his way to the fatal fight at Manzikert and after that the province was forever lost to the Empire.

Few churches from the period of the 4th to the 7th centuries have been preserved. Most famous are the rock churches and the dwellings of the hermits in the soft hills of tuff. Great congregational basilicas from the 6th and 7th centuries have been placed in the rocks at Cavusin and Ariclar. Most dated rock chapels have cells, mills, winepresses and refectories. The chapels that are dated before 843 and even earlier include SS Joachim and Anna and Nicetas the Stylite in Kizil Cukar and Saint Basil in Sinassos. The most important period of artistic production however occurred between the end of the Arab attacks on Anatolia and the Seldjuc conquest, and indicate how popular the region was as a monastic centre during the 10th century and the first half of the 11th century. Most important dated fresco cycles from this time are situated in Ayvali Kilisse or the church of Saint John (913-920) and the contemporaneous Güllü Dere, Tavsanli Kilisse and the Old Church in Toqali Kilisse and Kiliclar Kilisse in Göreme, all attributed to the "Archaic group" by Guillaume de Jerphanion, who seized upon aniconic traits such as crosses and ornaments and the great Pig House in Cavusin. The Dove-cote created in 965 by the founder and dignitary magistros Melias represents Emperor Nicephoros II Phocas and Empress Theophanu in the apse of the prothesis from the high Macedonian period. The new church in Toqali Kilisse in Göreme (Fig. 41) is dated to the middle of the 10th century, Direkli Kilisse to 976-1025 and Saint Michael to 1025-1028 near Hasan Dag, Eski Gümus close to Nigde and Saint Barbara to 1006-1021. Kurbas Kilisse (1060-1061) in Soganli and the column churches are dated to the middle of the 11th century. In architectural form, program and picturesque style these chapels reflect the tension between the cultural hegemony of the metropolis during these periods and the local artistic tradition.

Armenia

Christianity was introduced in Armenia as a state religion in 301 during the reign of Tiridates III, and Gregory the Illuminator was appointed its first bishop, consecrated by the bishop of Caesarea. Armenian art is divided into three main periods, the first between the introduction of Christianity and the Arabic invasion *ca* 301-750, the other during the time of the free Armenian kingdom *ca* 862-1021 and the third with pockets of Armenian power that had survived the Seldjuc, Georgian and Mongol reigns *ca* 1150-1500.

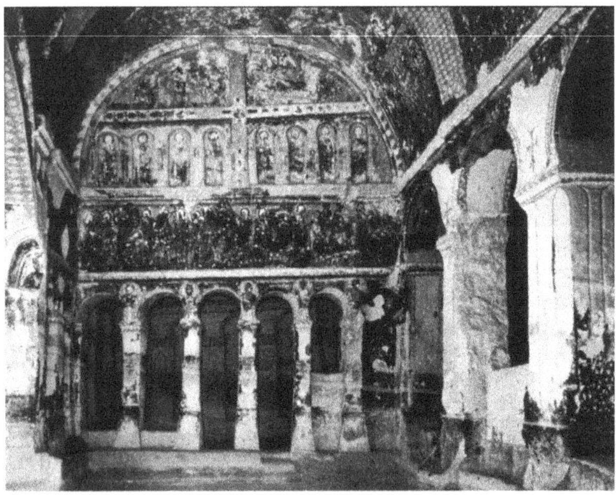

FIGURE 41. TOQALI KILISSE, GÖREME, CAPPADOCIA, MIDDLE OF THE 10TH CENTURY

Many constant elements return in the architecture. When Gregory the Illuminator converted pagan Armenia there were Hellenistic temples with broken or gabled roofs and Zoroastrian fire temples with towerlike structures covered by a dome. From the Hellenistic temple the Christian basilica was developed. Syrian influence from Kalat Siman is noticeable in the early Christian architecture. The churches were built with stone scraps and large finely composed blocks of tuff. They are vaulted and after the 6th century have domes of masonry. The exterior only hints at the disposition of the interior. The domes are enclosed in cones and pyramids and the vaults have gables. The apses are embedded in straight walls, deep niches indicate the place of the aisles and the apses. The apse buttressed or niche buttressed square is typical for the early domed churches.

The palace church in Zwarthsnotz (Fig. 42) is most famous, elevated by Katholikos Nerses III of Ishkhan between 643 and 652, a circular round-domed building of three floors with monumental proportions. The dome is 43 metres high with a diameter of 36 metres. The sanctuary was cross-formed but only the niche of the apse had a solid wall. The other three niches were open exedras each provided with arcades supported on six columns. Between the inner sanctuary and the walls of the cathedral there runs a circular ambulatory.

Achtamar (Fig. 43), on a little island in the southeastern corner of the lake Van, was the palace church for the Ardsruni kings of Vaspurakan and was built by the architect Manuel between 915 and 921. In the rich friezes of the exterior and reliefs with Christian and Islamic traits King Gagik I is seen as the founder with the model of the church. In churches from the period in between as the Holy Apostles in Kars *muqarnas*, Islamic stalactite vaults, are common.

The domed cathedral in Ani was elevated by the famous architect Trdat who repaired the collapsed dome in Hagia Sophia in Constantinople and was commissioned by King Smbat II shortly before his death in 989 for this project. It was built during the reign of his successor King Gagik I

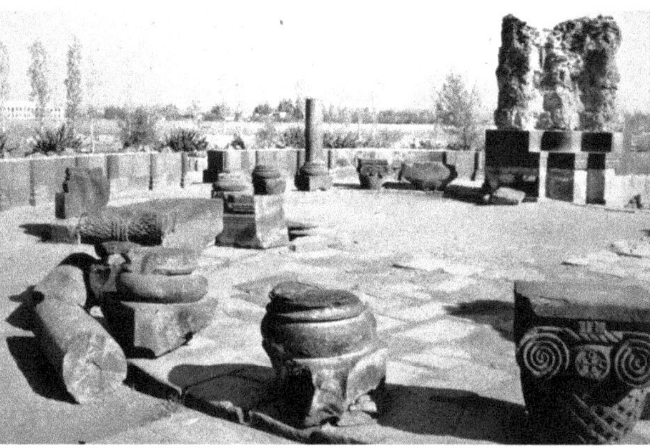

FIGURE 42. ZWARTHSNOTZ, ARMENIA, 641-661

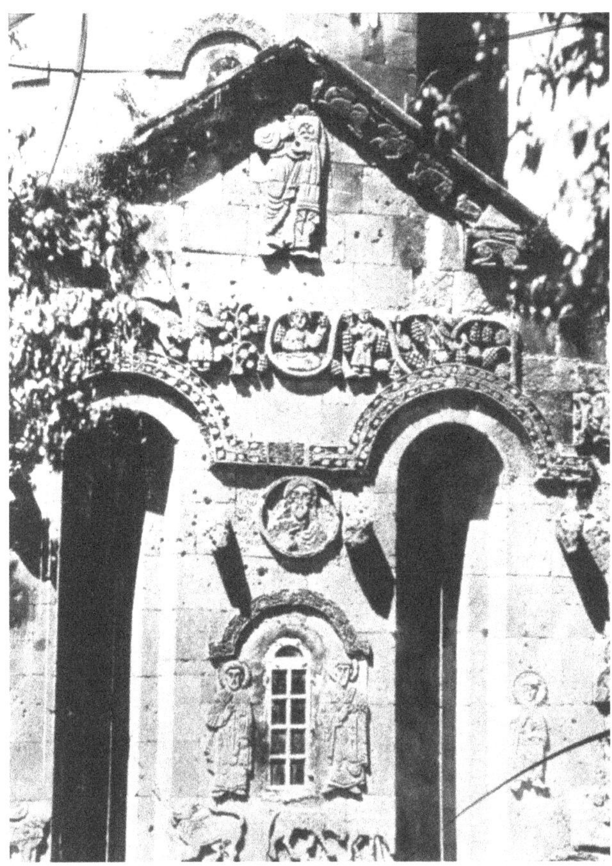

FIGURE 43. ACHTAMAR, ARMENIA, 915-921

(989-1020). The dome has like Hagia Sophia 40 windows in the base and is 30 metres in diameter and rises 55 metres over the ground. On the exterior there are blind arcades that herald the Proto-Renaissance in Italy.

The ivory triptych from the 6th century from the evangeliary from Etchmiadzin is famous, from 989 in the Manuscript department in the library Matendaran in Jerevan. The rich Armenian manuscript art has been published by Sirarpie der Nersessian.

Georgia

Iberia was converted to Christianity during the first half of the 4th century. Some churches from the early date exist as ruins, for instance Nekressi and Cheremi. Cheremi is square in form and is covered by the same type of domed roof that was found in the Mazdean temples. In the 5th century basilicas started to be built, for instance Sion in Bolinsk from 462-477, a building with three naves and a projecting altar apse. Five pairs of cross-formed pillars crowned with capitals sculpted in Sassanian style carry the ceiling. The narthex is lacking, but a big open gallery runs along the outer side of the northern wall, while a double baptistery was built along the southern wall. The ceiling had a central dome that later was copied in Djivari 586-587 and in Mskheta 604.

The typical Georgian basilica was developed into a complex in the 6th century where a trisect building body was united with three churches below a single roof. The central church is higher and wider than the lateral churches. During the 8th century the lateral churches were reshaped to porticos or exonartices. In the 7th century the dome was common in Iberia, for instance in Djivari and Mskheta and often adapted the pointed shape that is related to Armenia. Djivari (Fig. 44) was a tetraconch, a plan formed as a four leaf-clover, inscribed in a circle with arcade-formed apses that open towards the interior. The proportions are usually very large and the external walls are divided into three parts that emphasize the height of the building. Often each section of the building has been decorated with sculptures. The motifs were taken from a broad field of geometrical,

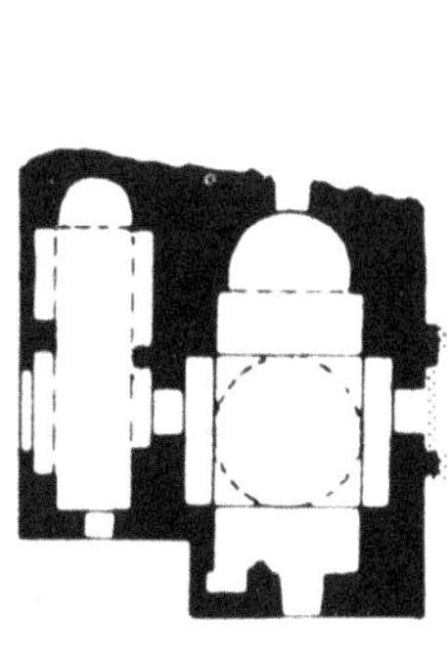

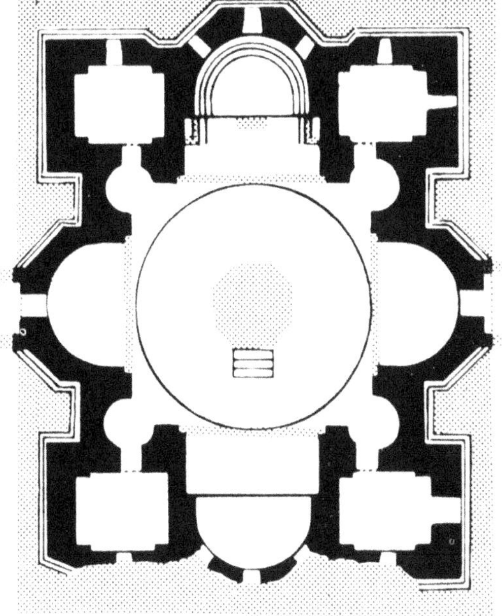

FIGURE 44. DJIVARI, GEORGIA, 7TH CENTURY

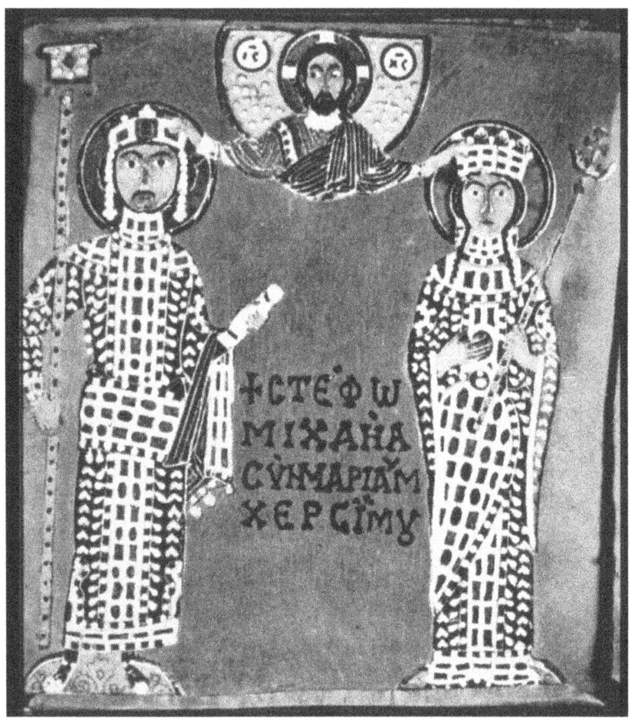

FIGURE 45. THE KHAKULI TRIPTYCH, TIFLIS, ENAMEL, 10TH-11TH CENTURY MICHAEL VII DOUKAS (1071-1078) AND MARY OF ALANY

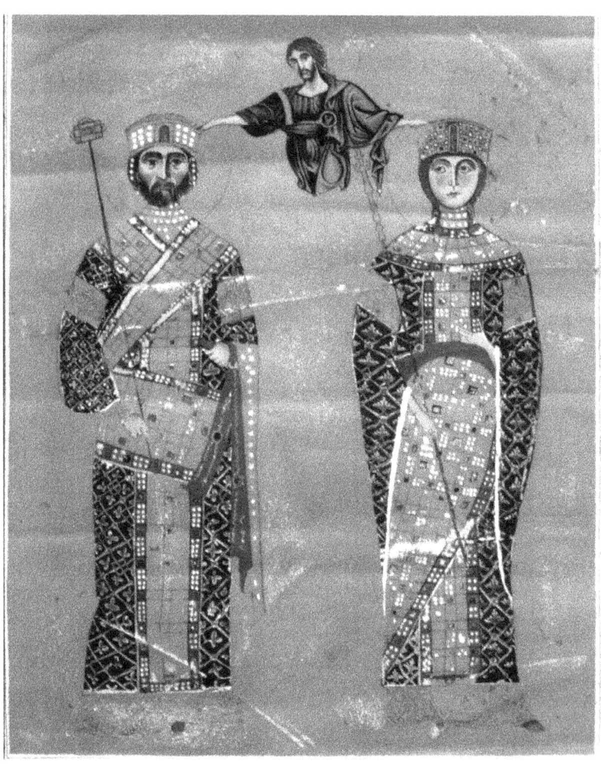

FIGURE 46. MS COISLIN 79, FOL 2 V, NICEPHOROS III BOTANEIATES (1078-1081) AND MARY OF ALANY, BIBLIOTHÈQUE NATIONALE, PARIS

vegetative, animal forms and figural scenes. Djivari is decorated on the exterior with a sculptural portrait of the Patriarch of Kartli Stefan I. The sculptures were executed both in high and low relief and each wall had its own cycle.

The sculptural style was closely connected to the exclusive embossed and chased pieces of metal that the Georgians produced with great skill from the early to late Medieval age. The sculpted stelae and altar railings of stone were both Sassanian and Christian in character. In enamel art Georgia appeared as a dignified rival of Byzantium. The technique is somewhat different in the production of the émail cloisonnée on gold and the final form of the enamel is more transparent than the Byzantine. The most famous enamels are preserved in the Georgian National Museum of Tiflis, of which the Khakhuli triptych seems to be the most important with both Georgian and Byzantine enamels. Decorated plates of chased metal cover the triptych, in the middle in red gold and on the sides there is an alloy of silver and gold. A Deesis icon with the Virgin in the middle descends from the first half of the 10th century. Of the image of the Virgin only the transparent enamels of face and hands remain. It differs from the Byzantine style by coarser facial traits. On the lock of the triptych there is a squared plate of enamel, a Byzantine work from Constantinople of Emperor Michael VII Doukas (1071-1078) and his consort the Georgian Empress Mary of Alany crowned by Christ (Fig. 45). She carries a Georgian sceptre of the same type that is found in the illumination MS Coislin 79, fol 2 v (Fig. 46) in the Bibliothèque nationale in Paris, where she originally was represented with the same Emperor, but after that Michael had been forced to resign from the throne and retire to a monastery and the young Empress was forced to marry the old Emperor Nicephoros III Botaneiates (1078-1081) to secure the status of her son, his head has been repainted over that of Michael on the miniature.

Some of the most splendid churches in Georgia are dated to the 11th and 12th centuries, when the country reached its peak of political greatness and economical prosperity. The cathedral in Kutais from 1003 and Msketha from 1040 have very high and wide domes and are spacious. In Khakhetia the palaces were two-floor buildings with an audience hall in the upper floor. They were illuminated by big closely-sited windows and it is supposed that they recall those of the Blachernae palace in Constantinople. The ruined palace in Gegat built in 1156 by George III, father of the mighty Queen Tamara (1184-1212) of Georgia was square in plan and enclosed a large central hall. Both brick and polished stones were used and ceramic roof slabs, perhaps influenced by Islamic art.

Until the 6th century the Georgian church was under Monophysitic influence and this perhaps explains why the earlier churches lack mural painting. When the Georgian church came under Byzantine jurisdiction mural paintings became common. The oldest are found in Djivari dated to 545-586. The Georgian masters developed their own style. The dome was often decorated with a cross in a medallion instead of the Byzantine Pantocrator image and a Deesis was placed in the apse instead of the Virgin, while the apse was treated as more important than the dome from the artistic point of view.

Miniatures are an important Georgian art. Most of them date from the 11th and 12th centuries. They were influenced by the Byzantine tradition both in style and iconography. Many were painted by monks who lived in the Georgian monastery Iviron on Mount Athos. Later Georgian masters produced secular miniatures that are closer to the Persian art, in particular numerous manuscripts in astrology between the 11th and 17th centuries.

Chapter 4

Byzantine sculpture

Statues reliefs ivory plates steatites

Of Byzantine sculpture very little is preserved. If we take the porphyry statue of the tetrarchs (Fig. 47) from the beginning of the 4th century which nowadays is exposed on the façade of San Marco in Venice and depicts the two augusti Diocletian and Maximinian, who resided in Milano and Nicomedia and the two caesars Galerius and Constantine Chlorus, the father of Constantine the Great, as a point of departure, we have entered Byzantium. Here the austere and somewhat brutal antique physionomy of the soldier emperor has stiffened into a mask and the figures are decoratively schematisized in geometrical patterns. We meet the same tendency on the Constantinian arch (Fig. 2) with some reliefs from the early Imperial period. It forms symmmetrical hieratic scenes that surround the official appearances of the emperor and emphasize his divinity and superhuman quality. Similar scenes are found on the Galerius' arch in Thessaloniki and on the Theodosius' obelisk in Constantinople.

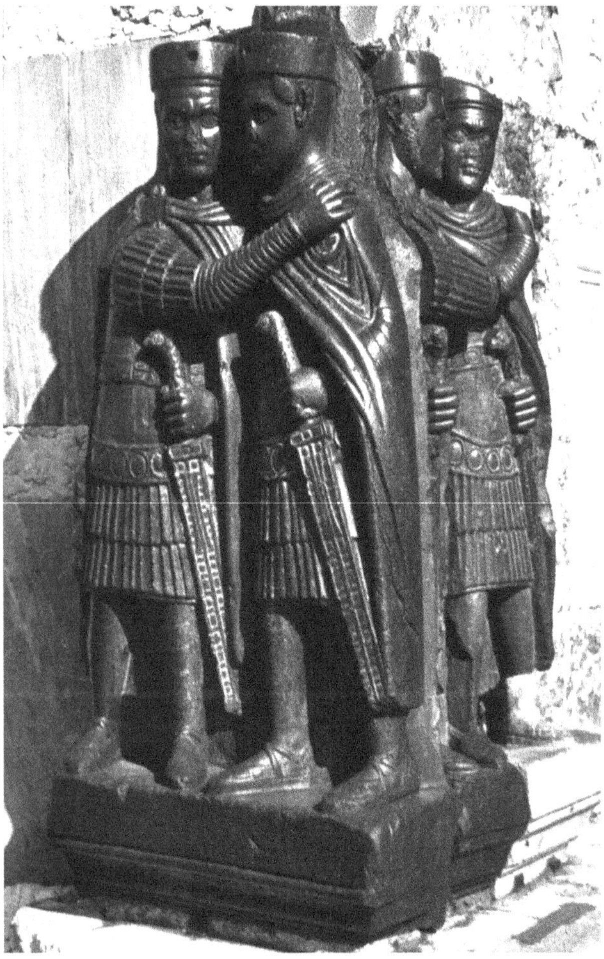

Figure 47. The Tetrarchs, San Marco, Venice, porphyry, beginning of the 4th century

The colossal portrait of Constantine the Great in the Palazzo dei Conservatori in Rome (Fig. 1) is the point of departure of the pneumatic imperial portrait. The Barletta statue (Fig. 23) is the only preserved free-standing bronze sculpture in the round. It represents most likely Emperor Markianos who ruled from 450-457. The exaggeratedly large and simplified form expresses the character of the supermundane ruling sovereign who unites the Roman Empire into a new entity. Andreas Alföldi divides the Late Roman imperial garment into three types: the costume of peace, the martial costume and the triumphal costume. We see the third variety represented here.

From the sources it is evident that triumphal columns erected in Constantinople carried imperial statues on the top. The statue of Constantine the Great in the Phoros forum in the form of Apollo carried Constantine's head in a crown of rays. The statue of Theodosius II (408-450) was erected on a column with spirals that represented his military triumphs in the Forum Tauri and on another column at the Arcadius forum. Justinianus' column was placed on the Augusteion with a horseman's statue that is similar to the statue drawn in the manuscript of Gregory of Nazianz's homilies, Par Grec 510 fol 409 v in the Bibliothèque nationale in Paris, that represents Julianus Apostata (361-363). It is also found on a drawing from the 14th century preserved in the Seraglio at Istanbul (Fig. 24), drawn by Mordmann. Emperor Justin I erected a column at the Deuteron, another close to Zeuxippos' baths and Phokas a column close to the Tetrapylon.

A relief statue of the coachman Porphyrios (Fig. 48) from the 6th century in the Archaeological museum at Istanbul shows the same heroic character. The bronze horses (Fig. 49) from a Helios quadriga now exposed on the façade of the entrance portal to San Marco in Venice could very probably have been part of the sculptural equipment of the Hippodrome in Constantinople. In research discussions there are different opinions about their origin. Some scholars maintain that they were sculpted by Lysippos in the 4th century BC.

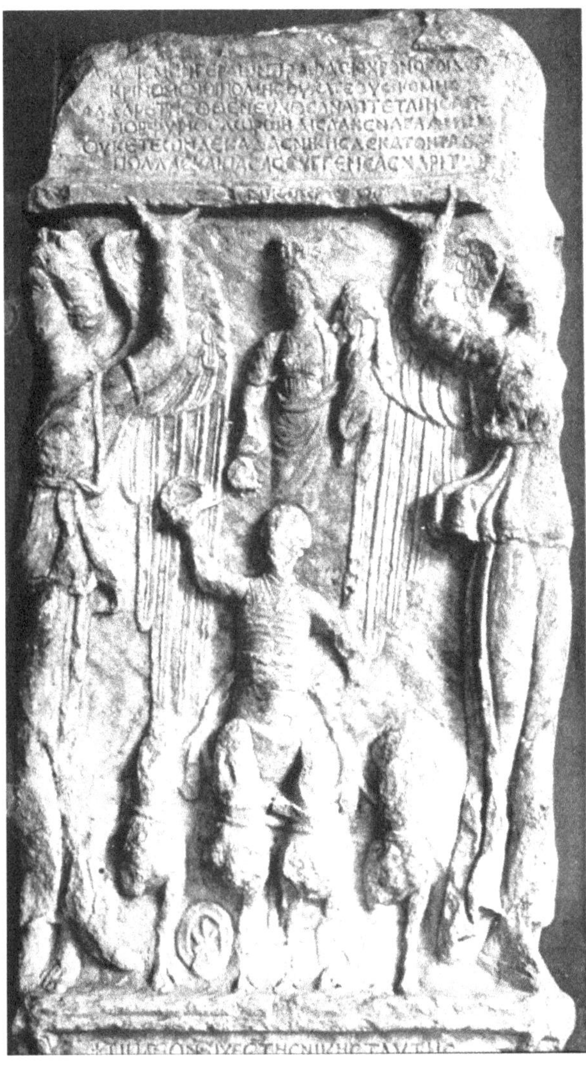

FIGURE 48. THE COACHMAN PORPHYRIOS FROM THE HIPPODROME IN CONSTANTINOPLE, THE ARCHAEOLOGICAL MUSEUM. ISTANBUL, 6TH CENTURY

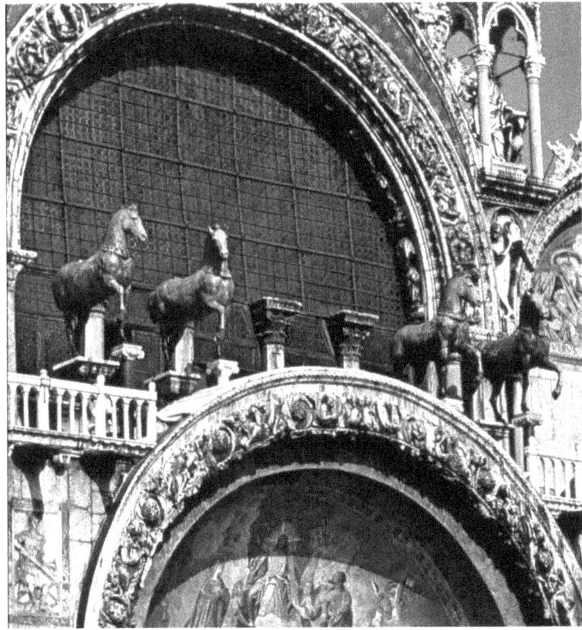

FIGURE 49. BRONZE HORSES, SAN MARCO, VENICE, 4TH CENTURY BC

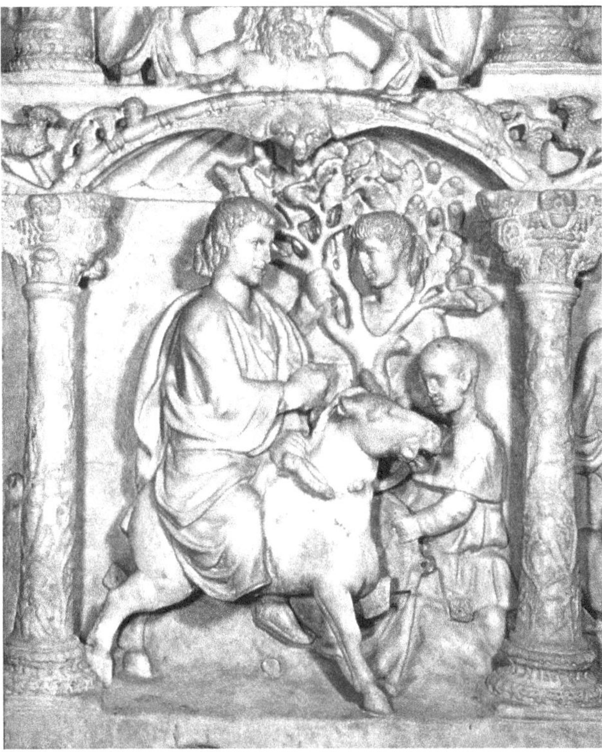

FIGURE 50. JUNIUS BASSUS SARCOPHAGUS, MARBLE, 359, THE VATICAN, ROME

In Late Antique relief, on sarcophagii, the figures of the New Testament appear in idyllic scenes with motifs of philosophers and shepherds recalling Greek sculpture. Constanzas' porphyry sarcophagus is decorated with Late Antique reliefs with playing putti and animal friezes. The Christian sarcophagus either shows a throng of figures with strong plasticity, or figures enclosed in divided scenes with a pronounced feeling for symmetry and proportion. Most perfect is Junius Bassus' sarcophagus (Fig. 50) *ca* 350 AD in Pentelic marble, which shows scenes from the Life of Christ, with a youthful beardless Christ in the Hellenistic spirit with picturesque polished surfaces where the antique frame is interrupted by alternating rounded and broken arcs.

The sculptural tradition continues in ivory. Since elephants were considered to be the cleanest of all animals, ivory symbolizes purity. The Lipsanothek in Brescia (Fig. 51) from about 360, in the Museo Civico, has scenes from the Old and New Testament with the same youthful Apollo-like Christ. Moreover, the antique frieze set against an ideal spatial background, a heritage taken from the Parthenon, as well as the division of small scenes into space shaping perspective pointing to the Middle Ages, shows dependence on sarcophagus relief and a step toward the liberation of Christian relief art. The guardians at the Holy Sepulchre from about 400 in the Trivulzio collection in Milan show new efforts to create real space.

Maximianus' (545-553) episcopal throne (Fig. 52) in Ravenna dates to the 6th century and is preserved in the

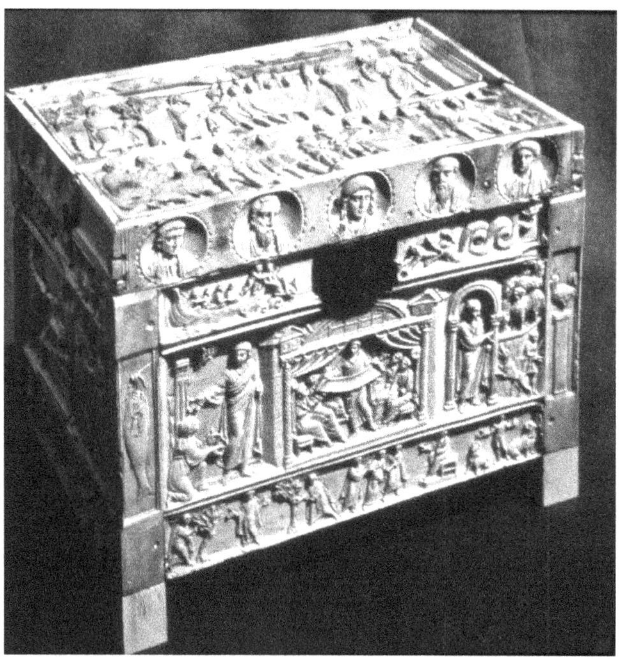

FIGURE 51. THE LIPSANOTHEK IN BRESCIA, IVORY, 360-370, MUSEO CIVICO, BRESCIA

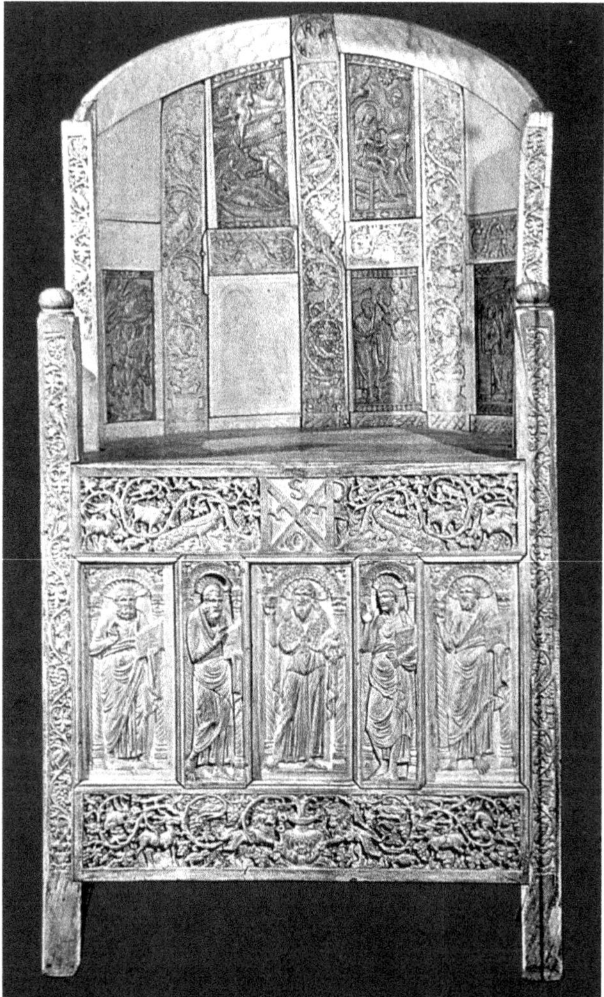

FIGURE 52. MAXIMIANUS' (545-553) THRONE, RAVENNA, IVORY, THE ARCHIEPISCOPAL MUSEUM, RAVENNA

Archbishop's palace. This is the only complete work of ivory that originates from the Byzantine period. On a monogram on the front side is written *Maximianus episcopus*. Originally there were 39 plates, of which some were double-sided, others framed by vegetative creepers with figures, 12 are lost and others have been replaced during the constant restorations, in particular the plates with Christ's Childhood and Miracles on the support for the back and on the back. Below the monogram and between the evangelists John the Baptist is placed, which could indicate that the throne was meant for the baptistery. Ten scenes from Joseph's life on the sides could point to the role of the Archbishop as superintendent, before the establishment of the Exarchate in Ravenna. Alexandria, Constantinople and Ravenna have been suggested as places of production. The depth of the relief and other stylistic traits vary from one iconographical group to another. The size, 1.24 metres high, and the type of construction – ivory plates attached to one another without a wooden frame – indicate that it is hardly the question of a bishop's throne. It has been suggested that it served as a stand for evangeliaries. Nothing is known about the throne in Ravenna before the 17th century.

From the schematic representations of consuls on the diptychs, with emphasized value perspective, that at the same time are portrait sculptures, another relief tradition emerges recalling the figures on the Ara Pacis, but of a more two-dimensional nature. It is important to compare the Rufus Probianus diptych from about 380 with Theodosius I's missorium (Fig. 53) from the same time honouring his decennalia, his ten years on the throne, in the year 388. This is a magnificent bowl in silver where he is enthroned together with his sons Arcadius and Honorius, and distributes the codicillus, a diptych with letters of appointment to grant office to a high official in the provincial government, and the Stilicho diptych with his wife Serena *ca* 395. The diptych of the Nichomachians and the Symmachians from around 400 shows a dependence on Greek grave stelae. The figures seem to sink into the surface and are reduced in their plasticity in such an inconspicuous way that the eye does not experience it as something unnatural.

Two silver bowls have been preserved from the rich production that imitates Persian metal sculpture, the silver bowl from Riha in Syria (Fig. 54) from the 6th century showing Christ distributing the Eucharist to his disciples, and the equestrian image of Emperor Constance II (641-668) from the 7th century that has Sassanian models. The big altar decoration in the bema of Hagia Sophia in Constantinople was made of silver and ornamented with precious stones. An artistic style reminiscent of this is found in the cathedral treasure in San Marco in Venice where the altar piece Pala d'Oro (Fig. 55) is preserved. It consists of different parts from the 11th to the 13th century and is made of gold with enamel encrustations as an iconostasis in miniature.

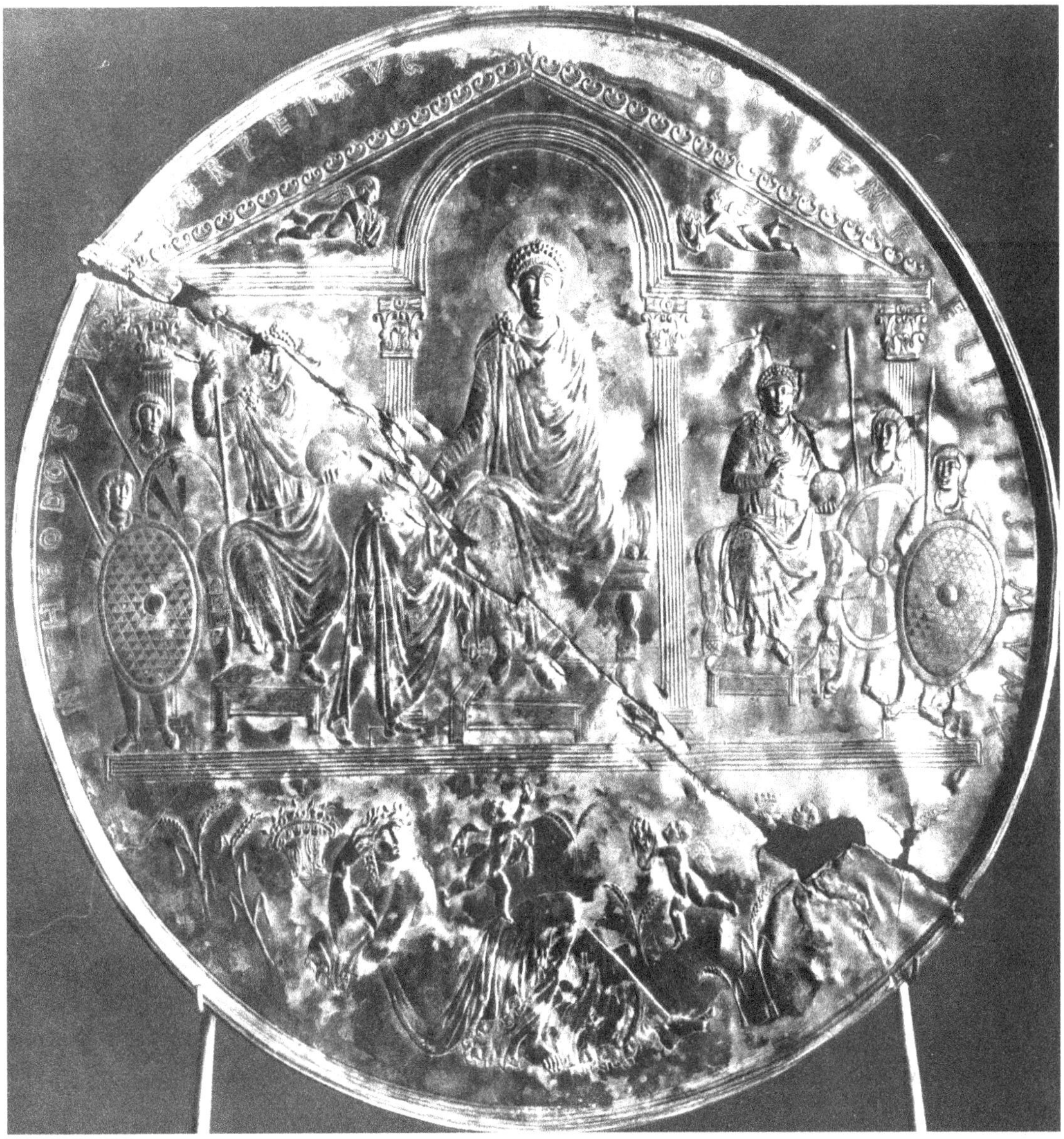

Figure 53. Theodosius' missorium, silver plate, 388, Real Academia, Madrid

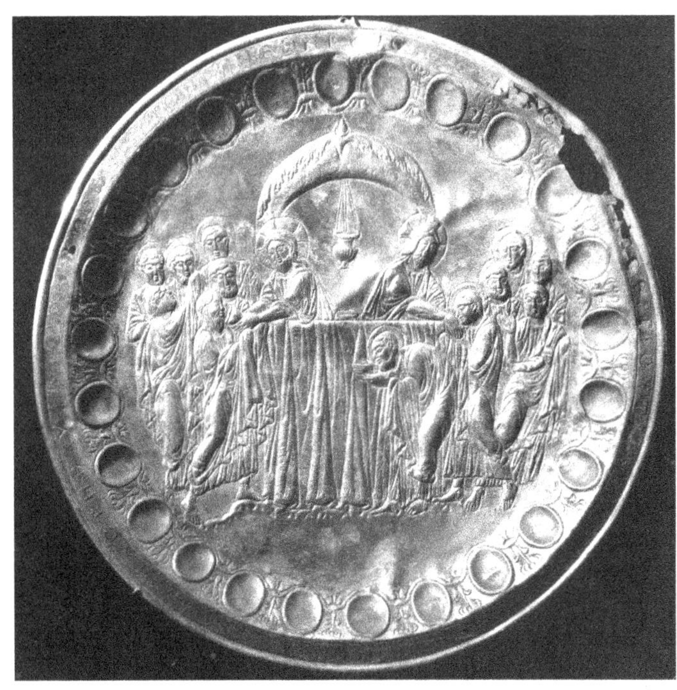

Figure 54. The Riha plate in silver, found in Syria, The Communion of the apostles, end of 6th century, Dumbarton Oaks collection, Washington DC

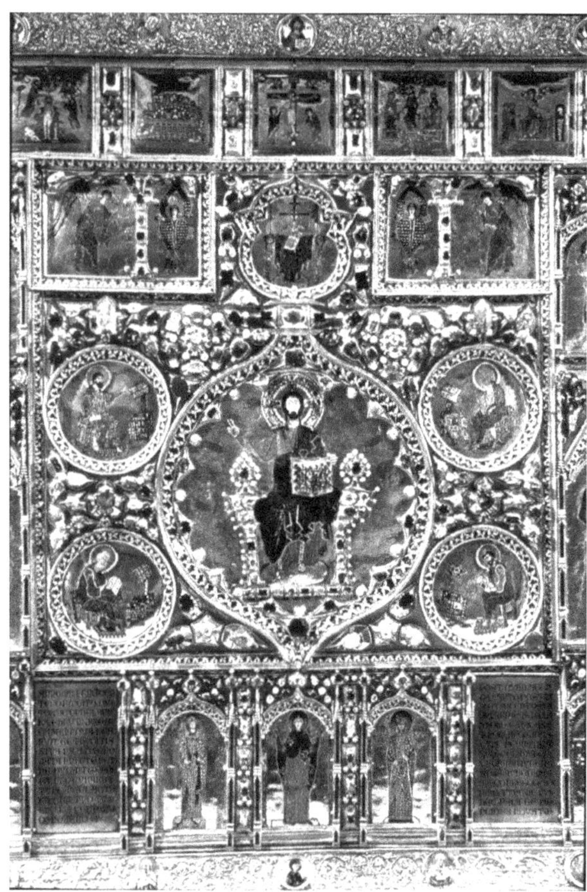

FIGURE 55. PALA D'ORO, ENAMEL AND GOLD, TREASURY OF SAN MARCO, VENICE, 11TH TO 13TH CENTURY

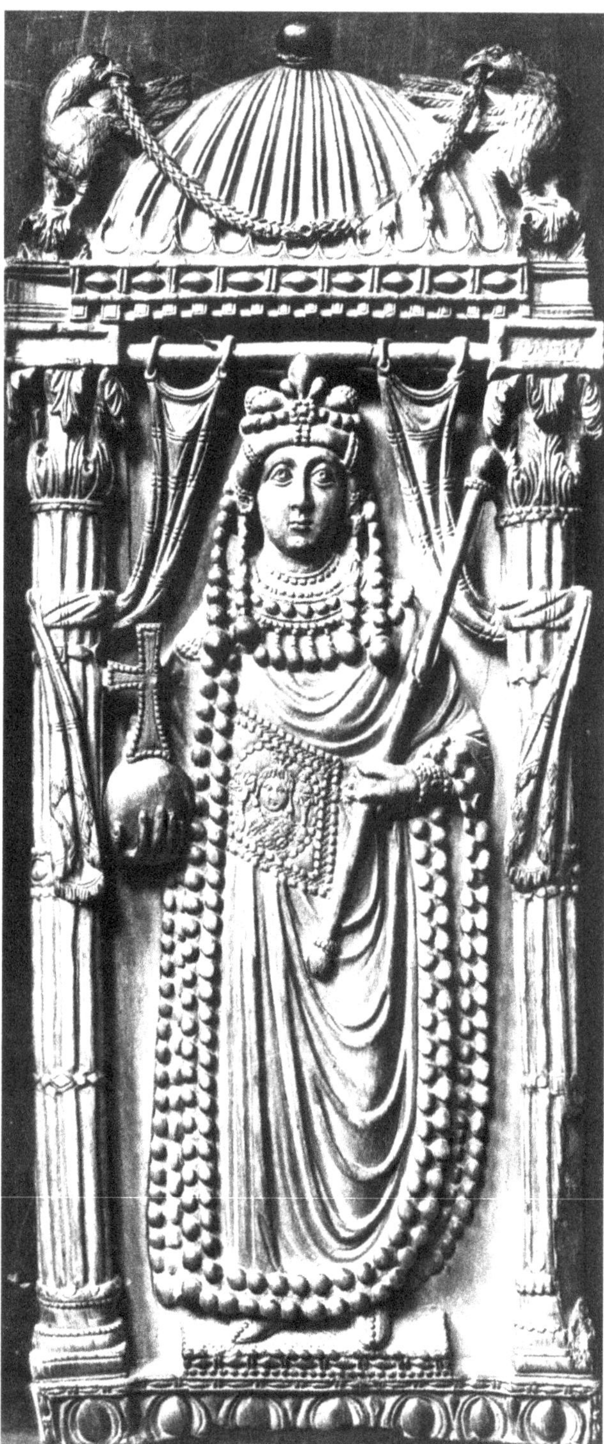

FIGURE 56. EMPRESS ARIADNE, MUSEO BARGELLO, FLORENCE, IVORY, *CA* 500

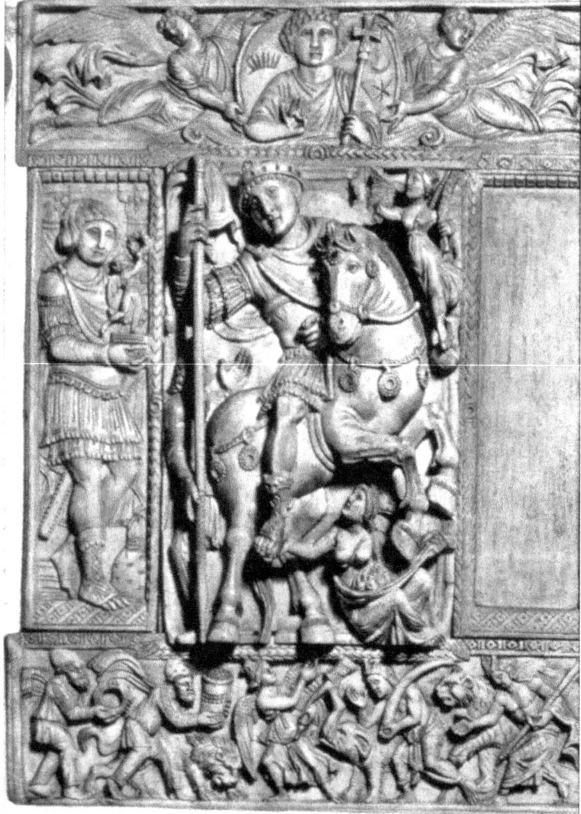

FIGURE 57. THE BARBERINI DIPTYCH, IVORY, LOUVRE, PARIS, *CA* 530

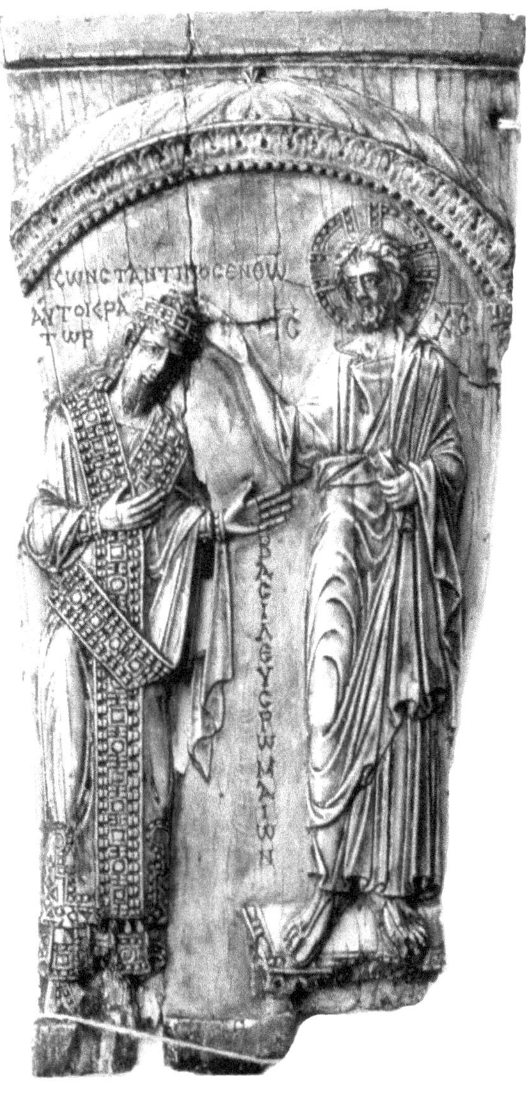

Figure 58. Constantine VII Porphyrogennetos (913-959) crowned by Christ, ivory, State Historical Museum, Moscow

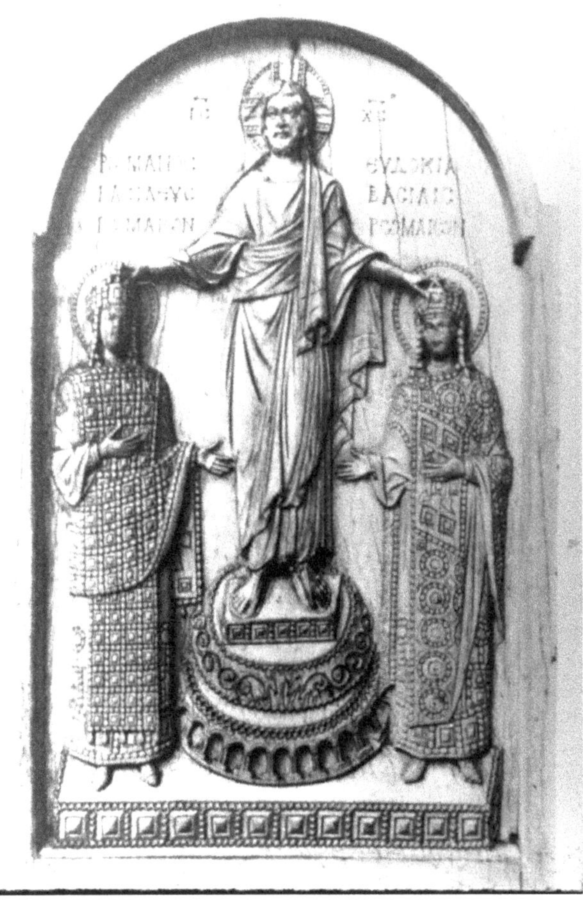

Figure 59. Romanos IV (1069-1071) and Eudokia, ivory, Cabinet des Médailles, Bibliothèque nationale, Paris

The ivory plate of the Empress Ariadne (Fig. 56) from about 500 in Bargello in Florence and another in the Kunsthistorisches Museum in Vienna demonstrate the mature Byzantine style, with its strict frontality, its ceremonial emphasis on the divinity of the augusta within the frame of the throne baldaquin with the insignia, the sceptre and the *grobus cruciger*, the cross-decorated world globe, and the theatral effect of the drawn draperies that make the divine parousia appear. On her splendid pearl-decorated chlamys the Empress carries a stylized portrait of her son Leon II (474) on the tablion with pearls, an application in cloth that shows the same frontal figure of the Emperor with the open jewel crown and the insignia that are found on the obverse side of his gold coins.

The most magnificent ivory plate of all, the Barberini diptych (Fig. 57) in the Louvre in Paris, the middle part of a pentaptyk, a plate in five pieces, that is supposed to represent Justinian I, shows the Emperor in three-quarter profile riding on a horse that has all the attributes of the horses in San Marco (Fig. 49), surrounded by antique personifications. To the sides stand court dignitaries who carry images of Nike, the goddess of victory, in their hands. Gaia, the personification of the fertile earth, is situated below and appears in value perspective, as well as an acclaiming Phrygian. Above is a symmetrical frame of a beardless Christ with angels with palms in their hands and below a register of barbarians carrying tributes.

On an ivory plate in the cathedral treasury in Trier from the 6th century a procession of relics is represented, that in the latest interpretation by Gary Vican was directed towards the Empress Pulcheria, the sister of Theodosius II. With lively richness of details and the profane scenes it demonstrates strong plasticity in the figures.

The ivory plates of the Macedonian renaissance have attracted great interest from scholars. The ivory plate in the Berlin Dahlem Museum, the upper part of a sceptre with the Emperor Leon VI surrounded by Christ and the Virgin in a mussel-shaped throne niche is dated to 886. Constantine VII Porphyrogennetos (913-959) (Fig. 58) crowned by Christ in State Historical Museum in Moscow is dated to the 10th century. The Romanos plate (Fig. 59) in the Cabinet des Médailles in Paris has been dated

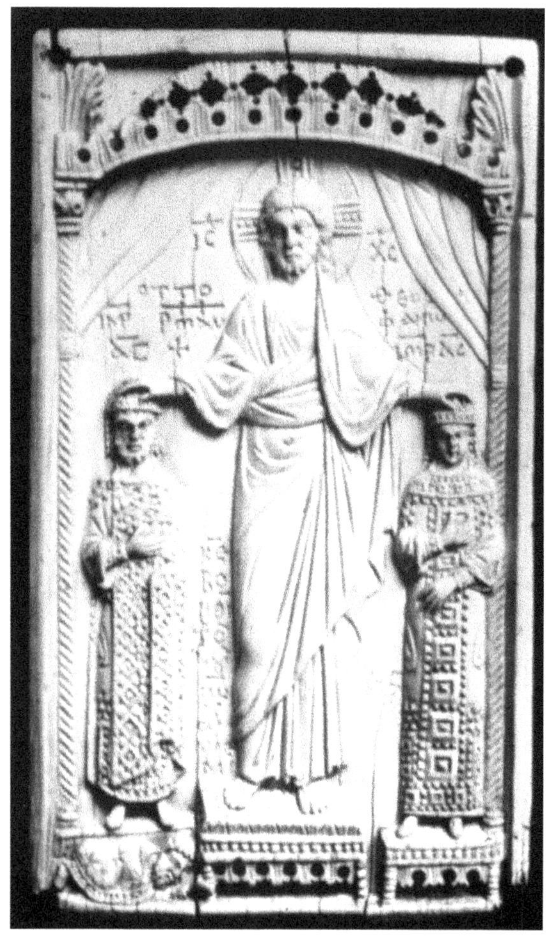

FIGURE 60. OTTO II (955-983) AND THEOPHANO, IVORY, MUSÉE CLUNY, PARIS

anew by Ioli Kalavrezou Maxeiner. According to Adolph Goldsmith and Kurt Weitzmann it represents Romanos II (959-963) the son of Constantine VII Porphyrogennetos and is dated to the 10th century. In the new interpretation it is considered to represent Romanos IV (1069-1071) and is dated around 1070. Charles Diehl originally suggested the first interpretation. The new one builds on a complex discussion about the title of the Empress Eudokia, *basilis Rhomaion*. One of the arguments is that Romanos is beardless and that Empress Eudokia Makembrolitissa had already reigned during the time of Constantine X Doukas (1059-1067). If this is correct it will have important consequences for the dating of the plates of the so-called Romanos Group.

The ivory plate of the German Emperor Otto II (955-983) and Empress Theophano (Fig. 60) carved in Italy from the second half of the 10th century must then have another Byzantine model that has disappeared. The Veroli casket (Fig. 61) from the 10th century demonstrates the Macedonian renaissance in its most pure form. The artistic program is totally antique, with scenes among others of the abduction of Europa.

Among the steatites that have been published by Ioli Kalavrezou Maxeiner in a corpus edition of the State

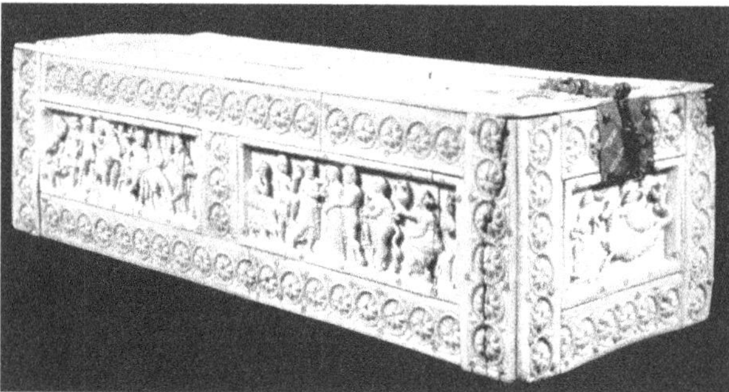

FIGURE 61. THE VEROLI CASCET, IVORY 10TH-11TH CENTURY, VICTORIA AND ALBERT MUSEUM, LONDON

Historical Museum in Stockholm is an example, found in Källunge parish on Gotland, that represents Christ's Crucifixion, the *Stavrosis* (Fig. 62). It is dated to the 12th century when the production of ivories had diminished and steatites experience a renaissance.

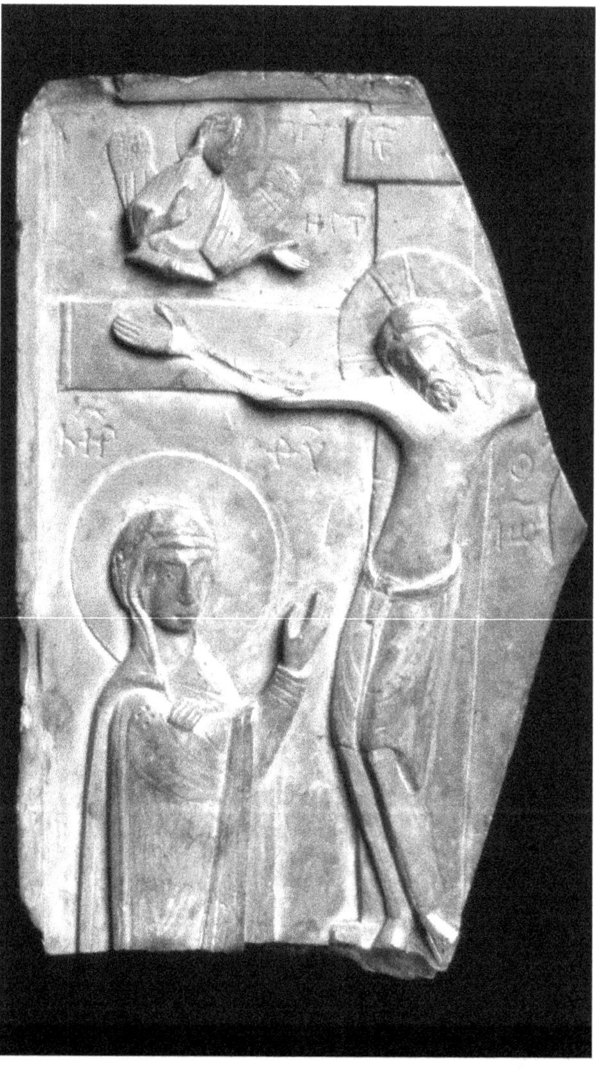

FIGURE 62. STAVROSIS, THE CRUCIFIXION, STEATITE, KÄLLUNGE, GOTLAND, 12TH CENTURY

CHAPTER 5

MOSAICS AND MURAL PAINTING

Pearl hosiery and artistic handicraft

During the period before Constantine the Great Christian art was principally burial monuments belonging to a Christian minority, mostly in Rome. Different types of crosses and Christ monograms are inscribed on the burial monuments or on oil lamps. The cross is identified with the Greek letter chi and the Christ monogram is associated with the fish symbol, corresponding to the Greek word *ichtys*, that was interpreted as Iesous Christos Theou Hyios Soter, Jesus Christ the Son of God, the Saviour. The characteristic iconography of Christ was developed in the Dura baptistery in the 3rd century AD and in the Roman catacombs in the 4th century. Christ appears on the sarcophagus mostly as the Good Shepherd and scenes from the Old Testament dominate, alongside for instance the Last Supper, which is represented on an antique Sigma table. Female orants are prototypes for the Virgin Mary.

The churches were decorated with mosaics or lime frescoes on the walls and the floors were covered with stone slabs, so-called *opus Alexandrinum*, or with marble mosaics. The Roman style differs at an early stage from the Syrian, which is more expressive. Mary with the Child from Coemeterium maius is very picturesque. Italian mosaics were influenced by eastern Hellenistic and in particular Alexandrian art. Blue and gold vary in the backgrounds. An abstract ornamentation with cross types and rosettes enclosed in star-shaped or six-edged figures indicate an influence from textiles.

Santa Maria Antiqua decorated during the pontificate of Pope Liberius (352-366) shows a limited colour range and primary colours with strong touches of orange. Saint John's baptismal church in Naples from the second half of the 4th century and San Aquilinus in Milan from the same time have other examples of early Christian mosaics.

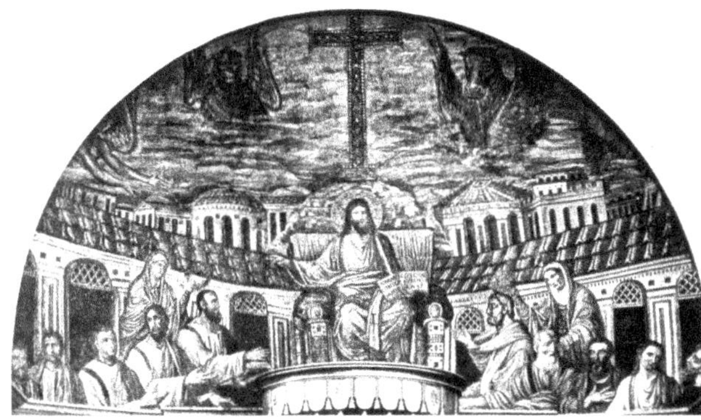

FIGURE 63. SANTA PUDENZIANA, MOSAIC, ROME, BEGINNING OF 5TH CENTURY

The apse mosaic in Santa Pudenziana (Fig. 63) during the pontificate of Pope Innocentius II (402-417) constitutes the breakthrough of the mature Christian mosaic. In the background appears the heavenly Jerusalem and the Cross decorated with jewels on Golgotha. The four beings from the vision of Ezekiel, who are interpreted as the four evangelists, are looking down at the enthroned Christ. To the right is seen Saint Peter with a woman who represents the Jewish Christian church, Santa Pudenziana, and to the left Saint Paul with the pagan Christian church, Santa Praxedis. In the architectural coulisses the influence from Pompeii is revealed. Christ is depicted bearded in the Oriental version. The suggestive image with its peculiar perspective is characterized by mysticism. In Santa Sabina during the pontificate of Pope Celestin (422-432) these two churches are also represented as *Ecclesia ex gentibus* and *Ecclesia ex circumsione* and also the Hetoimasia, the empty throne.

In Santa Maria Maggiore (Fig. 64) the tendency is more sober. It is attributed to the pontificate of Pope Sixtus III

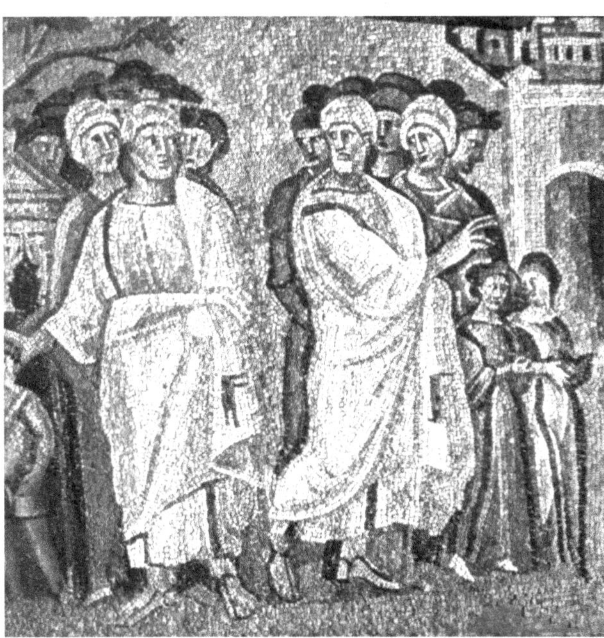

FIGURE 64. SANTA MARIA MAGGIORE, MOSAIC, 432-440, ABRAHAM AND LOT, ROME

(432-440). On the clerestory wall of the central nave there are fields with Old Testament scenes, on the triumphal arch united scenes with the Virgin Mary and the Childhood of Christ. The apocryphical gospel of Matthew might have influenced the iconography on the scenes on the triumphal arch that are more dogmatic, perhaps they were created immediately after the council of Ephesus in 431. The Old Testament scenes are narrative with a picturesque background and the scenes that describe the Life of the Virgin Mary and Christ are continuous in a way that recalls the Roman 2nd century, for instance the columns of Trajan and Marcus Aurelius. The Hetoimasia with evangelist symbols is depicted. Mosaics from the first half of the 5th century are found in Santa Matrona in San Prisco, showing the Hetoimasia and the evangelist symbols, and in San Ambrogio in Milan.

The mosaics in Thessaloniki reflect the art of Constantinople. Saint George's rotunda (Fig. 65) from the second part of the 5th century owns the earliest preserved monumental mosaics in East Rome. In the niche vault of the wall, birds, stylized plants and geometrical figures recall the art of Syria and Cilicia as it is reproduced in Santa Constanza in Rome. The lower part of the dome shows architectonical compositions of great complexity that form backgrounds for the figures of saints in unusual positions. The Pompeian style and Alexandrian mosaics have been proposed as the inspiration, but it might also reflect real architecture that has been lost. Saint Demetrius (Fig. 66) has mosaics preserved in fragments from the 7th century that show the title saint surrounded by spiritual and secular hierarchs, Bishop John who repaired the church in 654 and the Eparch Leontius. San Vitale in Ravenna, the baptisteries, San Apollinare in Classe and San Apollinare Nuovo have been treated above in the chapter on architecture.

Floor mosaics have been preserved in great variety in the Near East and North Africa. Scenes from the Old and New Testament are in principle avoided and instead geometrical patterns, birds, the zodiac, the seasons, flood landscapes and hunting scenes are depicted. The Nile scene in the 5th century floor in the cathedral in Aquileja (Fig. 67) shows fishing cupids that symbolize the priests. A popular scene in Syria in Cilicia is the Messianic paradise, the prophecy of Isaiah. A rustique version is found in Asyas (Eleousa Sebaste), another from the 5th century in Misis (Mospuestia) with relations from the history of Noah and Simson. In the Great palace in Constantinople there is a suite of profane floor mosaics preserved from the 6th century with idyllic scenes and animal motives (Fig. 68).

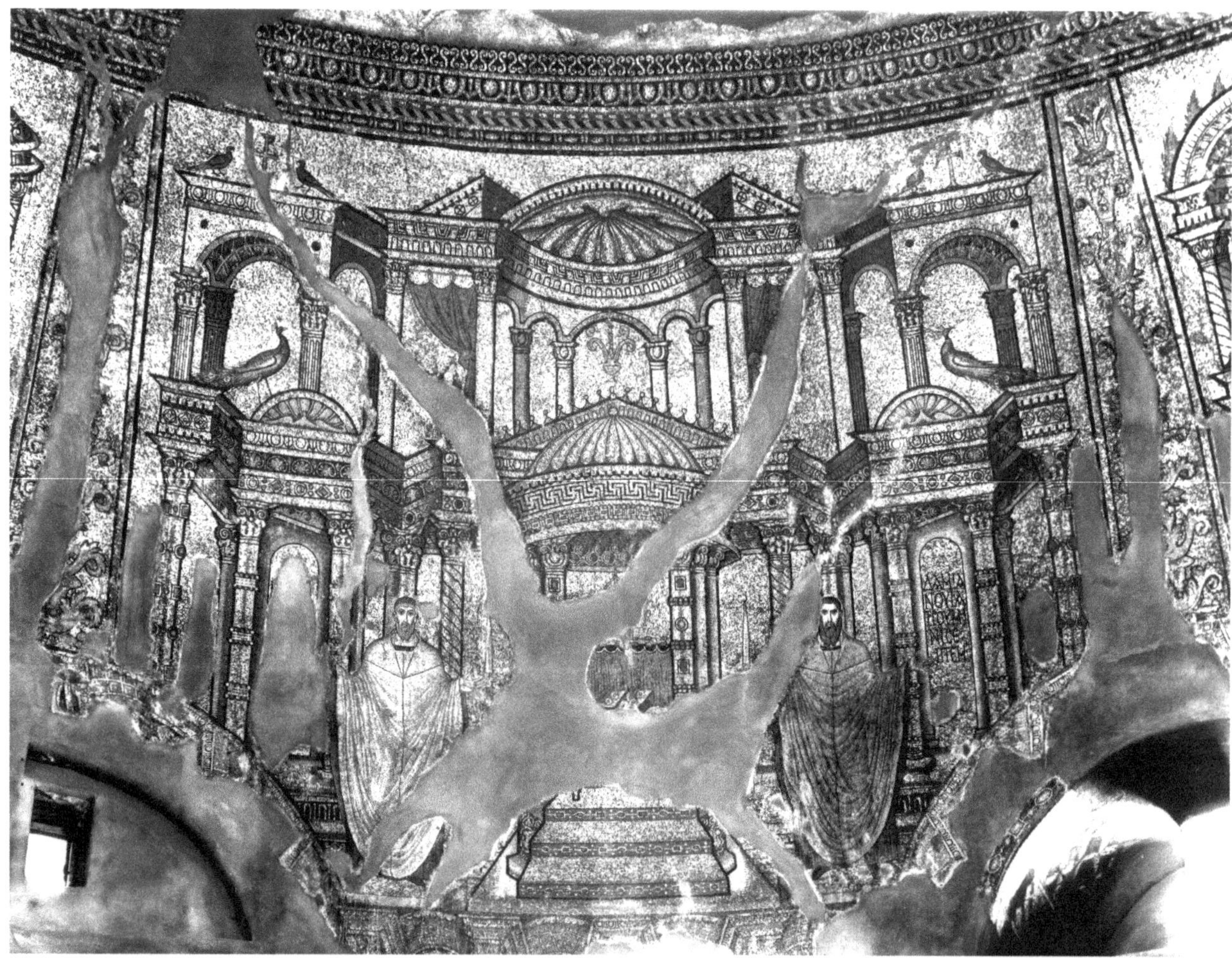

FIGURE 65. THE ROTUNDA OF SAINT GEORGE, MOSAIC, SECOND HALF OF THE 5TH CENTURY, THESSALONIKI

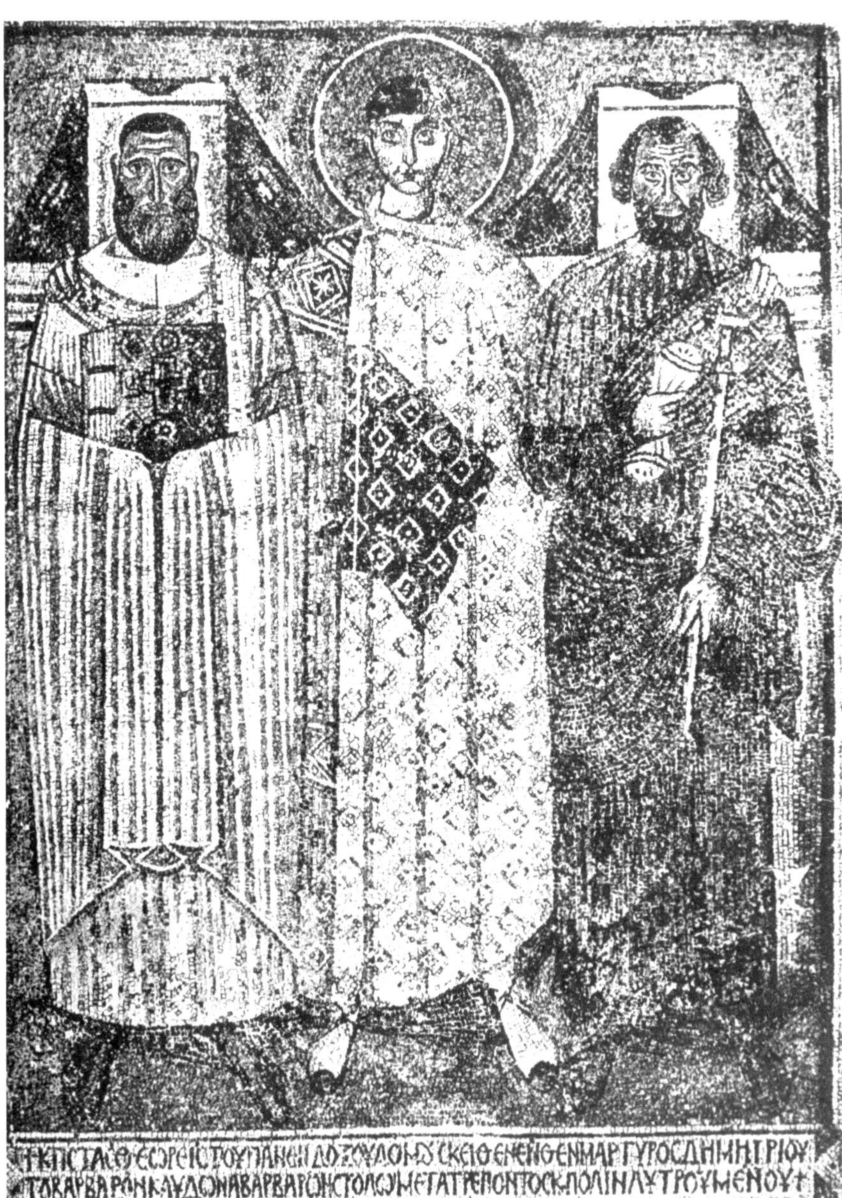

FIGURE 66. SAINT DEMETRIUS, MOSAIC, THESSALONIKI, *CA* 635

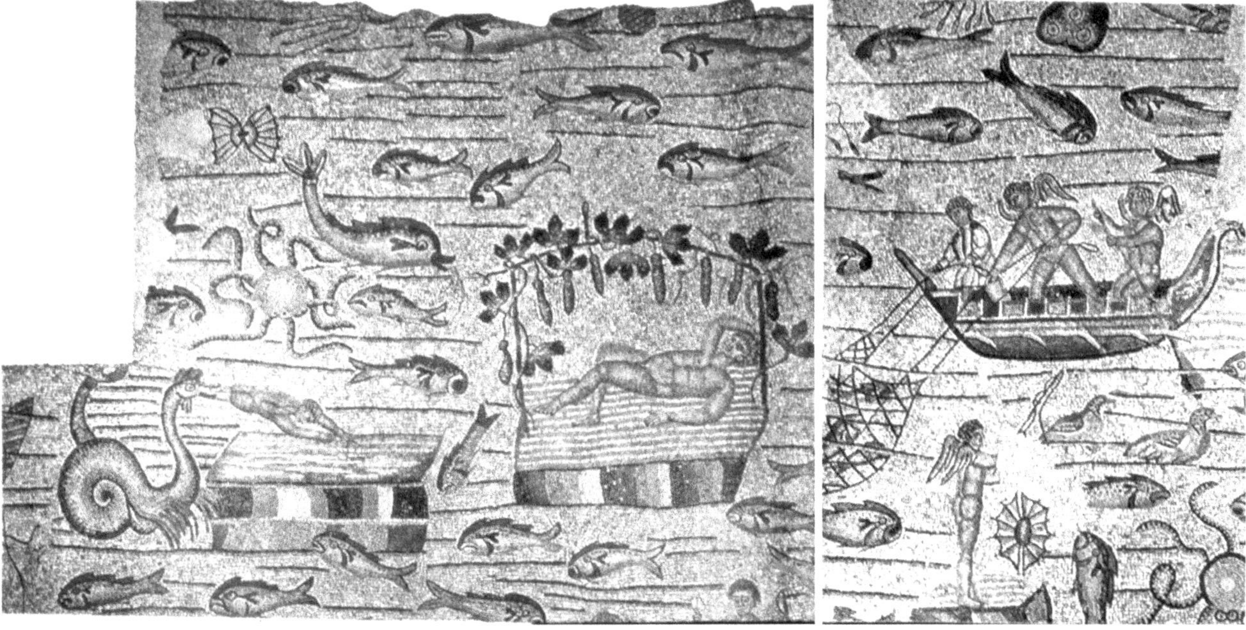

FIGURE 67. AQUILEIA, MOSAIC, THE CATHEDRAL OF AQUILEIA, 5TH CENTURY

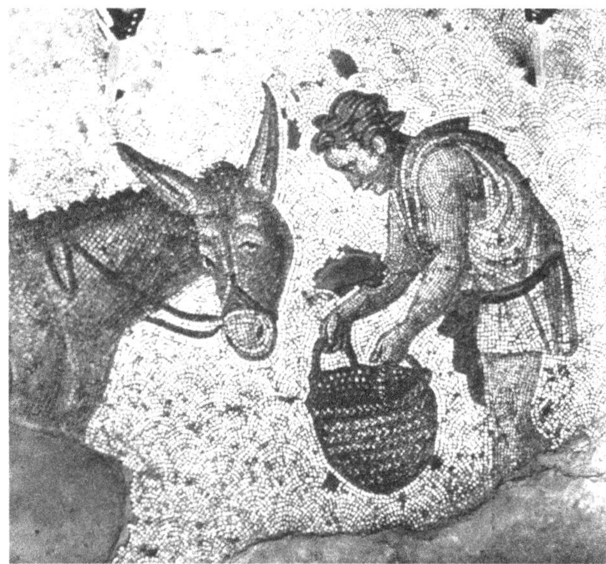

FIGURE 68. THE GREAT PALACE MOSAIC, CONSTANTINOPLE, 6TH CENTURY

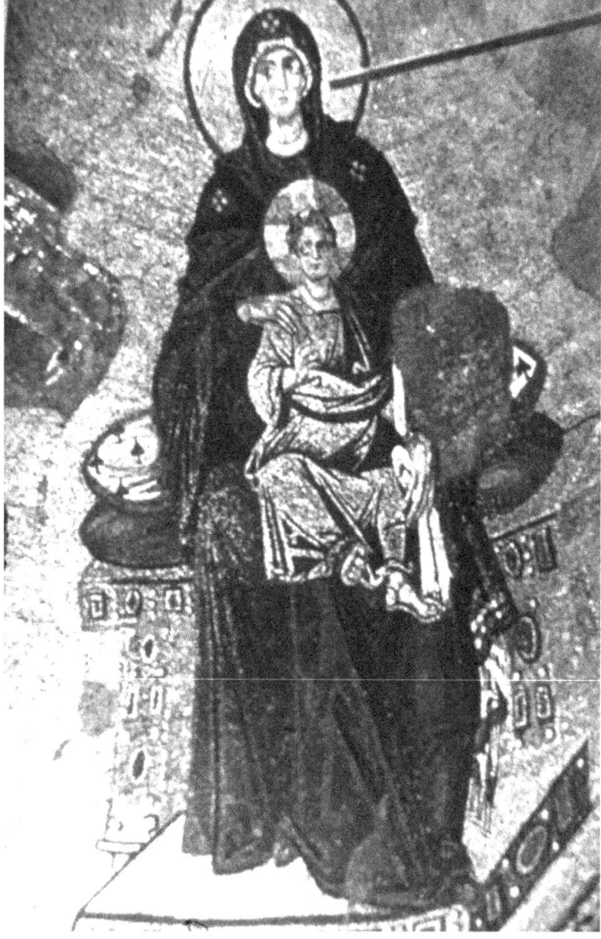

FIGURE 69. THE VIRGIN IN THE APSE MOSAIC IN HAGIA SOPHIA, CONSTANTINOPLE, 867

In Hagia Sophia in Constantinople mosaic art reaches its absolute pinnacle during the 9th century when the apse is decorated with its paradigmatic madonna image, a Maria Kyriotissa with the Christ child on her lap, in around 867 (Fig. 69). About this image the Ecumenical Patriarch Photios has in an ekphrasis in a homily (nr XVII) in the cathedral formulated the interpretation in rhetorical metaphorical language. The Virgin is represented as the prototype of the living icon. At the entrance of the central nave Christ is enthroned in a lunette surrounded by the Virgin and the Angel Gabriel in round tondo medallions. In front of Christ an anonymous emperor lies on his face in proskynesis, presumably Emperor Basil I the Macedonian (867-886), who in this way tries to expiate the offence against the image of the holy Incarnation that was proclaimed by the Iconoclasts. About 913 Emperor Alexander is depicted in full imperial Macedonian attire. At the entrance of the inner narthex Emperor Constantine the Great is represented with the model of the city Constantinople in his hand and Emperor Justinian I with the model of the cathedral Hagia Sophia in his hand surrounding the Mother of God with the Child (Fig. 70). This mosaic originates from the later half of the 10th century and the portraits of the emperors depict the portrait of the ruling emperor at that time. In the 11th century the magnificent ktitor image is created on the southern gallery of Emperor Romanos III Argyros (1028-1034) and Empress Zoe in front of Christ with a foundation document (Fig. 71). After having drowned Romanos in the palace in 1034 and finally married Constantine IX Monomachos in 1042 as her third husband the Empress had the image retouched. The head of the new Emperor was placed on the mosaic and a new inscription was added. The head on the image of Christ was given his personal features and also Zoe's face was renewed. The originally frontally turned imperial couple now turn their faces in three quarter profile towards Christ in an attitude of penance. About 1118-1120 the second ktitor image in the south gallery was made of Emperor John II Comnenos (1118-1143) and Empress Irene together with their son Alexios (Fig. 72) who died in 1120. Further into the southern gallery there is a magnificent Deesis scene with Christ surrounded by the Virgin and John the Baptist (Fig. 3) that is dated to the end of the 12th century or to the 13th century.

The dome that was decorated with a naked cross has now been painted over with Turkish quotations from the Quran. Below the splendid archangel from the 9th century are situated the four cherubim who surround the throne of God. Already in early times there were mosaics in the private apartment of the Ecumenical Patriarch on the lower floor, a Deesis is preserved in fragments. Rows of saint bishops decorated the north and south walls in the central nave. Of these only fragments survive. This type of decoration became a model for the future.

Another series of mosaics with the Pantocrator image from the Middle Byzantine period are found in Fethiye Camii (Fig. 73) in Constantinople and in the Greek monastery church Hosios Loukas in Stiris in Phokis, in Daphni and in Nea Moni on Chios.

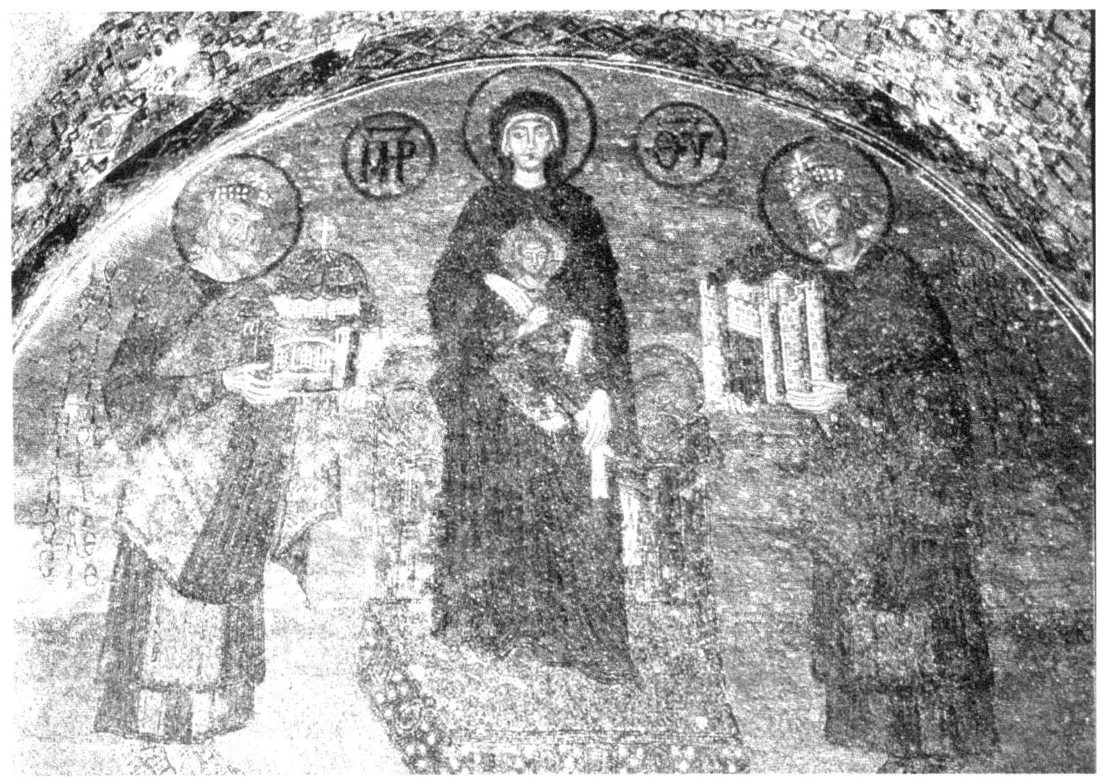

Figure 70. Justinian I and Constantine the Great in the entrance vestibule in Hagia Sophia, Constantinople, mosaic, 10th century

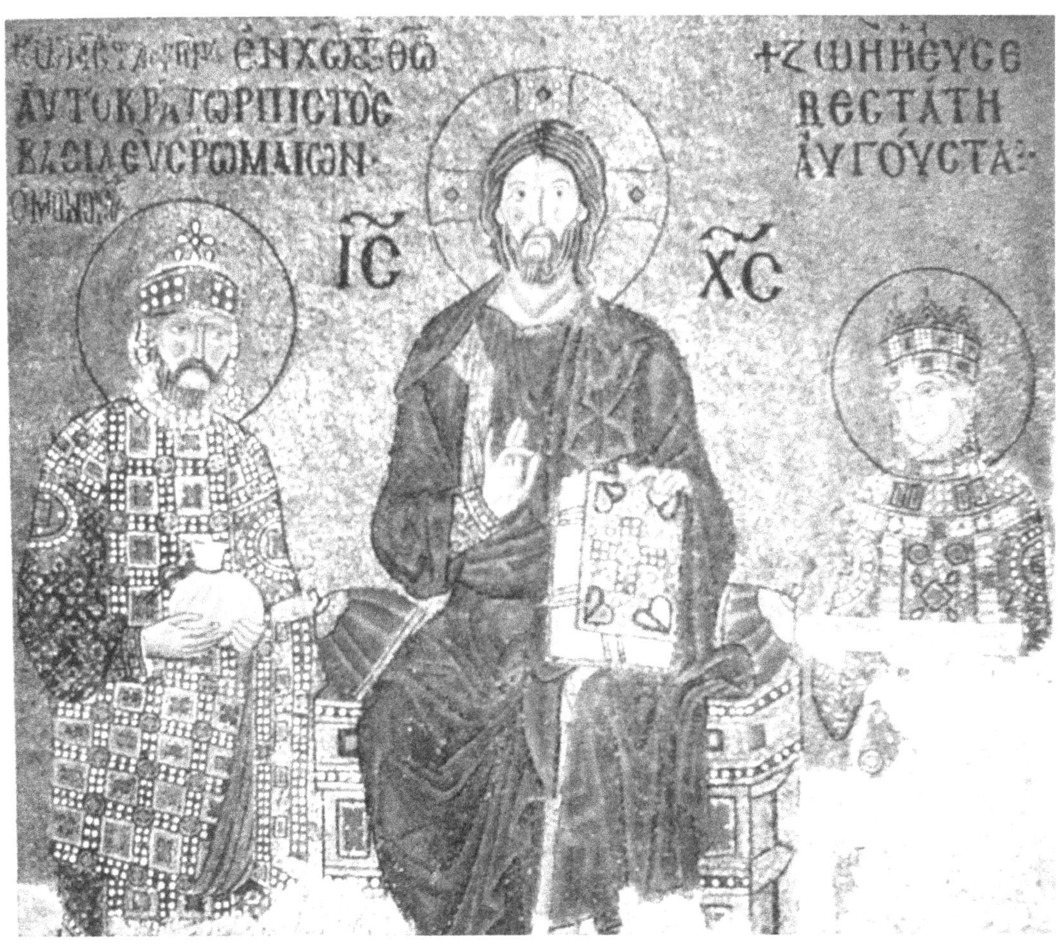

Figure 71. Constantine IX Monomachos and Zoe, mosaic, Hagia Sophia, Constantinople, *ca* 1030

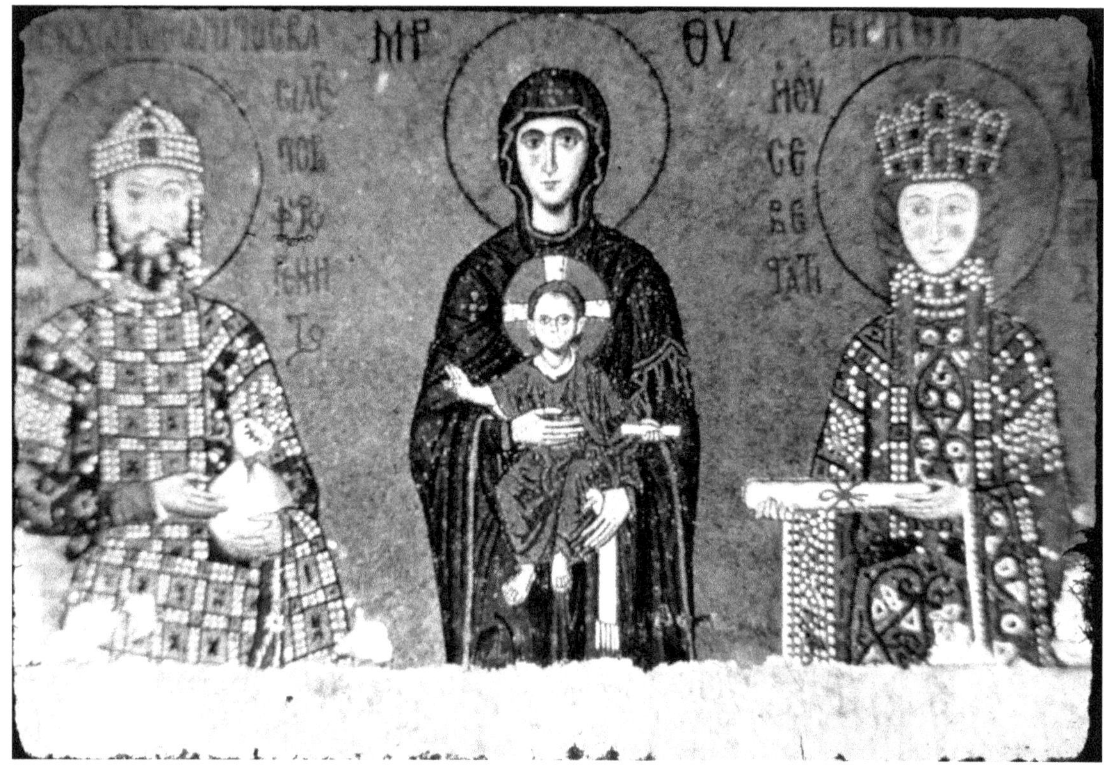

FIGURE 72. JOHN II COMNENOS (1118-1143) AND IRENE, MOSAIC, HAGIA SOPHIA, CONSTANTINOPLE *CA* 1120

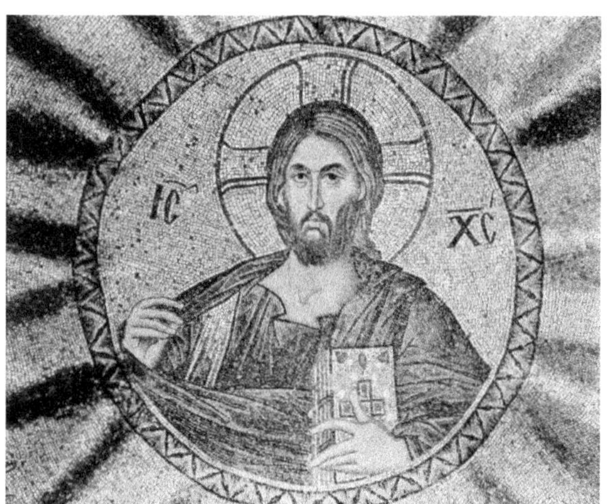

FIGURE 73. FETHIYE CAMII, MOSAIC, CHRIST PANTOCRATOR, 11TH CENTURY

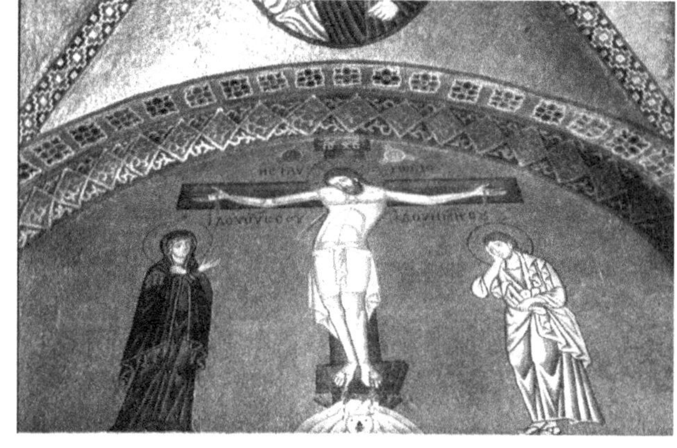

FIGURE 74. HOSIOS LOUKAS, MOSAIC, 11TH CENTURY

Hosios Loukas is a monastery and a place of pilgrimage with the miraculous tomb of the holy Loukas the younger. The oldest church is a small cross inscribed in a square inaugurated to the Theotokos, the Mother of God. Different theories about its foundation have been suggested. One maintains that it was built by Krinites Acrotas 946-955 who was a military strategos over the thema Hellas and resided in Thebe. Charalambos Bouras on the contrary attributes the church to the patronage of Romanos II about 960. It lacks paintings. In the katholikon (Fig. 74) the oldest mosaic program was executed from the 10th to the 12th century. The larger church was built on a martyrium for the holy Loukas who died in 953. It has a domed octagonal nucleus with squinches under the main dome. 140 images of saints are found in the decoration. Doula Mouriki dated them to 1020. In the narthex there are christological mosaics in strict symmetry and in the main nave icon-like pictures. Bouras dated the katholikon to 977-1031, Manolis Chatzidakis to 1011 and Eustathios Stikkas considered that the ktitor was the Emperor Constantine IX Monomachos (1042-1055).

Daphni is a monastery dedicated to the holy Virgin. The mosaics in the katholikon (Fig. 75), the church of the monks, originate from the end of the 11th century. The church is a Greek cross with an octagon. The date of the building activity is unknown but 1048 is a terminus ante quem. This year a priestmonk called Dionysios in

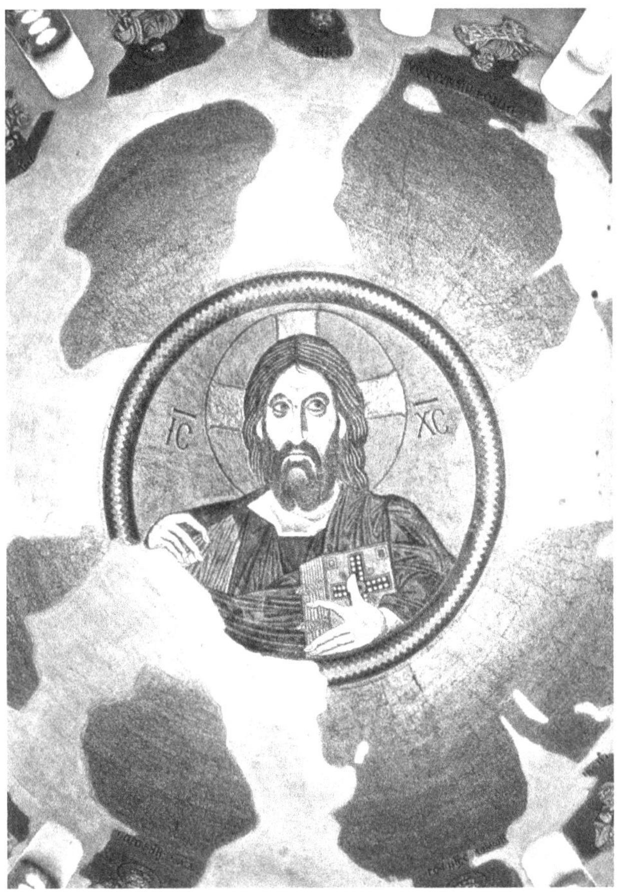

FIGURE 75. DAPHNI, CHRIST PANTOCRATOR, MOSAIC, END OF THE 11TH CENTURY

Daphni is recorded as celebrating mass in Hosios Loukas. The mosaics use tesserae, mosaic cubes of silver that illuminate the gold. The Pantocrator image in the dome is dominating. Four church feasts in the arcs below the dome depict Christ's Life. A fine cornice of marble accentuates the classical style.

Nea Moni (Fig. 76) was founded before 1042 by the local hermits Nicetas and John. Emperor Constantine IX Monomachos was its patron and provided the church with rich privileges and land. It was built during his reign and was decorated with mosaics between 1040 and 1055. The main nave is a rectangular room built in receding brick technique below a segmented dome on an octagonal drum. The inner narthex and the bema are covered with local red marble and mosaics of Constantinopolitan origin. In the apse a Virgin as orant is depicted and in the squinches of the drum eight church festivals. In the inner narthex cupola there is found the oldest known specimen in mosaics of a Virgin surrounded by military saints and martyrs. Here a paradigmatic Middle Byzantine iconographical program is developed that covers the interior with the whole salvation history. Christ Pantocrator dominates in the dome.

The destroyed cathedral in Nicea belongs to this group, as well the suite of mosaics in the cathedral in Torcello (Fig. 77) in Italy from the 11th century with an imposing representation of the Last Judgment and a standing Virgin as orant in the apse. In San Marco in Venice survives an iconographical program that evidently decorated the church

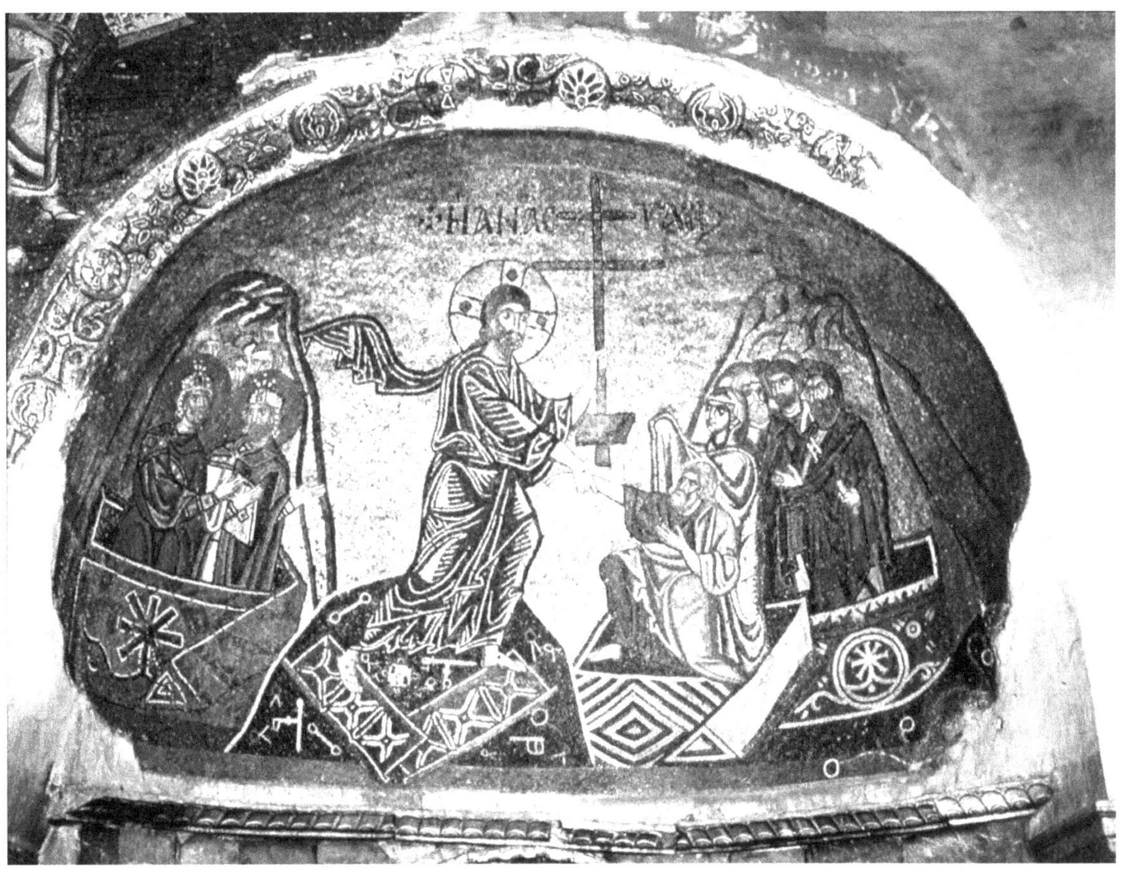

FIGURE 76. NEA MONI, CHIOS, MOSAIC, 1042-1055

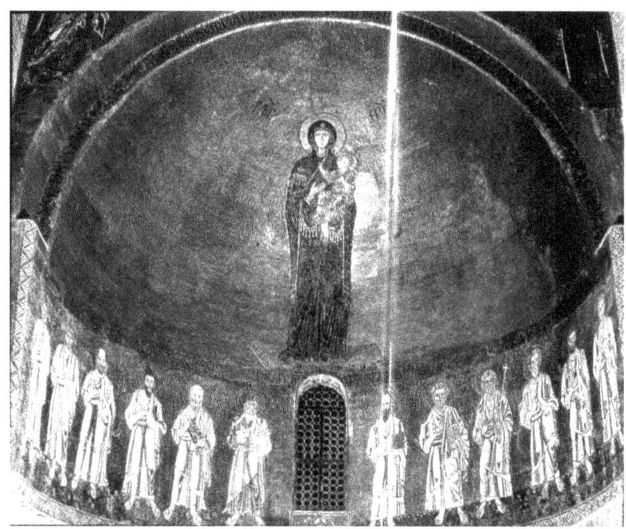

FIGURE 77. TORCELLO, MOSAIC, 11TH CENTURY

of the Holy Apostles, Apostoleion, in Constantinople. Its Genesis suite has been interpreted by J J Tikkanen as originating from a model that is preserved in the British museum, the Cotton Genesis (Otho B VI), a fragmentary manuscript from the 5th or 6th century partially destroyed by fire.

The mosaics on Sicily demonstrate the last offshoot of Late Comnenian art. It was created by invited Greek masters who also trained indigenous talents. The oldest mosaics in Cefalù and Cappella Palatina originate from the time of Roger II. Christ dominates in semi-figure in the apses and in Palatina's dome sitting on a throne surrounded by archangels. In Cefalù the Virgin as orant stands in the apse surrounded by loros adorned archangels with imperial coronation girdles and below there are standing apostles with names in Greek and Latin inscriptions. In Palatina the *horror vacui* principle is applied, the fear of the vacant space, and below the stalactite decorated ceiling in the central nave the mosaic completely covers the space. Christ dominates on the west wall sitting between the standing apostles Saint Peter and Saint Paul and with two angels in semi-figure above. The scenes from Christ's Life, the Church Fathers and female martyrs are followed by cycles from the Old and New Testament. The style is forceful with clear contours, classical draperies and an energetic expression. In Martorana the expression is intensified to manneristic distortions in particular in the sitting Pantocrator in the dome surrounded by kneeling archangels. The figures are elongated and the drapery inorganic. The Koimesis scene and Roger II who is crowned by Christ (Fig. 33) and the proskynesis by the ktitor George of Antioch in front of the Virgin is depicted in austere unplastic forms.

In Monreale the Late Comnenian art reaches its summit. The Hellenistic illusionism that at different times returned to Byzantine art here celebrates its triumphs. Christ in the central apse (Fig. 35) has evident similarities with the central image in the Deesis in the southern gallery of Hagia Sophia in Constantinople and below enthroned is a Theotokos Panachrantos, the Immaculate Mother of God, who is also inspired by the image in the apse in Hagia Sophia surrounded by loros adorned archangels. The cycles of Christ's Life that have here been extended with many genre scenes from the miracle repertoire are severely restored. The models are all destroyed and the most important were found in the church of the Holy Apostles in Constantinople. The rich narrative joy brings about very complex architectural coulisses and scenes of landscape.

The landscape is developed into stylized hieratic coulisses in the Norman stazas in a manner that has taken influence from Saracen art with prototypes in Persian textile art.

On Crete a rich monumental painting is developed. The monastery church of the Virgin in Myrokefalia, that was founded by John Xenos was decorated with frescoes in the 11th century. Panteleimon in Pege has paintings from the early 12th century and during the Venetian dominance the Byzantine tradition continued to be favoured in Santa Anna in Amari *ca* 1225 and in Saint George in Skavopoula from the same century where the provincial version of Comnenian painting remained. For the rest Crete shows close connections with the monastic centres in Asia Minor rather than with Constantinople.

In Kastoria the Hagioi Anargyroi basilica originates from the early 11th century, dedicated to the poor miracle-working doctors Cosmas and Damianos. It was redecorated in the 12th century by Theodor Lemniates. Among the masters one is notable who also worked in Kurbinovo. During the third quarter of the 12th century also a church with one nave was built for Saint Nicholas by the official magistros Nicephoros Kasnitzes decorated with a cycle of church festivals. There is found an icon with the ktitor represented in proskynesis. In the narthex the life cycle of Saint Nicholas is depicted.

On Cyprus there are mosaics already in the 6th and 7th centuries in Kiti and Lythrantessori. Three domed basilicas, Hagios Lazaros in Larnaka, Hagios Barnabas in Salamis and Hagios Barnabas and also the Hilarion in Festerona and Hagia Paraskevi in Geroskipos originate from the time before the Byzantine conquest of the island in 965. Hagios Nicholas tis Stegis from the 11th century was built as a cross in a square and has frescoes in the katholikon with a cycle of the church festivals. In the 12th century an icon of the saint was installed together with an image of the founder of the monastery between the lateral room and the diakonikon and the central nave. Later during the 12th century a Last Judgment was painted in the narthex.

Mosaics and frescoes from the time before the Arabic assault 648-649 decorate the apses of the Early Christian churches. Panaghia Karakaria in Lythrangomi, Panaghia

Kyra at the village Livadi and Panaghia Angeloktistos, the church decorated by angels, in Kiti at Larnaka have the Mother of God enthroned in the apse. This painting is an offshoot of contemporary painting in Constantinople. Cyprus is an autocephalous church that became independent from the jurisdiction of the Ecumenical Patriarchate in Constantinople in the 5th century. In 965 the island was liberated from the yoke of the Arabs by Emperor Nicephoros II Phokas and became a Byzantine province. Cyprian painting during the 11th and 12th century also reflects the tendencies in the capital. At the end of the 12th century appears the Madonna of Passion. The island was not influenced by Arabic art.

The oldest frescoes in Hagios Nicholaos tis Stegis (Fig. 78) at Kakopetria recall the frescoes in the Sophia cathedral in Ochrid in the Balkans. Frescoes from the beginning of the 12th century have a primary position. Panaghia Forbiotissa in Asinu, the church of the Trinity in the Chrysostomos monastery in Kutzuvendis, Panaghia Theotokos in Trikomi, the entrance hall and the south west part of Hagios Nicholaos tis Stegis that have classicizing tendencies are calm and dignified. The Cyprian frescoes from the 11th and 12th centuries are similar to contemporary painting in Greece, in the Balkans, in Bulgaria and in Russia and demonstrate the universality of this pictorial style.

In the middle of the 12th century a new phase of the development of Cyprian Byzantine painting was inaugurated. The destroyed Panaghia Afendika at the village Kutsuvendis and the frescoes in the church of the Apostles in Perachorio show this new stylistic phase. In the first church a Christ's Entombment is depicted, Epitaphios threnos, a pillar saint, the fragment of a Christ's Crucifixion and a Taking down from the Cross in picturesque colours with lively emotional expressions. The frescoes in the church in Perichorio are characterized by baroque swift movements and voluminous masses of cloth.

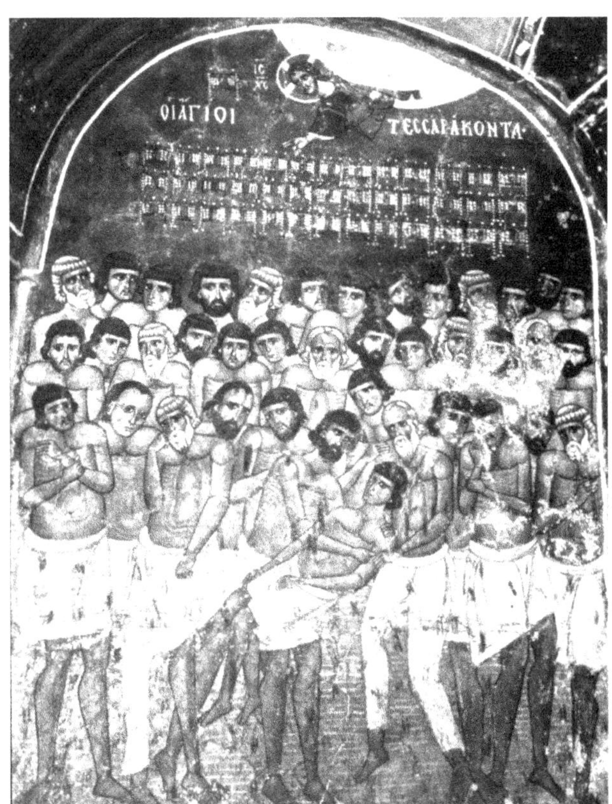

FIGURE 78. HAGIOS NICOLAOS TIS STEGIS, CYPRUS, BEGINNING OF 11TH CENTURY, THE FORTY MARTYRS

At the end of the 12th century the splendid frescoes in the Hagios Neophytos hermitage Enkleistra in the Paphos district were created, dating to 1183. The frescoes in Panaghia tou Arakos at Lagoudera from 1192 belong to this group just as the church Christos Antiphonitis, Christ who answers prayers, at the village of Hagios Ambrosios. Common elements of style for these frescoes are elegant elongated figures, dignified gestures and fluttering draperies of cloth. They have Constantinopolitan origin. A similar stylistic painting is found in Hagioi Anargyroi in Kastoria in Greece, in Saint George's church in Kurbinovo in the Balkans and in Saint George's church in Staraja Ladoga in Russia.

The oldest preserved Cyprian icons date from the second Byzantine period on Cyprus (965-1192). The oldest icon depicts Cosmas and Damian with a fine modelling of the incarnate. It is damaged and recalls the Thaddeus icon on Mount Sinai. A fragment of a Koimesis scene in the church of Saint Michael in Lafkoniko show apostles with wide open eyes, energetic facial traits and powerful contours, an eastern tradition that recalls the manuscript Par Grec 510 in the Bibliothèque nationale in Paris, Gregory of Nazianz's homilies from the last quarter of the 9th century. These are the only preserved icons from the time immediately after iconoclasm.

During the reign of Emperor Alexios I Comnenos (1081-1118) a Mother of God Eleousa, the Merciful, protecting patron for the Kykkos monastery in Constantinople, was sent to Cyprus. This icon was attributed to the evangelist Luke. She gave rise to a type of Hodegetria, the Virgin that shows the way pointing at the Child, that is called Kykkotissa.

In the 12th and 13th century a characteristic Cyprian tradition of icons was developed that Doula Mouriki called the "maniera cypria" with elements of the Byzantine tradition of the 12th and 13th centuries. Linear decorative elements were combined with an expressive tendency that gave the faces a vivid expression. Cinnabar red was abundantly used in the background, on the costumes and in different ornamental details, but the icon lacked the monumentality and the illusionistic character that was typical for the contemporary art in the capital of the Empire. The superficial surface quality and the linear tendency might be explained by the lack of contact with the centre of the Empire and by influence from different indigenous ethnic groups with East Christian tradition, in particular Syrian and Armenian.

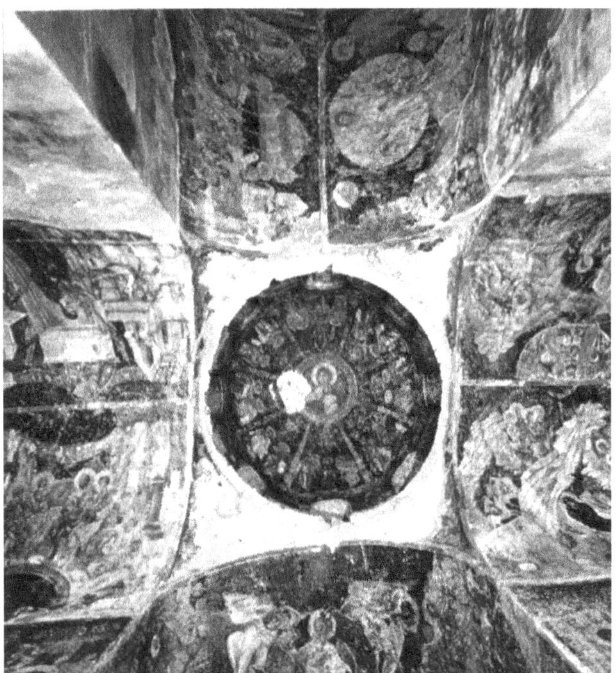

FIGURE 79. PERIBLEPTOS, MISTRA, FRESCO PAINTING, THE BIRTH OF CHRIST, MIDDLE OF 14TH CENTURY

The painting in Mistra that was founded by the Latins in the middle of the 14th century shows the late prosperity of Paleologian art in the monasteries Brontocheion, Peribleptos and Pantanassa. Here the Neo Platonic philosopher Gemisthos Plethon worked. Brontocheion is a domed church with five naves, three apses and a narthex. Peribleptos (Fig. 79), a domed church, a cross inscribed in a square, with three naves and three apses depicts Christ Pantocrator in the dome. The church is rich in paintings of Christ's Life, the Divine Liturgy, the Sleeping Emmanuel and the Koimesis, the Dormition of the Virgin, the Last Judgment and the Hetoimasia, the empty throne. Pantanassa has three naves with three apses and a narthex. On the second floor a cross in square is developed with galleries. The frescoes depict Christ's Life and miracles and the Acathistos hymn, the homage to the Virgin.

Most important for the development in particular in Russia is Kariye Camii (Fig. 80) with a parekklesion, an added chapel filled with mosaics, among others the Mother of God with the Child reminiscent of Hellenistic art and the fresco painting with the story of salvation and an original Last Judgment scene from the 14th century that transforms the whole cosmos. The apocalyptic angel rolls out the celestial cloth.

The icon painting with its origin in the mummy portraits from Egypt among others from Faijum with its strong realism and the encaustic technique is a continuation of the antique portrait art. Crosses and relics were venerated already in the 4th century. The first trace of veneration of icons is mirrored in the 5th century in writings of Augustinus and Epiphanius. During the first half of the 6th century a proskynesis in front of an icon is mentioned. Not until the second half of the 6th century do indications of the veneration of a number of icons increase. The idea that the icons were miracle-working was developed during the period of the 6th to the early 7th centuries.

Pre-Iconoclastic icons are foremost preserved in Rome and in the collections of the Saint Catherine's monastery on Mount Sinai. The Russian archimandrite Porphyrios

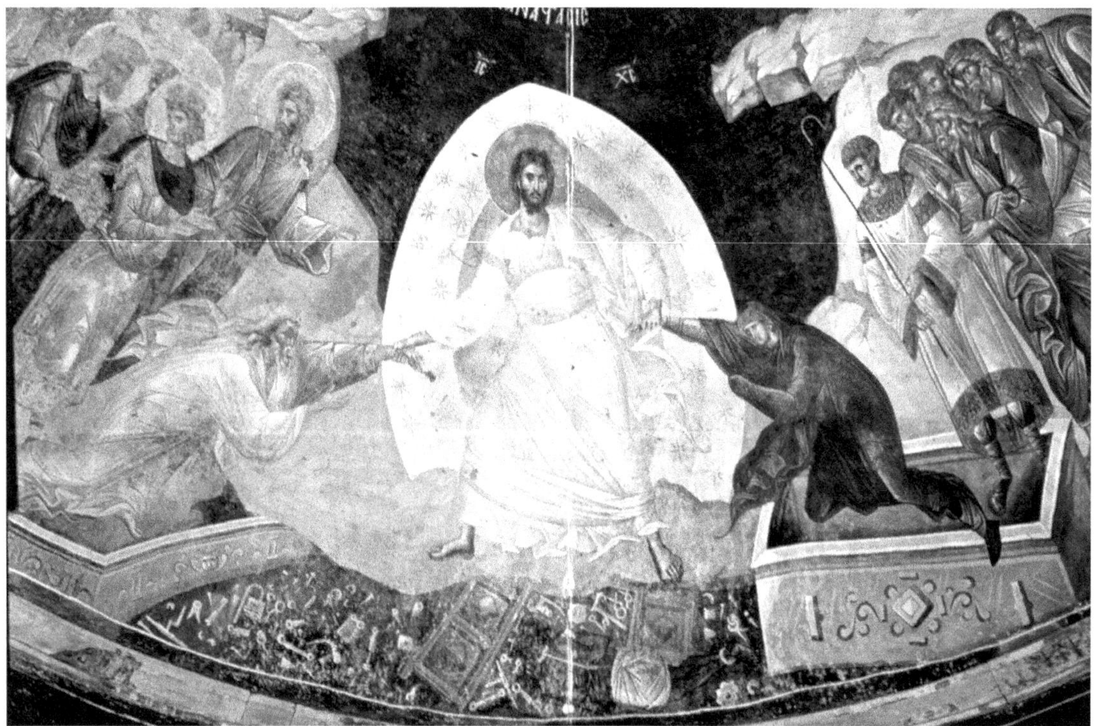

FIGURE 80. KARIYE CAMII, THE ANASTASIS, FRESCO PAINTING, CONSTANTINOPLE, 14TH CENTURY

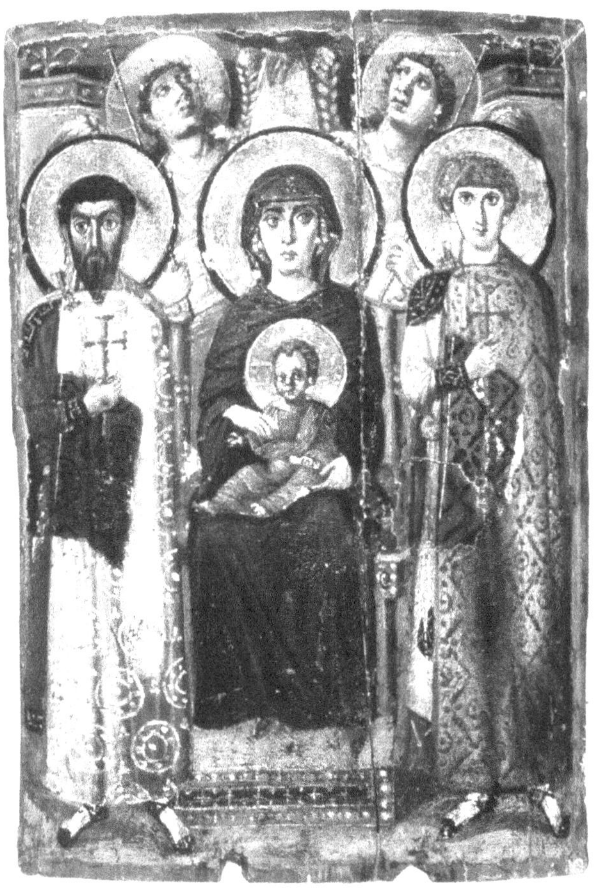

FIGURE 81. THE ICON OF THE VIRGIN AND CHILD, SAINT CATHERINE MONASTERY, MOUNT SINAI, 6TH CENTURY

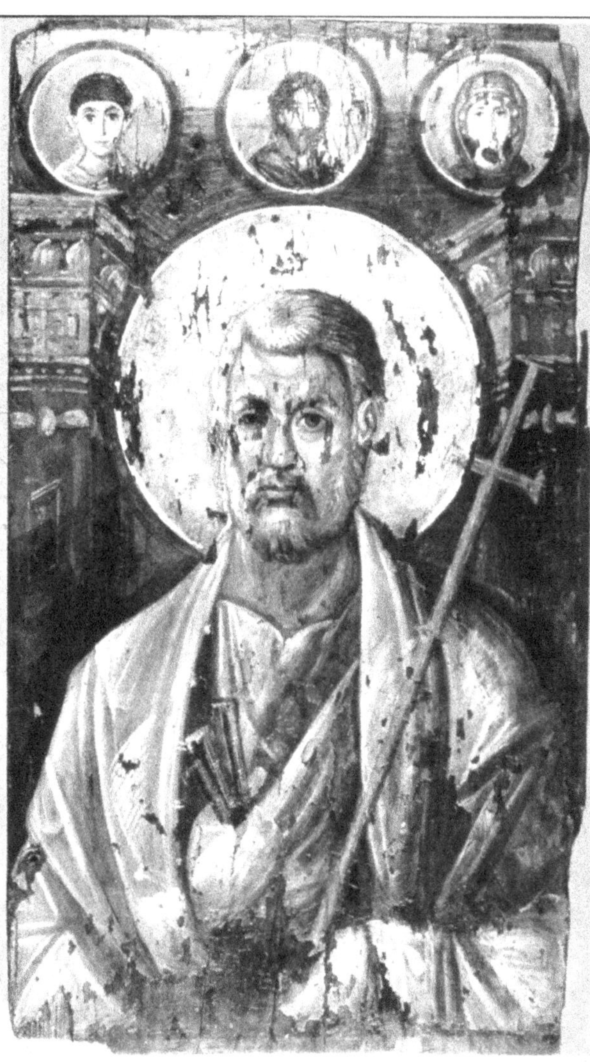

FIGURE 82. THE ICON OF SAINT PETER, SAINT CATHERINE MONASTERY, MOUNT SINAI, 6TH CENTURY

Uspenski brought four icons from Sinai to Kiev in the middle of the 19th century. Georgios and Maria Soteriou discovered new icons from Pre-Iconoclastical times in the same monastery. Two are of excellent quality and originate from Constantinople. An enthroned Virgin in encaustics is sitting with the Child in her lap, surrounded by the soldier saints Theodore and George as two pylons, while two angels placed in a second spatial layer look up towards God's hand, that sends a beam of light towards the head of the Virgin (Fig. 81). The saints are dressed as imperial dignitaries with a strictly frontal position. Mary has more freedom of movement. She looks to the left and turns her knees towards the right. The movement is intensified in the Christ Child who draws in his legs as a baby, but has a face with a high forehead like an adult. Deep olive coloured shadows emphasize the divinely super-real in the figures. Theodore is sunburnt and George pale in his face. The pasted coloured faces of the angels give them an ethereal celestial character. The draperies are softly modelled and plastic.The icon is dated to the 6th century.

The almost lifesize icon of Saint Peter (Fig. 82) shows the apostle in a niche holding a cross stick in his left hand and a bunch of keys in his right. He fixes the beholder with a penetrating glance. The spiritual tension that is expressed in the whirls of his hair and beard is controlled by the firm grip of his hand that expresses collected energy. Three busts in medallions above represent Christ, who turns his head to the side surrounded by the Virgin Mary and a youthful saint, presumably John the Evangelist. The costume of Saint Peter is painted in illusionistic technique in the antique painting tradition. Because of the lustrous lights that are ornamentalized the icon is dated to the 6th century. These two icons appear to be the most remarkable early icons besides the Madonnas in Santa Maria Antiqua, Santa Maria Nuova, Santa Maria in Trastevere (Fig. 83) and the famous acheiropoietos, the reprint of Christ's face in the Sanca Sanctorum in the Vatican and the cathedral in Genoa, that are "not made by human hands". The famous Hodegetria, the Virgin with the Christ Child who points to the road of salvation, that was preserved in the Studios monastery in Constantinople and was brought to the Chora, where is was cut into pieces by the Moslems in 1453, was considered to be the original first icon according to the legend painted by the evangelist Luke as a real portrait.

The belief in the miracle-working effect of the icons contributed to the creation of an opinion against the

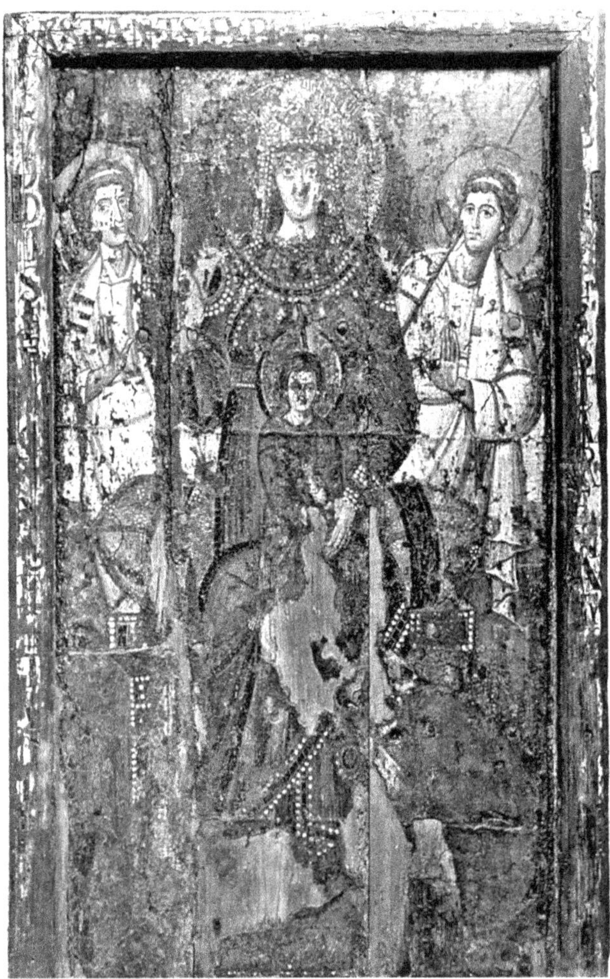

Figure 83. The Virgin of Santa Maria in Trastevere, Rome, 7th century, icon

existence of the sacred image. During the rulers of the Isaurian dynasty from Armenia that was influenced by the Islamic prohibition against sacred images a bloody war broke out in Byzantium in the 8th century about the essence and the existence of the sacred images. In 726 the famous Christ icon on the entrance portico Chalke, the Bronze Gate, to the Sacred Palace was destroyed on the command of Emperor Leon III and this became the starting-point of the persecution of the icon-friends, the iconodules, of which many became martyrs. The monasteries associated themselves with the image-defenders, the iconodules, but the army had a mission to destroy all sacred images in the empire during the time that the iconoclasm, the image controversy, continued. The Pantocrator image was replaced by simple crosses, the only permitted picture formula. Only in the periphery of the Empire on Mount Sinai and in Rome, which stood under the protection of the Pope who actively defended the image cult, could a few sacred images be saved. A council in Nicea, Nicenum II, in the year 787, convoked by the Empress Irene and the Ecumenical Patriarch Tarasius, defined the liturgical position of the images. Irene replaced the demolished Christ image on the Chalke gate with a new one and let the large cross that the Iconoclast emperors had put there remain. The icon was demolished again by Emperor Leon V the Armenian in 815 and was not replaced until 843, after the death of the last Iconoclast Emperor Theophilos, when the image cult was restored in Byzantium. Iconoclasm was declared to be a heresy, a false doctrine, and each Orthodox believer was obliged to venerate the sacred images, which had their authorization thanks to the Incarnation of Christ, the Divine Word. Thanks to this event the matter had become divine and there was no humiliation for holy persons to be depicted in an image.

During the time after the Iconoclasm the classical image program was developed, that decorates the iconostasis, the successor of the templon, *scenae frons*, the antique scene curtain. Rows of saints, apostles and martyrs follow the register of the twelve church festivals and around the Royal Gate and the two lateral doors show the Annunciation and the icon of Christ and the Theotokos.

Three exceptional specimens of Byzantine handicraft with silk- and pearl hosiery are preserved in the Sanca Sanctorum in the Vatican and in Orushejnaja palata, the Vestiary in the Kremlin in Moscow. It is the famous "Dalmatique de Charlemagne", (Fig. 84) a magnificent sakkos, a sacred episcopal vestment, with representations of the Blessed in paradise on the front and the Transfiguration of Christ on the back from the end of the 14th century and the two sakkos vestments "Metropolitan Photios' Little sakkos" and "Metropoltian Photios' Big sakkos" (Fig. 85), the former from about 1339 and the latter from about 1415. According to the decision of the Second Nicene council here is represented an army of confessors of the faith, polemic theologians, martyrs and ascetics, who all belonged to the pentarchy, the five original patriarchates that administered Christianity: Rome, Constantinople, Antioch, Alexandria and Jerusalem. Greek patriarchs and Roman popes stand beside each other and both these sakkoi have the Nicene Creed that extends over the clavi, the Roman borders of the officials on the toga praetexta. Photios' Little sakkos is a specimen of mass production, while the Big sakkos was commissioned by the Russian Grand Prince Vassilii Dmitrievich, on the occasion of the marriage of his daughter Anne to the young Byzantine Emperor John VIII Palaiologos, from the famous pearl hosiery workshop in Hagia Sophia in Constantinople. She was one of the child empresses in Constantinople who was forced to leave her native country for this overwhelming task at only eleven years old. She died in the pestilence in 1417 and it is claimed that John never ceased to mourn her.

In the area of artistic handicraft Byzantium appears as a superior culture. Textiles and metal bowls with émail cloisonnée and émail champlevée were brought as triumphal booty to the west after the fall of Constantinople in 1204 and were preserved in particular in the cathedral treasury in San Marco in Venice. In Sens, Auxerre, Laon and even in Roskilde in Denmark are preserved triumphal textiles in purple with double eagles among other motives.

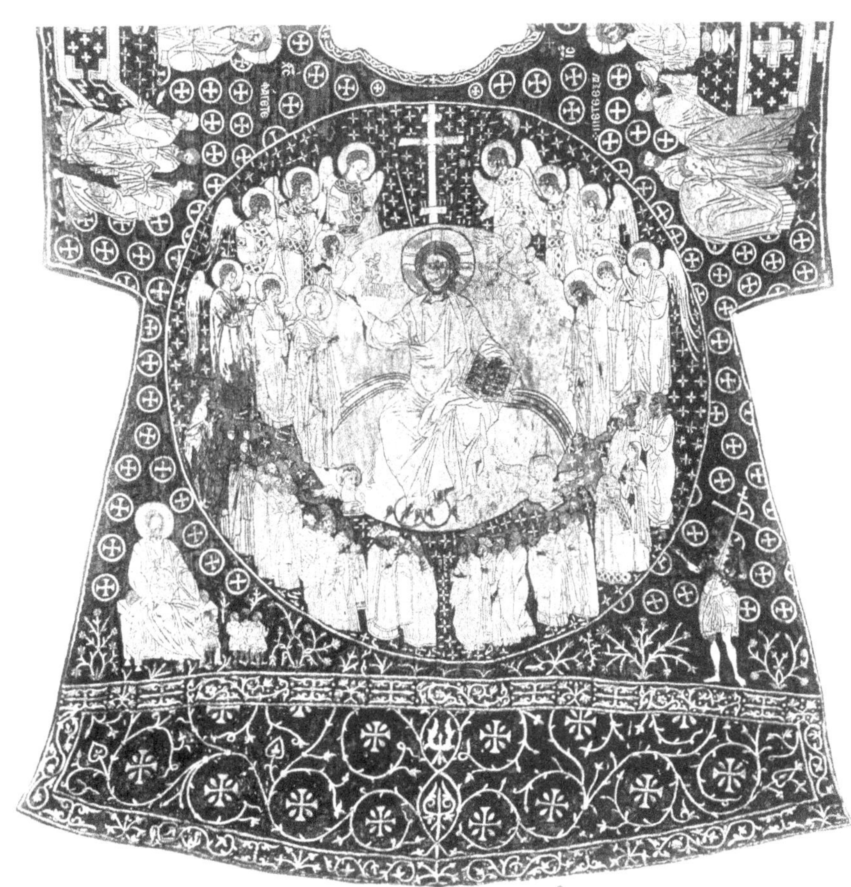

Figure 84. "La dalmatique de Charlemagne", saccos, Sancta Sanctorum, The Vatican, Rome, end of 14th century, the Chosen in paradise

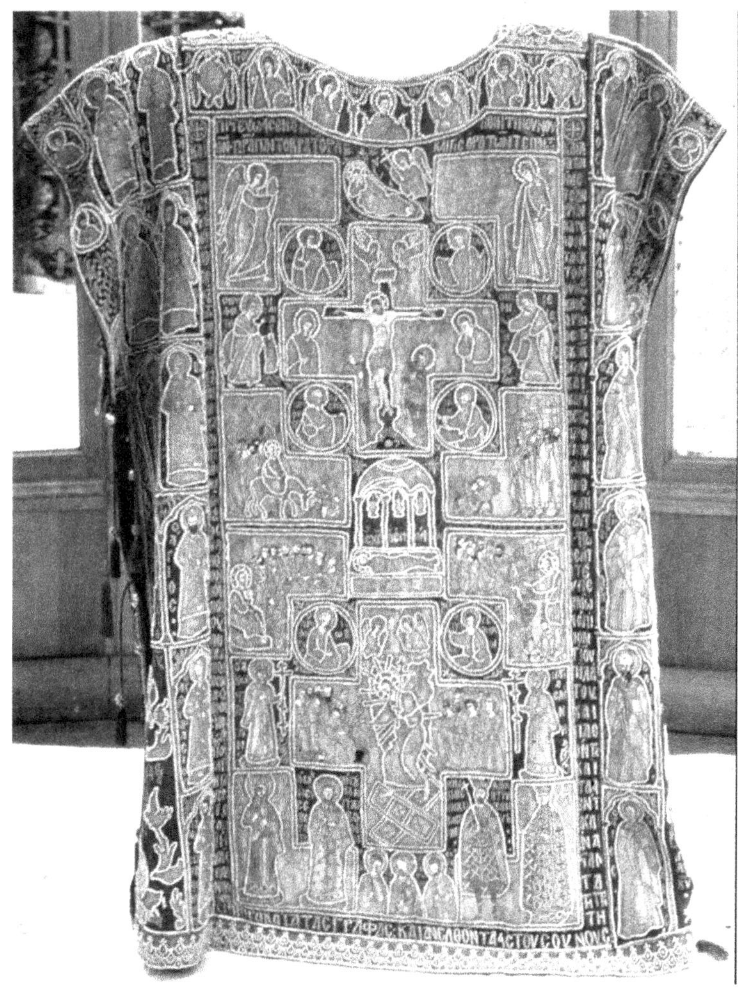

Figure 85. Metropolitan Photios Big sakkos, Orushejnaja palata, the Kremlin, Moscow, 1415, front

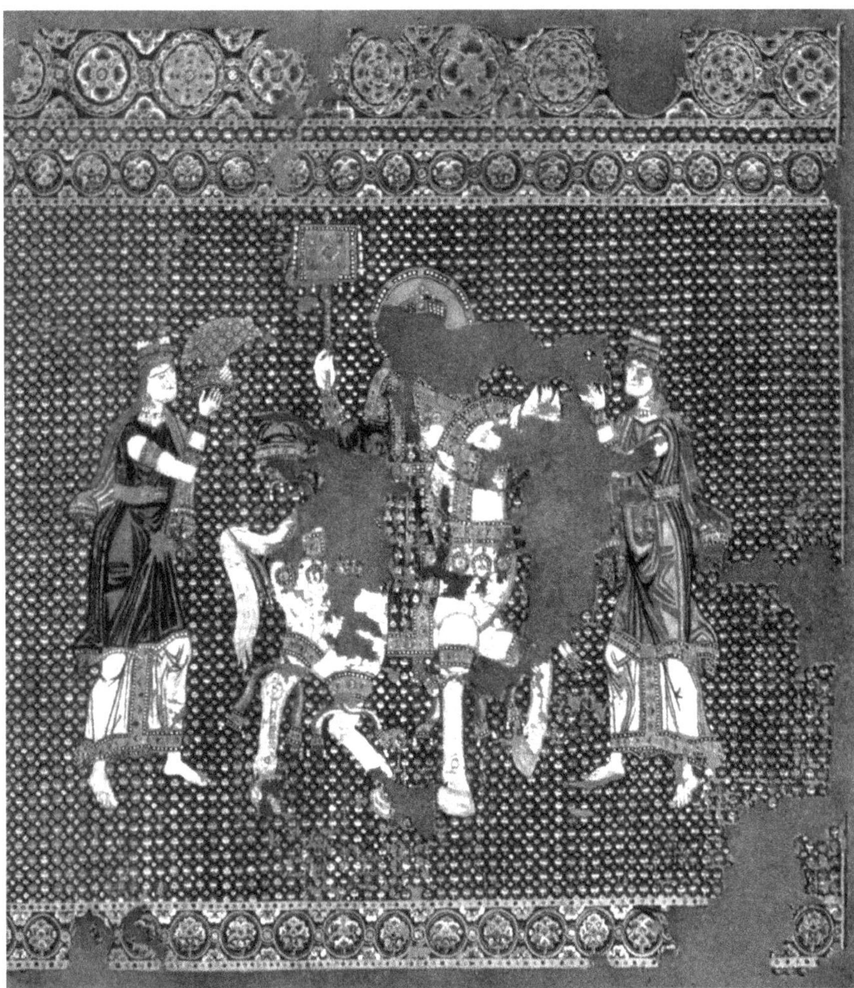

FIGURE 86. THE TAPESTRY OF BAMBERG, CATHEDRAL TREASURY, BAMBERG, *CA* 1064

Famous is the tapestry in Bamberg (Fig. 86) from *ca* 1064 that was brought home by bishop Gunther as a gift, presumably showing Emperor John I Tzimiszes (969-976) on horse surrounded by the two town goddesses of Constantinople.

The art of handicraft is one of the most brilliant branches of art in Constantinople with models from Persia and Syria. The red silk industry in Tyros gave inspiration to the imperial purple colour that was used for textiles in the Late Antique tradition.

Chapter 6

Manuscript illuminations

From rotulus to codex – magnificent manuscripts as gifts and liturgical mass production

In antiquity the book was a roll, in Greek called *eleitarion* and in Latin *rotulus* and *volumen*. It was made of leaves of papyrus pasted to long rolls, wound around a stick. The text was usually written only on the inside of the roll. In the 4th century AD the roll was replaced by the more easily handled bound book, the *codex*, but the rotulus continued to be used for the registers of the tax collectors and in the sacred liturgical context. The most famous antique rolls are the torah rolls with Old Testament texts that are preserved in the Ark of the Covenant in the synagogue.

The liturgical rolls that were written on parchment or paper could be 12 metres long and the text was copied in short sequences parallel to the short side. The oldest preserved specimen is the Ravenna roll from the 7th century. Most numerous are the liturgical rolls that originate from the 11th century, but only few of them have illustrations. They are often introduced with an author portrait of the founder of monastic life, Saint Basil the Great, or the Church Father John Chrysostom. A specimen from Jerusalem has initials with historical representations, marginal vignettes and an image of Constantinople. Another specimen in Moscow belonged to the Studios monastery in Constantinople. A 12th century roll in Athens, Nat Bibl 2759, depicts Saint Basil the Great and John Chrysostom in front of an altar in a church with several domes. It is reminiscent of the frontispiece, the entrance leaf, to the manuscript of John Kokkinobaphos Par Gr 1208 (Fig. 8) from the first half of the 12th century in the Bibliothèque nationale in Paris. There are also imperial chrysobulls in rotulus form.

While the papyrus roll was often illustrated with lines and thin water colours the codex was painted with thick gouache. The most important and famous preserved rotulus is a 10.64 metre long roll of parchment, Vat Pal Gr 431 (Fig. 87), a unique roll from the 10th century recording the history of Joshua with continuous horizontal illustrations of episodes from the first ten chapters of the Joshua book, preserved in the Vatican library in Rome. The text is written below on the page and is

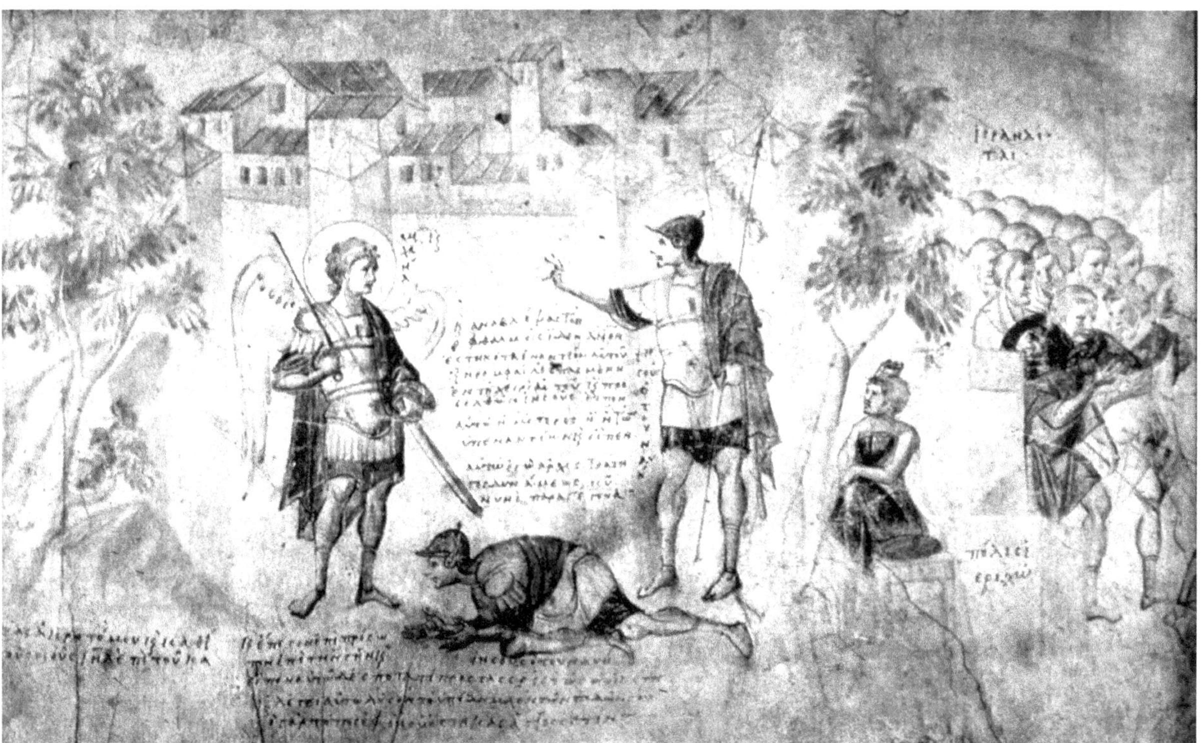

Figure 87. The Joshua roll, Biblioteca Vaticana, Rome, Vat Pal Gr 431, Joshua and the angel, first half of the 10th century, illumination

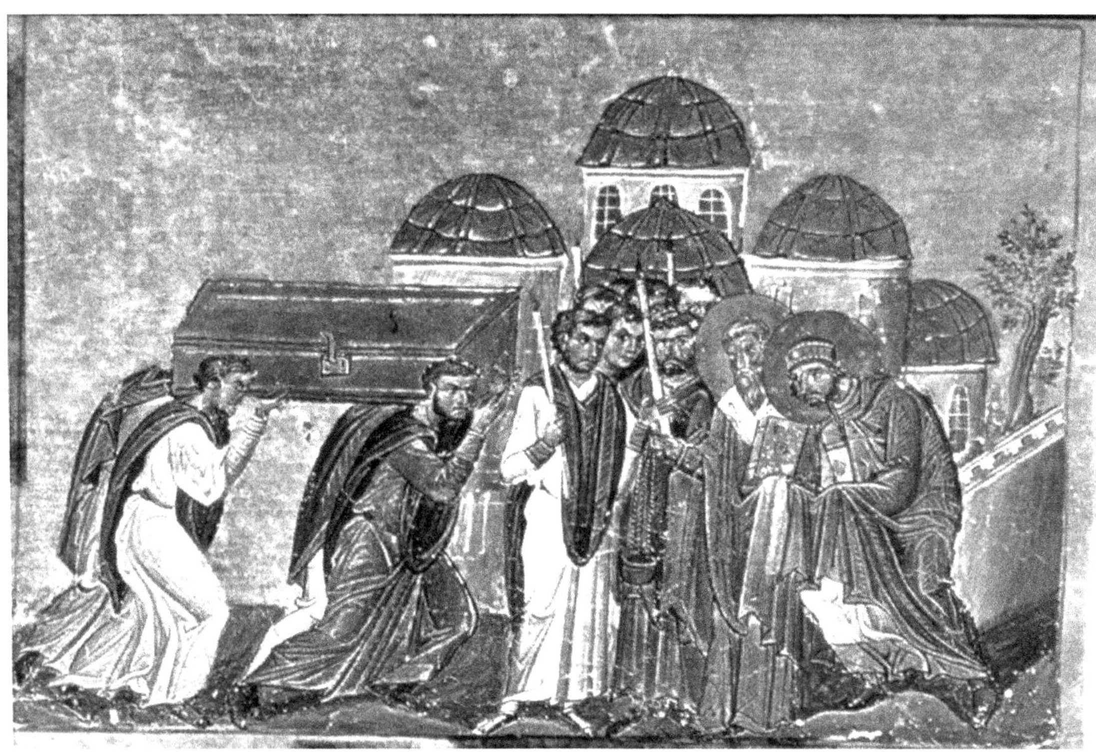

Figure 88. The Menologion of Basil II (976-1025), Biblioteca Vaticana, Rome, Vat Gr 1613, The translation of the relics of Saint John Chrysostome to the church of the Holy Apostles in Constantinople, illumination

subordinate to the miniatures. These are painted with a brush technique that is unusual in Byzantium and leaves large fields undecorated. Against this neutral background landscapes are depicted, personifications and the exploits of Joshua, the archetypical Old Testament general in pastel-like colours against trees and rocks, that recall the 2nd Pompeian style. This style and the Palestinian frame suits well the symbolic representation of imperial exploits on the battlefield. Proskynesis, falling down to the earth, is inflicted on the enemy. Cyril Mango proposes that the Joshua roll is a copy from a 7th century original, that glorifies the exploits of Emperor Heraklios. Michael McCormick proposes instead the exploits of Emperor Constantine VII Porphyrogennetos or Emperor Nicephoros II Phocas. If it earlier was considered to depend on the frieze-like scenes of the column of Trajan, Otto Mazel argues that it is an innovation that expresses the martial mentality of the Macedonian era. The roll has script on the back. It was preserved in Padua at the beginning of the 15th century and is today cut into 15 arbitrary pieces.

The codex consisted of books that were made of papyrus, parchment or folia of paper, pasted together one by one with pattern drawings, that indicated how the text should be distributed. It was now possible to write more text than on the roll. Because they were written on both sides, verso and recto, the front side and the back side, the book was easier to handle. The codex perhaps originates from the note pad of the Roman merchant in parchment, that in its turn originated from small codices, bound together, and waxed wooden plates for everyday use. It was used by the Christians from the 2nd century AD for Bible texts. Eusebius of Caesarea, the biographer of Constantine the Great, relates that the Emperor gave an order that 50 books of the Bible should be copied for liturgical use in Constantinople. From the 4th century on it replaced the rotulus as preserver of liturgical texts. Because the book was easy to consult it made the codification of the Roman legislation possible in the 5th and 6th centuries. For the artists the possibility arose for creating entire page miniatures.

The number of Greek manuscripts that have been preserved total only about 55,000, of which 40,000 are Byzantine. Most of them are preserved in the form of a codex. Few of them originate from the time before the 10th century, when the minuscule script was introduced, and thereby the amount of manuscripts increased drastically. Most of them were liturgical and theological treatises. Books were expensive in Byzantium. A manuscript from the 9th century of 400 pages cost according to Nigel Wilson 15-20 nomismata, corresponding to the half of a yearly income for an official according to Cyril Mango. Private libraries had seldom more than 25 books. Books were acquired by loans or commissions of copies from the scriptoria, the writing workshops. The monasteries Studion, Hodegon and Galesios had important scriptoria in the 14th and 15th centuries. Other people boasted that they lacked the need for books, because they knew the Holy Writ by heart, as for instance the Holy Anthony.

The manuscripts were decorated by writers and illuminators. In general the text was written first and the pictures added afterwards. An unusual specimen where

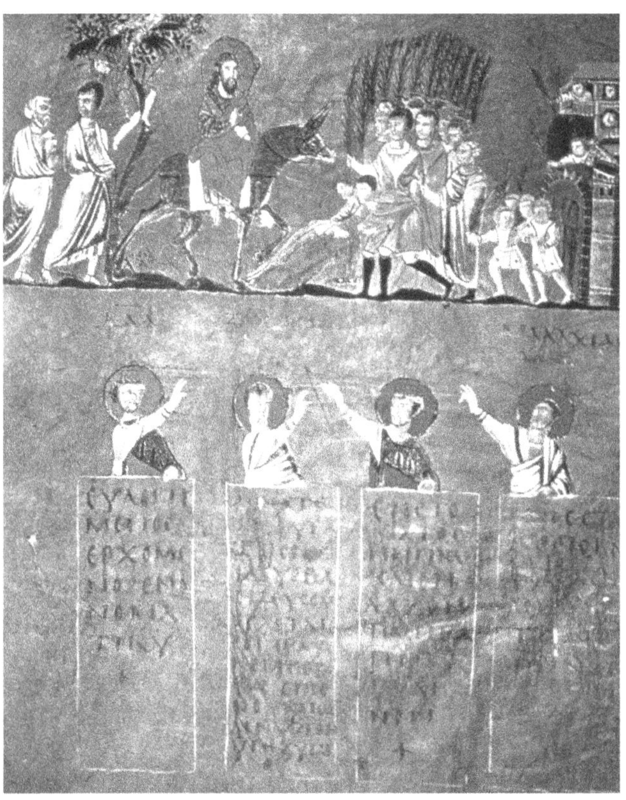

FIGURE 89. THE CODEX ROSSANENSIS, CATHEDRAL OF ROSSANO, ILLUMINATION, 6TH CENTURY, CHRIST'S ENTRANCE INTO JERUSALEM

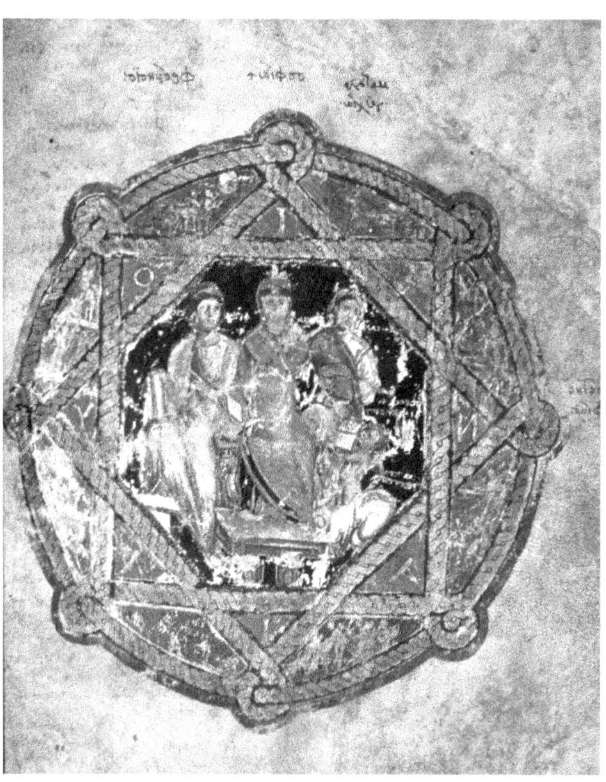

FIGURE 90. JULIANA ANICIA, FRONTISPIECE OF THE DIOSCURIDES MANUSCRIPT, NATIONALBIBLIOTHEK, VIENNA, MED GR 1, FOL 6 V, 512, ILLUMINATION

the illustrations precede the writ is the Menologion of Basil II in the Vatican, Vat Gr 1613 (Fig. 88), from the 10th century. The motif was first drawn and was then filled with the finishing coat. Most decorated manuscripts are Biblical with the Psalter and the Gospels as the principal motif, and further the Lectionaries with chosen texts from the Bible. Menologia and Church councils, theological treatises and monastery texts such as the Typikon, the rule, John Climakos' Celestial Ladder and the novel Barlaam and Ioasaph are illustrated. The secular texts were more seldom decorated, exceptions are the chrysobulls with the image of the emperor.

The only historical text with images that is preserved is the Skylitzes chronicle from the 12th century in the Biblioteca nacional in Madrid, Vitr 26:2, a copy that was made in Norman Sicily in order to be presented as a gift at the court. To this manuscript corresponds the Bulgarian Constantine Manasses' chronicle in the Vatican library, Vat Slav 2, and a copy of the Russian version of the Georgios Hamartolos' chronicle in the National Library in Moscow Fol 173, nr 100. Scientific manuscripts, like the Dioscurides in Vienna and Nicander, have images and diagrams. A fragment of an Ilias from the 5th century is preserved in Milan with Byzantine illuminations in the margin.

The few manuscripts from Pre-Iconoclastic times, the Codex Rossanensis (Fig. 89), the Rabbula Evangeliary (Fig. 93), the Wiener Genesis from the 6th century and the Cotton Genesis in London, are painted in a soft picturesque tone that is Hellenistic in its origin. The Dioscurides manuscript in Vienna from about 512 is dedicated to Juliana Anicia (Fig. 90), the daughter of the Emperor of West Rome. She is enthroned in the image as a female patrician, surrounded by personifications of Generosity and Prudence. A genius gives her thanks from the city quarter Honoratae in Constantinople, where she had built a church. In the manuscript a thousand pharmaceutical plants are reproduced, since Dioscurides was a doctor of medicine.

Only one manuscript of Ptolemaios remains from the time of the Iconoclasm in the Vatican. From the 9th century the Chludov psalter originates in Moscow, D 129, in the State Historical Museum, dated 829, Gregory of Nazianz's homilies in Paris, Par Gr 510, the Sacra Parallela and Par Gr 923 in Paris. The 10th century is the summit of illuminations. The classicizing Psalter Par Gr 139 (Fig. 91), Leo Sakellius's Bible, the Joshua roll (Fig. 87), the Menologion of Basil II in the Vatican (Fig. 88) and the Stavronikita evangeliary are the most famous manuscripts from this century. The style and iconography in the 11th and 12th centuries is innovative, for instance the Theodore Psalter and the Codex Ebnerianus and the decoration of the title frames, the initials and the canon tables then reach their peak. Also the province created manuscripts in the early Paleologian era.

Byzantium influenced Armenian, Georgian, Syrian and Coptic scriptoria. Byzantine illuminators painted

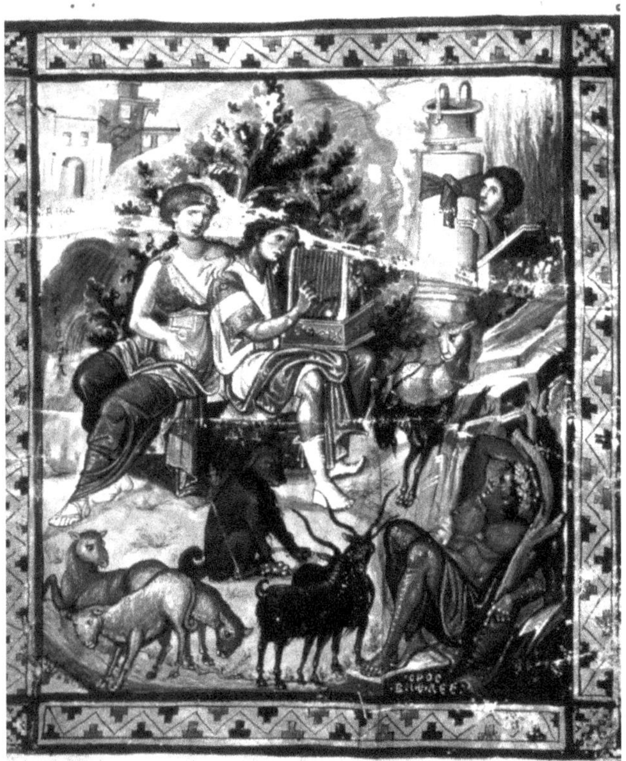

Figure 91. Par Gr 139, David in the desert, illumination, Manuscript department, Bibliothèque nationale, Paris, early 10th century

evangeliaries in Georgian and Arabic and the Slavic editions imitated the Byzantine. Moslem artists copied scientific Greek treatises.

The *Octateuch* consists of the eight first books of the Old Testament, the five Books of Moses, Joshua, Judges and Ruth, The *Pentateuch* has only the Books of Moses. Six illustrated specimens have been preserved. The Laur Plut 5, 38 in the Bibliotheca Laurentiana in Florence from the middle of the 11th century has miniatures that run until the Expulsion from the Paradise. Vat Gr 746 and Vat Gr 747 in the Vatican library in Rome originate from the 12th century like the Smyrna A 1, nowadays Topkapi Gr 8 in the library of the Seraglio in Istanbul. The Vatopedi 602 on Mount Athos belongs to the late 13th century.

The *Psalter* is a liturgical manuscript with 150 psalms from the Psalter attributed to King David accompanied by odes, so-called canticles. From the 3rd century on the Psalter was the most important book of prayer for the Christians, used as an antiphone dialogue between the deacon and the choir during the liturgies. It was considered to be the utmost weapon against the demons. 84 illustrated psalters are preserved, the oldest originates from the 9th century. They are so-called Psalters of the margin, i.e. monastic and theological or "Aristocratic" psalters with illuminations in the margin.

Among the psalters that were illustrated in the margin the three oldest are the Pantokrator 61 from Mount Athos, Par Gr 20 in Bibliothèque nationale in Paris and the Anti-Iconoclastic Chludov psalter in Moscow. They continued to be produced unto the 14th century, as for instance the Walters Gr 733 in Baltimore. They were copied by Bulgarians, Serbians and Russians, such as the so-called Hamilton psalter Gr 78 A 9 in Berliner Kupferstichkabinett and the Serbian psalter, Slav 4, in Bayerische Staatsbibliothek in Munich.

Aristocratic psalters are those that illustrate whole pages with images as frontispieces. Par Gr 139 (Fig. 91) from the 10th century is the most famous. Some illustrate commentaries like the Vat Gr 752 and the Vat Gr 927 in the Vatican Library and the Gr 62 in the Bodleian Library at Oxford, that shows interesting connections to the representations of David on silver bowls from the 6th century.

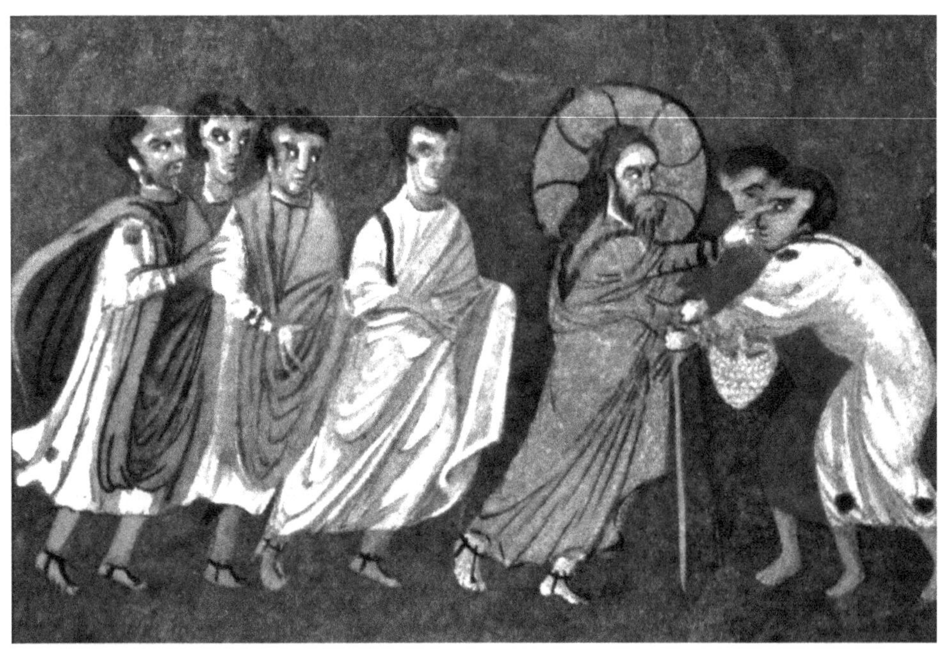

Figure 92. The Sinope fragment, Codex Sinopensis, Ms suppl: grec 1286, fol 29, 6th century, illumination, Bibliothèque nationale, Paris

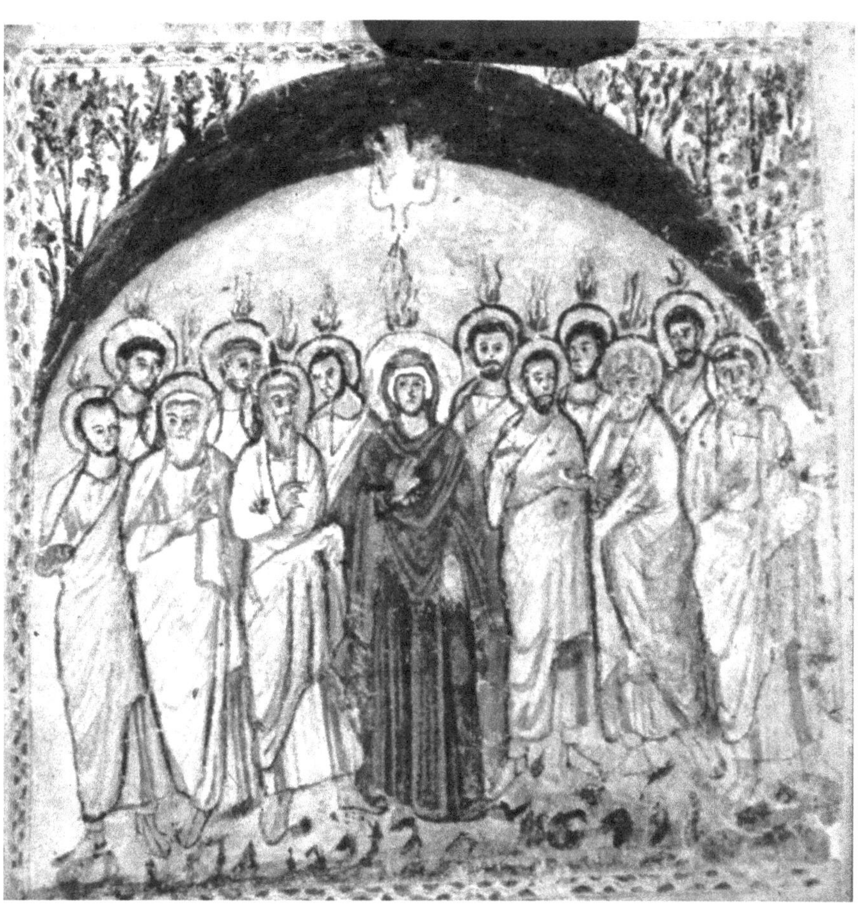

FIGURE 93. THE RABBULA EVANGELIARY, 586, BIBLIOTECA LAURENTIANA, FLORENCE, ILLUMINATION, PENTECOST

The *Tetraevangelia* are collected works with the four gospel texts and should not be mixed up with the Byzantine gospels, that are Lectionaries, i.e. they contain only the gospel texts that are read during the liturgies. From Pre-Iconoclastic times in the 6th century only three originate, the Codex Rossanensis (Fig. 89) and the Sinope evangeliary Par Gr 1286 (Fig. 92) in the Bibliothèque nationale in Paris and the Syrian Rabbula evangeliary dated 586 (Fig. 93). After the Iconoclasm the uncials, the big letters, were abandoned, and small letters in minuscule writ became common. The evangeliaries contained a preface and Eusebius' letter to Karpianos about the redaction of the canon tables. The canon tables contain the Bible passages that coincide with one another, decorated title frames and initials and author portraits. The most innovative were created in the 11th and 12th centuries. Many are preserved in the decorative style.

The gospels or lectionaries were first and foremost used at the liturgical celebration of the Eucharist. The first part has gospel texts for the moving cycle in liturgical order, the other part, the *Synaxarion*, contains readings for each day of the year from the vitae, the saints lives.

The *Menologion* contains the vitae of the saints for every day edited monthly. The earliest are dated to the 9th century. Symeon Metaphrastes, a logothete, an officer of the finances, at the imperial court in the second half of the 10th century and presumably monk at the end of his life composed an edition during the late 10th century with 150 texts in 10 volumes. It lays out the standard model for menologia that are illustrated. Nancy Patterson Sevcenco has studied these Metaphrastian menologia. In the Kongelige Bibliothek in Copenhagen is preserved a Metaphrastian menologion, Ms Gr 167. The so-called Imperial menologia have saints lives with a finishing acclamation of the emperor and in great part copy the Menologion of Basil II, Vat Gr 1613 (Fig. 88). It is as a matter of fact a Synaxarion for Constantinople for the months September to February with 430 miniatures on a gold ground. 15 illuminations lack texts. The balance between the text and the image is total. It depicts great ecclesiastical feasts, translations of the relics of saints, prophets and saints in exquisite landscapes or in front of elaborated architectural frames. Scenes of martyrs and torture are very realistically depicted and violent. Every miniature has in the margin a name of the artist in genitive, 8 with the words *tou graphou* and the name of the painter – Pantoleon, George, Menas, Symeon, Michael the younger, Nestor, Michael of Blachernae and Symeon of Blachernae. The artist who has illuminated the Psalterion of Basil II, Marc Gr 17 (Fig. 94) in the San Marco Library in Venice is also called Pantoleon, both manuscripts from the last quarter of the 10th century. The illuminated Imperial menologia from the 11th century imitate this menologion.

The Wisdom of Solomon Ms Gr 6 from the 10th century in the Kongelige Bibliothek in Copenhagen is a magnificent manuscript produced for presentation as a gift. It belonged

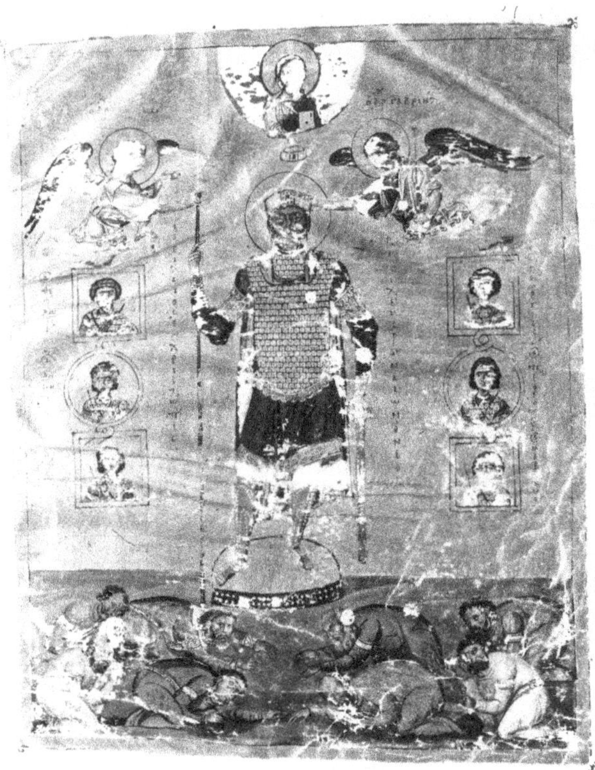

FIGURE 94. BASIL II (976-1025) IN MARC GR 17, SAN MARCO LIBRARY, VENICE, ILLUMINATION

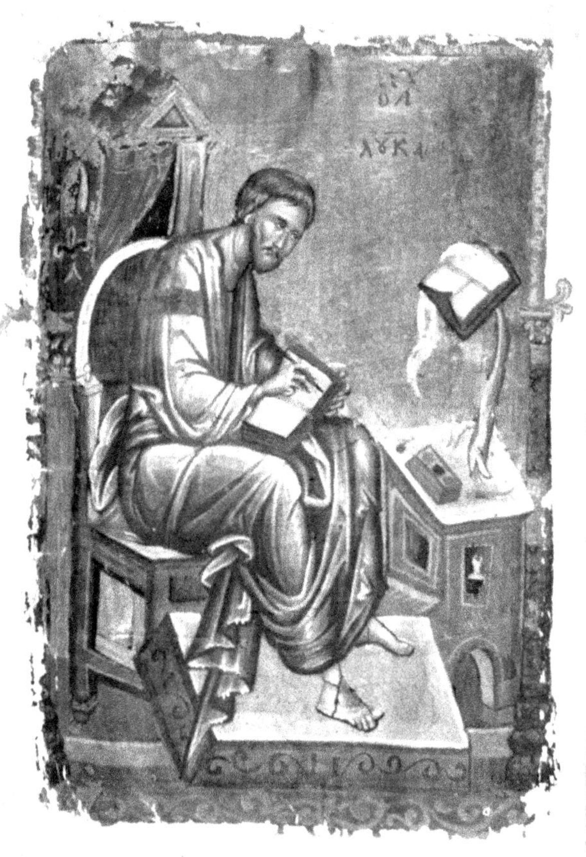

FIGURE 95. MS GR 9, THE EVANGELIST LUKE, ILLUMINATION, UPPSALA UNIVERSITY LIBRARY CAROLINA REDIVIVA, 1300

to the famous Late Byzantine admiral Loukas Notaras, who together with his sons was brutally murdered after the fall of Constantinople by the Turkish sultan. The manuscripts in Carolina Rediviva in the university library in Uppsala Ms Gr 4 from the 11th century and Ms Gr 9 (Fig. 95) from around 1300 are specimens of liturgical mass production of evangeliaries that were used every day in the monasteries with scolia in the margin indicating which gospel texts should be read and when.

Chapter 7

Painting in the Balkans and in Scandinavia

A very rich monumental painting was developed in the part of the Balkans that corresponds to the former Yugoslavia particularly in the Late Byzantine period. Serbia and Macedonia have the richest artistic heritage from this time. In Studenica, Sopocani, Mileseva, Gracanica, Kurbinovo, Pec, Decani, Mateic, Markov monastir and Staro Nagoricino the large program of representing Christ's Life with elements of genre scenes was depicted.

In Nerezi Macedonian painting was developed in the church of Saint Panteleimon in the late 12th century. It was founded in 1164 by Alexios Comnenos, the son of Theodora the Porphyrogenita, a domed cross form in brick. Frescoes from the cycle of the suffering of Christ show one of the earliest Epitaphios Threnos representations in monumental painting, the dead Christ on *lit de parade*. In the narthex and the narthex chapels hagiographical illustrations are depicted. The style is expressive, like in Kurbinovo and in Kastoria.

Kurbinovo in Macedonia has a church of Saint George about whose founder nothing is known, but on the back of the altar there is an inscription that confirms that the decoration was begun on the 25 April 1191. The form of the church is only one nave with a wooden roof, an apse in the east and a narthex in the west. It is constructed by mortar and stone sherds, polished in the exterior and painted with an imitation of cloisonné shaped brick like Kastoria. The interior is decorated with paintings from the Great Feast cycle. The master of Kurbinovo was evidently active in the second phase of the decoration of the Anargyroi church in Kastoria. The style of the painting relates to the concave forms that are typical for the monumental painting of the late 12th century with exaggerated details of the figures and strong tonal contrasts in the incarnate, that give the images an expressive intensity that is lacking in contemporary painting outside Macedonia.

Studenica is a monastery near Usce in southern central Serbia, founded 1183 by Stefan Nemanja (1167-1196). Nemanja's brother, Sava of Serbia, abbot in 1208, introduced in his typikon the monastery rules from the Euergetes monastery in Constantinople. The building of the church of the Virgin was started by Nemanja and finished by his son as a burial church, since Nemanja had retired to Mount Athos. It has finely worked local marble. Nemanja's body was brought from Mount Athos to Studenica in 1208. The church mixes Romanesque and Byzantine elements. The frescoes were made in 1314. The Pantokrator image in the dome is surrounded by four evangelist symbols, cherubim with wings in fire and the Divine Liturgy and the Eucharist. Eight Old Testament prophets carry script rolls that relate to the Resurrection. 34 busts of the ancestors of Christ refer to his earthly life as God's Son. In the pendentives and the upper zones of the walls evangelist portraits and ten church festivals are depicted. In the lower zone the Life of the Virgin is represented. On the south wall straight across the Nemanjid saints Stefan Nemanja, Sava of Serbia and the Virgin with the Child surrounded by saints, the portraits

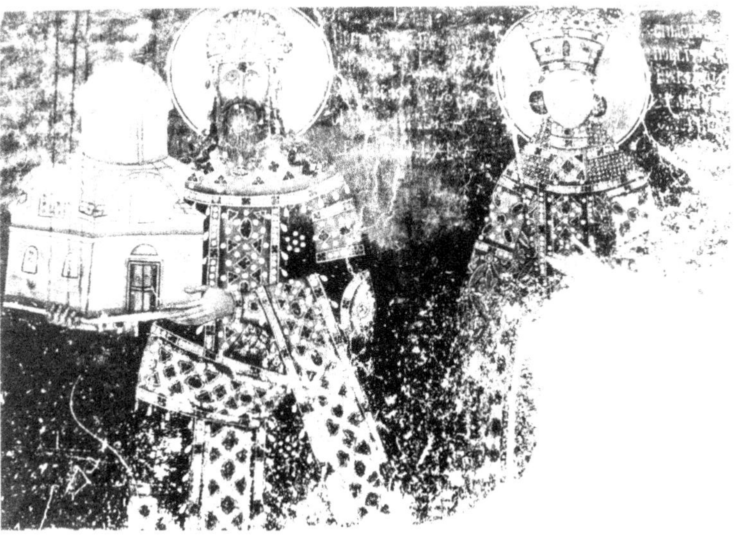

Figure 96. Kral Milutin and kralaina Simonis, Studenica, fresco painting, Serbia, 1314

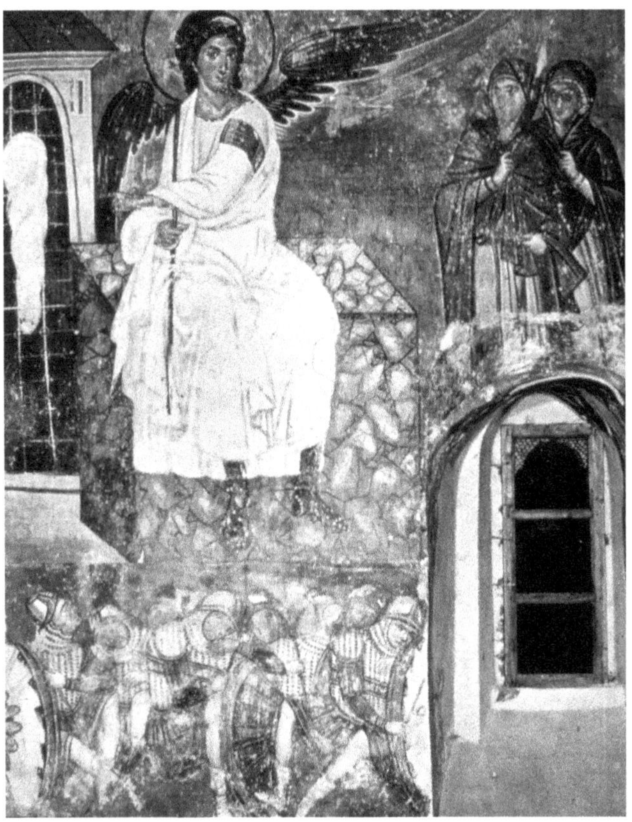

FIGURE 97. THE ANGEL ANNOUNCING CHRIST'S RESURRECTION, MILESEVA, FRESCO PAINTING, SERBIA, *CA* 1228

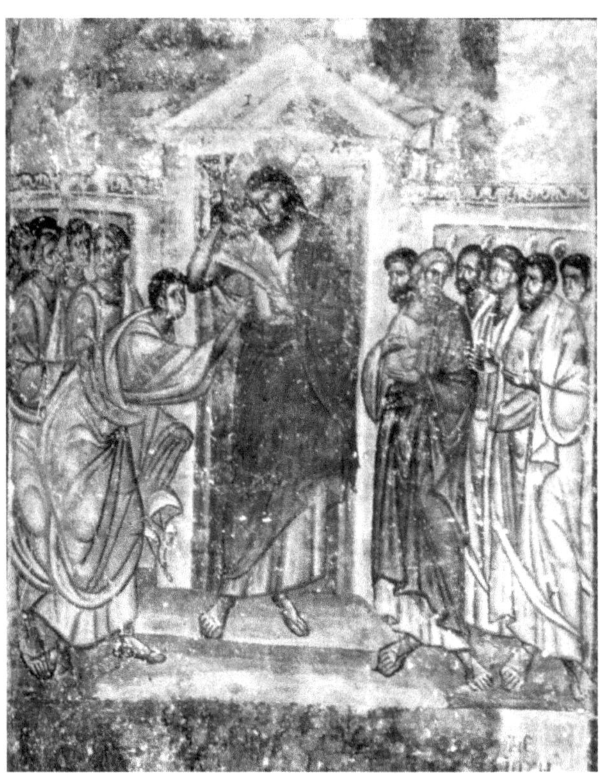

FIGURE 98. THOMAS AND CHRIST, SOPOCANI, 1265, FRESCO PAINTING, SERBIA

of Kral Milutin and his queen Kralaina Simonis (Fig. 96) are reproduced as parallels to the ancestors of Christ. A great number of bishops in the sanctuary in busts, in semi-figure and officiating in the liturgy emphasize the tradition of the Orthodox church and its liturgical importance. Here appears the master Eusthatios of Thessaloniki. The modelling is exerted in rich tones of ochre, red, green and white. The heads of the individualized saints in the lower zone recall the cathedral of Saint George in Staro Nagoricino, from where the masters originate.

A painted Greek inscription in the dome dates it to 1208/1209. In the frescoes there is a conscious effort to imitate mosaics. In the background leaves of gold are used. The Crucifixion scene has a blue background with stars in gold. From the late 13th century originates a large solemn dead Christ, Epitaphios Threnos, that differs from the nervous configuration in the Byzantine art of the 13th century. A painted inscription in Serbian in the exonarthex dates it to 1233/1234. Four scenes from the life of Stefan Nemanja and his translation from Chilandar to Studenica make up the oldest example of historical painting in Serbian monumental painting.

Mileseva (Fig. 97), a monastery in the south-western part of Serbia close to Priepole, was founded in 1220 by Prince Vladislav, son of King Stefan the First Crowned. The katholikon is dedicated to the Ascension of Christ and has a Byzantine plan, a nave with short cross arms as bema, a dome on pendentives and three semi-circular apses. The frescoes were presumably painted before 1228 with a typical Byzantine image program, but with an unusual choice and distribution of the scenes. The portrait of the ktitor and of his ancestors are situated in the nave. In the narthex there is a portrait of an unidentified Byzantine emperor, perhaps John Doukas Vatatzes (1222-1254) beside Constantine the Great and his mother Helen. This is the only case in Serbian art where the Byzantine emperor is represented as superior. Two artists have collaborated there, most likely Greek, with accentuated linear volumes and a combination of red and blue, something that only sophisticated classical painters could create. The background is either blue or ochre coloured with leaves of gold that imitate mosaic cubes. These frescoes are forerunners of the Paleologian painting and particularly important because few paintings remain in Constantinople from the same time. Vladislav's tomb in marble stands in the nave in front of his portrait. An exonarthex with two lateral chapels and frescoes with the Last Judgment were added in 1236 in order to house the relics of Saint Sava of Serbia.

Sopocani (Fig. 98) close to Novi Pazar in Serbia is a Trinity church, that was founded in 1255 by Stefan Uros I (1243-1276) as a cathedral. It later became the katholikon for the monastery and burial church for Uros and his parents. Stefan the First Crowned (1217-1228) was transferred from Studenica in 1266. The church is a basilica with one nave with a dome over the cross middle similar to Studenica in its plan of stone with a round apse. It has

Romanesque traits and was at the end of the 13th century extended with two chapels that flank the narthex, an open exonarthex and clock towers in the west. The exonarthex was decorated with paintings before 1346 during the time of Stefan Uros IV Dusan (1331-1355). At the period 1342-1345 two chapels were included on the northern and southern side of the main nave between the eastern cross arm and the western narthex chapels with a common roof for all the chapels.

The frescoes in the nave and the narthex are counted as the most excellent masterpieces of medieval monumental painting. They illustrate the transition from the Late Comnenian to the Paleologian art. The masters are unknown. Between 1263 and 1268 these paintings were executed in a time from which few monuments are preserved in Constantinople. The frescoes are partly made in a linear narrative style of the type of the Late Comnenian manner in the narthex, the upper parts of the main nave and the pendentives below the dome, and partly of Greek masters in a new heroic style. The Koimesis on the west wall, stately compositions, monumental single figures and massive architectural forms take models from the Paleologian works of the late 13th and the 14th century. The background recalls Studenica and Mileseva. It imitates gold mosaics with leaves of gold on a yellow ground. The program is traditional, with several princely portraits, councils and cycles of the Last Judgment in the narthex. 18 scenes from Josef's Life were created in order to emphasize the influence of the vitae of the Serbian princely brothers Stefan Nemanja and Sava, written by Domentijan. A fresco shows Anne Dandolo, the wife of Stefan the First Crowned and the mother of Uros I on *lit de parade*. In the southern narthex chapel the historical painting is developed, showing the translation of the remains of Stefan Nemanja from Chilandar on Mount Athos to Studenica. The chapel associated with the main nave was dedicated to Saint George and Saint Nicholas and decorated with scenes from their lives.

The Koimesis church in Gracanica (Fig. 99), a monastery close to Pristina, originally an Annunciation church, was begun in 1310 during the time of Serbian Kral Stefan Uros II Milutin on the site of a destroyed church from the 11th century basilica. The master builders originated from Thessaloniki or Epiros. It is a domed cross church in a square in the main nave. The bema is flanked by great lateral chapels with cupolas in the north and the south and by ambulatory wings and an inner endonarthex. Another two cupolas cover the corner arch of the inner narthex. This characteristic five cupola scheme is a well-balanced composition with elongated proportions. In the exterior there is a reserved application of brick work in cloisonné form. The church was decorated with paintings before 1321 in the standard version of the ecclesiastical program of decoration during the Paleologian era with Old Testament prefigurations and liturgical themes in the bema. The foundation document of Kral Milutin and a deceased Serbian bishop is reproduced in a writ in the southern chapel. The portraits of the Nemanjid dynasty as a family tree inspired by the Root of Jesse are depicted in the inner narthex. The style of the masters Michael, Astrapas and Eutychios indicates a certain interest in the human anatomy and uses both natural and reversed perspective. The church was perhaps from the beginning destined to be a burial church for Milutin, who was actually buried in the Banjska monastery, and continued to serve as such for local bishops and important personalities.

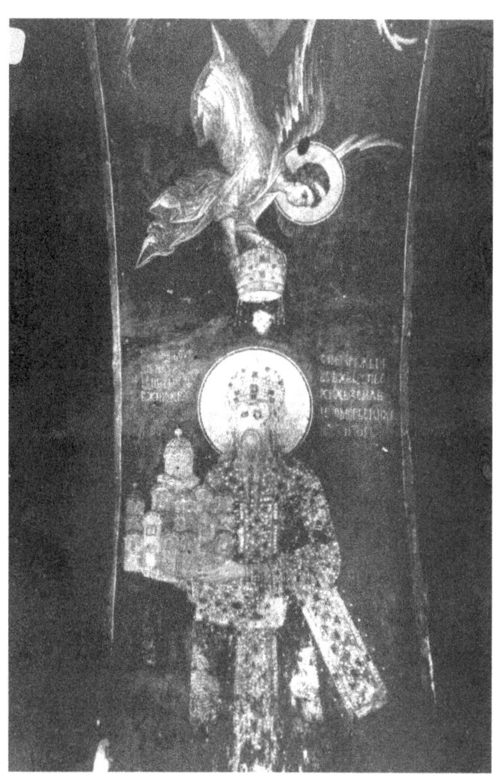

FIGURE 99. GRACANICA, KRAL MILUTIN CROWNED BY CHRIST THROUGH AN ANGEL, FRESCO PAINTING, 1318-1321

Staro Nagoricino near Kumanovo is a Saint George monastery built by Kral Stefan Uros II Milutin in 1313 according to an inscription on a plate placed over the western entrance of the church. Another inscription dates it to 1316-1318. An ambitious fresco program that includes usual Byzantine themata, shows scenes from Christ's Suffering, the Miracles and Parables of Christ in the nave. Also Saint George's Life is depicted there, the Life of the Virgin Mary in the prothesis and the Life of Saint Nicholas in the diakonikon. The iconostasis in marble has icons in fresco of Saint George Diassoritis and the Virgin Pelagonitissa. In the narthex 365 scenes are developed from the calendar of the church, for the first time illustrated in Serbian art. This number of episodes with a didactic character threatens the balance between the narrative and the pictorial. The program and the style is repeated in Gracanica.

In the peripheral Scandinavia, Byzantine fresco painting made its appearance only in the 12th century, foremost in the churches on Gotland Garda and Källunge (Fig. 100,

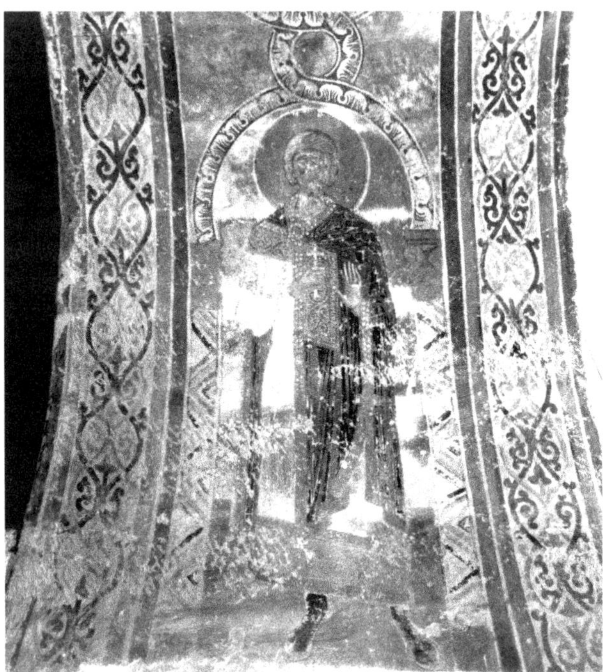

Figure 100. Saint Boris, Garda church, fresco painting, Gotland, third quarter of the 12th century

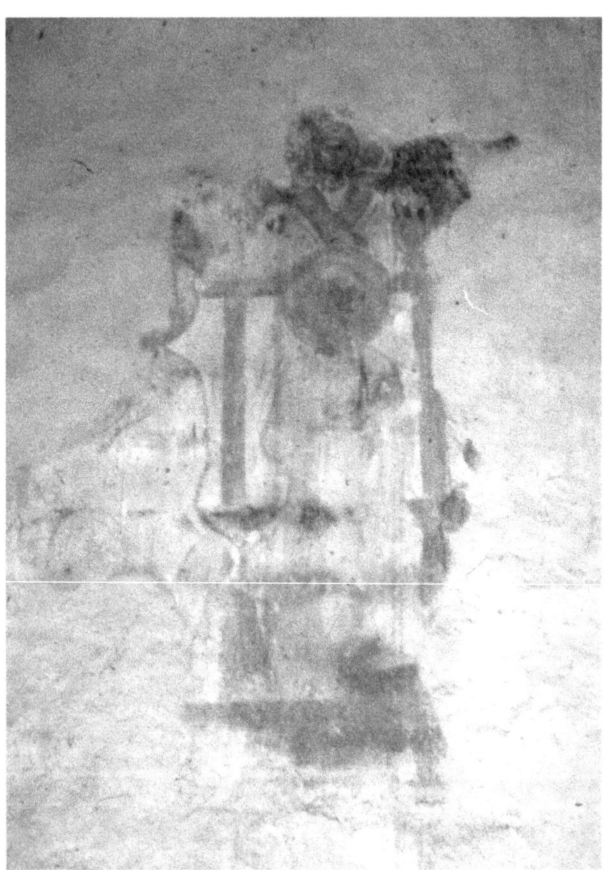

Figure 101. Last Judgment fragment, Källunge, fresco painting, Gotland, third quarter of the 12th century

101). There an authentic Late Comnenian fresco cycle is represented with Christ's Life as the principal theme, with the Forty martyrs below the ceiling logs and the Theotokos in the apse surrounded by archangels. Both churches have motifs of the Last Judgment on the west walls. The angels carry the imperial pearl-studded coronation girdle, the loros, and the thrones of the apostles are ornamented with pearls. The angels in Källunge have a blue nimbus. The apses were long ago demolished and only the entrance portal remains. The Byzantine arabesque is depicted both in Garda and Källunge.

Also in Torpa church outside Eskiltuna on the loft over the star vaults built in the 15th century there is a Byzantine fresco cycle with Christ's Life as the theme. The church is connected to the cult of Saint Eskil and the paintings were most likely commissioned by a workshop of the Crusaders belonging to the Order of the Johannites in the 12th century, that decorated the nowadays destroyed monastery in the vicinity.

In Gotland Russian Byzantine paintings have been preserved from wooden churches with fragments of the Last Judgment in Eke, Dalhem and Sundre churches (Fig. 102) from the 12th century. In order to explain the existence of Byzantine paintings so far away from the borders of the Empire, the intensive colonisation that was carried through from Russia towards the northwest primarily for commercial purposes must be referred to.

In Visby the Saint Lars church was erected with inspiration from the commercial courtyard in Novgorod in a plan that the church of the Apostles in Constantinople originally had as a prototype. Oleg I Ioannisian at the Hermitage in Saint Petersburg has identified the similarities with the Paraskevi church in the commercial courtyard in Novgorod.

A Late Comnenian plate of steatite from the 12th century has also been found in the vicinity of the church of Källunge in Gotland (Fig. 62), an iconostasis in miniature that was used by priests who accompanied the tradesmen and stayed over the winter in liturgical contexts at the celebration of the Eucharist. It depicts a Stavrosis scene, Christ's Crucifixion, with Mary and the disciple John and the archangels Gabriel and Michael. Aside from that, the glass windows in Gotland that were painted by masters from the Sachsonian-Westphalian school in the 1250s, have elements of Byzantine ceremonial art. This is most evident in the Pantocrator images that appear in Endre (Fig. 34) and Dalhem with models in the glass-painting that was made in Constantinople at the same time and that has been developed in the apse paintings in Sicily in Monreale and Cefalù.

In the National Museum in Stockholm is preserved an icon of the Pantocrator from the end of the 14th century (Fig. 103) of Constantinopolitan origin in an austere heroic style with compact volumes and rich colouring. It belonged to the Harald Bagge collection and was bought by the museum in 1917.

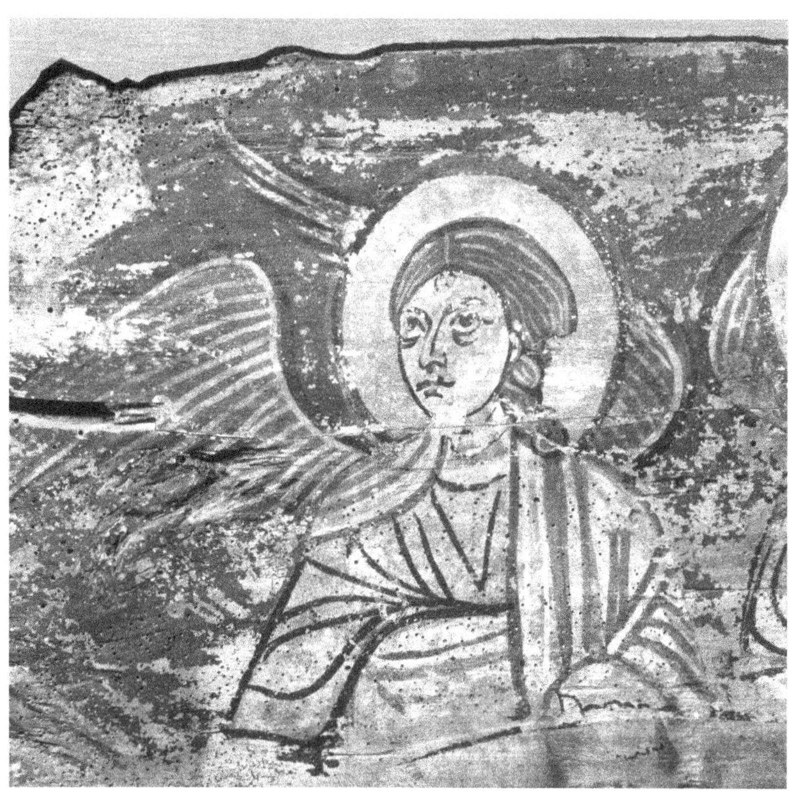

Figure 102. An angel of the Last Judgment fragments, Sundre, Gotland, painting on wood, first half of the 12th century

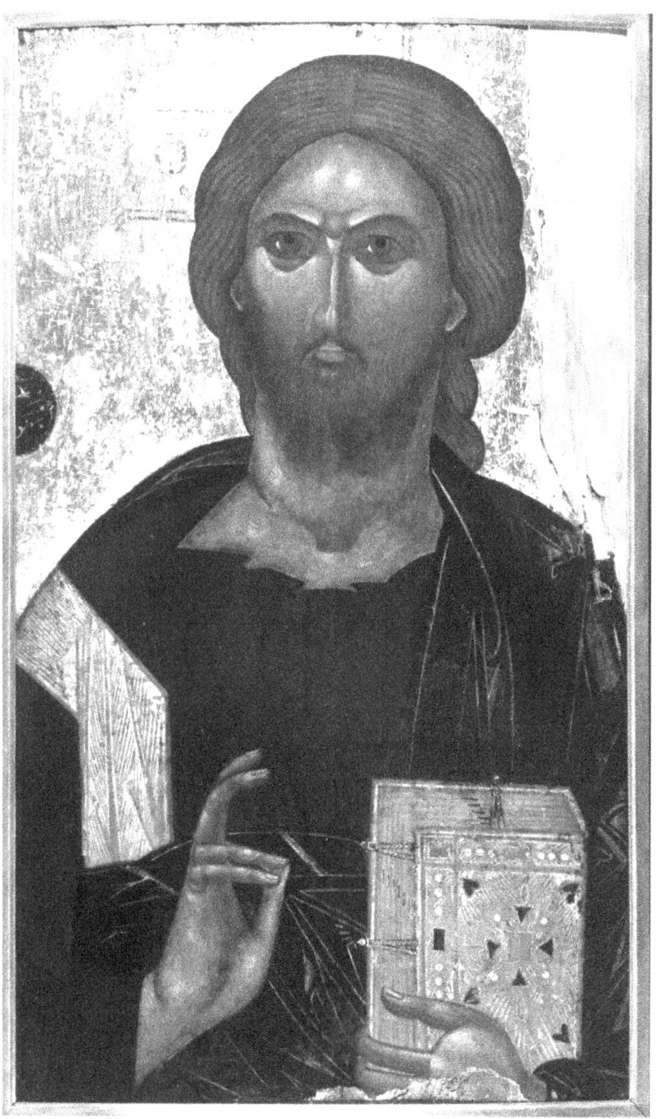

Figure 103. Icon of the Pantocrator, Nationalmuseum, Stockholm, 14th century

Chapter 8

Rus′

Kiev a New Constantinople – Moscow the Third Rome – the New Jerusalem

The Byzantine empire extended its hegemony to the areas north of the Black Sea during the Macedonian era in the 10th century. The Northmen had started to penetrate into Russia already during the 8th century and established their commercial activity in Staraja Ladoga in northern Russia and then continued through the impenetrable forests to Volga and the Dnepr. Thus the top stratum of the Russian state became populated by Russified Northmen. In the 10th century Rus′ was included in the Byzantine Commonwealth. Great Prince Vladimir the Saint was baptized together with the Russian population in Kiev in 988 and thereby the Greek influence on the arts, church administration and education became dominant.

The Russians had tried to conquer Constantinople in 860, 911, 941 and 1043 and were transformed into commercial allies. Already the Princess Olga, Igor's widow, had been baptized at the court of Constantine VII Porphyrogennitos in 956. In the 10th century the Church of the Tithes, the Desjatinnaja was built, the Cyrillos monastery and the Peterskaja Lavra and in 1036-1054 the great cathedral Saint Sophia was built by Great Prince Jaroslav Mudroj, the wise, who had married the Swedish Princess Ingegerd, daughter of King Olof Skötkonung, the first baptized Swedish king. In Russian she was called Irene and was canonized as the nun Anne. Great Prince Jaroslav, the son of Vladimir the Saint, devoted himself to Greek learning and invited a monk from Mount Athos to found monasteries in Kiev. Novgorod was a principality a short time before Kiev. It was situated to the south of Staraja Ladoga, a Viking period emporium, that was founded in the 750s, from which point of departure the Northmen penetrated into and colonized Russia along the rivers Volga and Dnepr.

Russified Varangians formed, together with their retinue, the druzhina, the governing stratum in Rus′. The Saint Sophia cathedral in Novgorod (Fig. 104) from 1034 has five domes and five naves and is situated at the river Volkhov. Straight across lies the commercial town with Jaroslav's commercial courtyard and the Gotlandian commercial courtyard with the many commercial churches. Aside from that Novgorod has a great richness of churches from the 12th century, among which the Spas Nereditsa, the Saviour church, is of great interest for iconography in the churches of Gotland. Saint Sophia in Kiev (Fig. 105) has 13 domes, five naves and open

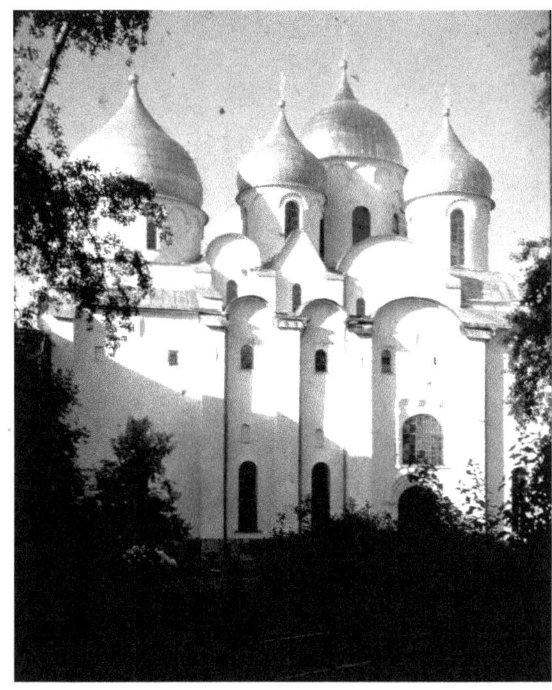

Figure 104. Saint Sophia, Novgorod, 1034

galleries that symbolise the dignity of the prince as *isapostolos*, the thirteenth apostle. In the interior there are Greek mosaics and Russian frescoes, which among other things show Christ surrounded by the founders Vladimir the Saint, Princess Olga and Jaroslav and Ingegerd with four daughters and three sons on the west wall in the nave. In the apse the great Mother of God as orant is depicted in mosaic, the Annunciation, the forty martyrs in the arcade arches of the central dome and Christ who distributes the Eucharist to his disciples. The rest of the church is covered by frescoes.

Cyril Mango has published the *Building of the Churches of Kievan Russia* by P.A. Rappoport and there the author demonstrates how the Byzantine building technique was adapted to the Russian climate. In the small principalities Vladimir and Suzdal, Jaroslavl, Galich and Smolensk provincial traditions were developed in the architecture. Andrej Boguljobskij, the son of Dmitrij Dolgorukij, the youngest son of Vladimir Monomach, became Great Prince in Vladimir in 1157 and built a palace and the

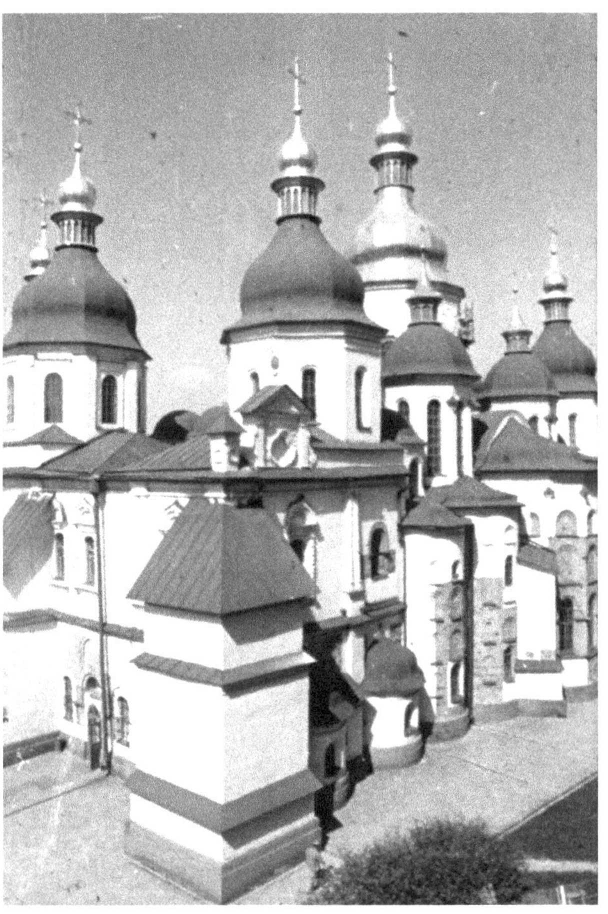

Figure 105. Saint Sophia, Kiev, *ca* 1050

Pokrov church, the Protecting Cloak of the Virgin at the river Nerl. The town Vladimir at the river Kliasma has the most important buildings from the 12th century, the Saint Dmitrij cathedral (Fig. 106) with frescoes made by a Greek painters workshop that worked there in 1198. Of this painting only the Last Judgment on the west wall remains. In the Uspenskij cathedral, the Dormition of our Lady, the famous painter monk Andrej Rublev worked in 1408 together with his assistant Daniil Tjornyi. Of this activity there remains the gigantic iconostasis with the romboid forms and a Last Judgment representation with authentic female portraits.

The wooden churches with their many onion cupolas are famous. Particularly splendid is the Kishi church from the 18th century in Russian Carelia. The Carelian wooden churches have been studied by Lars Pettersson.

Aristotele Fioravanti from Bologna erected the Uspenskij cathedral (Fig. 111) in the Moscow Kremlin in the 1470s. Alisio Novi from Milan built the Archangelskij cathedral there in 1505-1509, the burial church for the tsars inaugurated to the Archangels. Also the clock tower of Ivan Velikij 1505-1508 was erected by Italian architects and the Kolomenskoe church outside the city 1530. As a reminder of the conquest of Kazan, Ivan the Terrible commissioned the colourful cupola church of Marie Protection at the grave, Vassilij Blachennij (Fig. 107), on

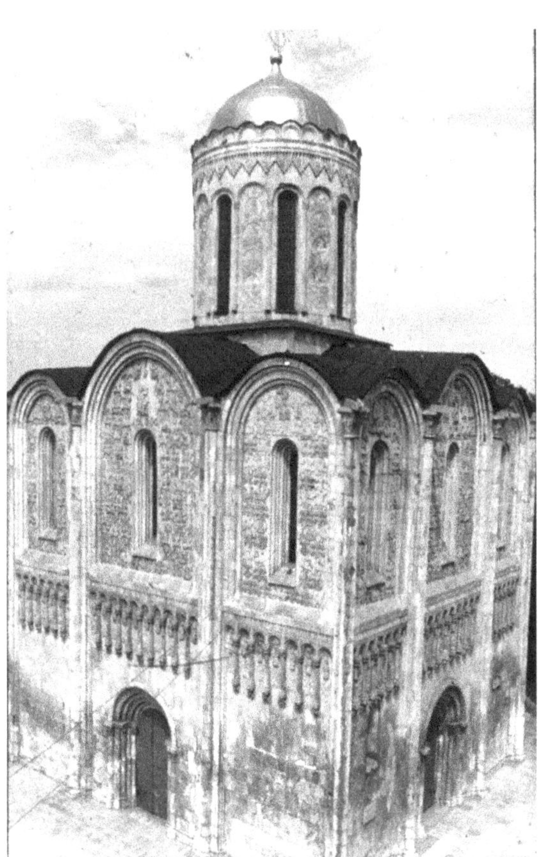

Figure 106. Saint Dmitrij Vladimir, 12th century

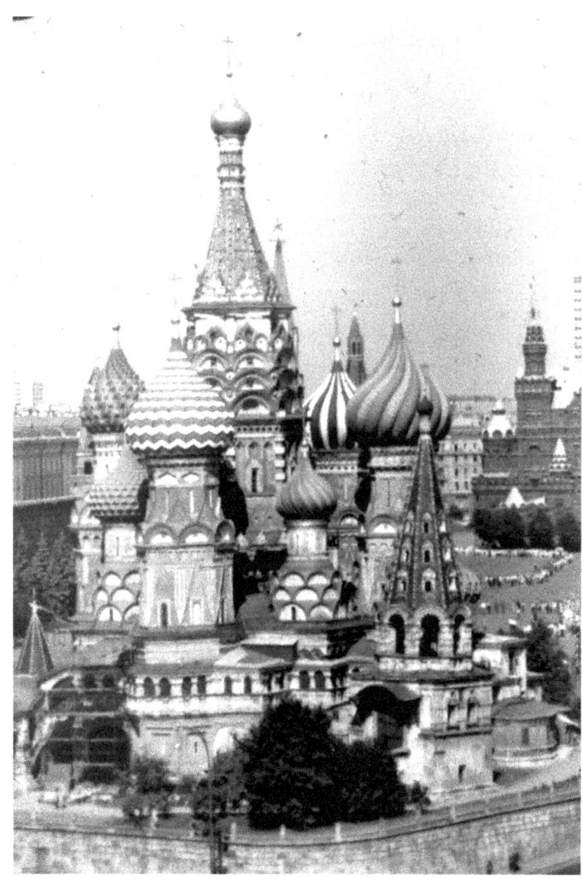

Figure 107. Vassilij Blachennij, The Moscow Kremlin, 1555-1560

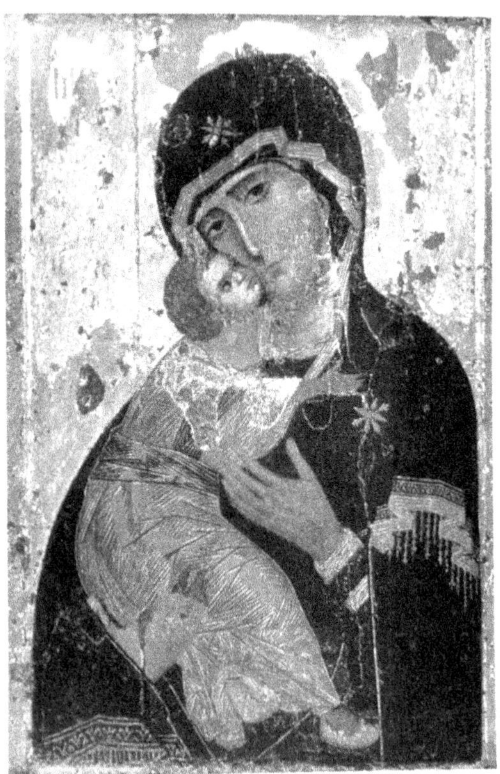

FIGURE 108. BOGOMATER VLADIMIRSKAJA, ICON, TRETJAKOV GALLERY, MOSCOW, 11TH CENTURY

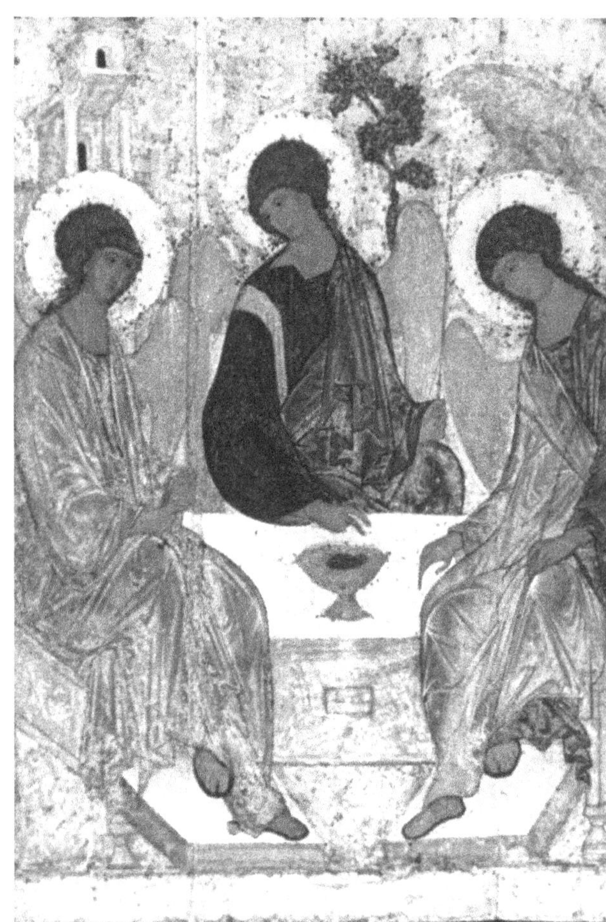

FIGURE 109. THE TRINITY BY ANDREJ RUBLEV, TRETJAKOV GALLERY, MOSCOW, 1425

Red Square outside the Kremlin in the 1550s and according to the legend he had the two architects Barma and Posnik strangled in order to prevent a repetition of this style of building which was unique.

Rublev had been the pupil of a Greek master Theophanes, who is called Feofan Grek in Russian and who first decorated the church of the Transfiguration of Christ in Novgorod in 1378 with an image of the Trinity and a frightening Christ Pantocrator in the dome. His picturesque style is characterized by light accents and strong expressiveness. He then participated in the execution of the great iconostasis in the Annunciation cathedral in the Kremlin together with Rublev.

The Russian painting schools that developed after the first known Russian icon painter Alypij, who lived at the end of the 12th century, introduced the tradition from individual local schools in Novgorod, Pskov, Moscow, Tver and Suzdal. In Staraja Ladoga also a Greek painters workshop painted the frescoes of the Saint George cathedral and a Russian decorated the Spas Nereditsa in 1198 situated outside Novgorod.

Some icons are particularly famous: the Bogomater Vladimirskaja (Fig. 108), the Mother of God from Vladimir with the child at her cheek, a Greek Eleousa, the Mother of Mercy, that was brought from Constantinople in the 12th century and later on partly has been repainted, the Virgin Blachernitissa from Jaroslavl in the Trejakov Gallery in Moscow from the 13th century with the large size that is a Greek Platytera holding the Christ Child in front of her breast in a tondo "More voluminous than the universe", because she has given birth to the Divine Word, the Logos in her womb. Further was the Virgin of Don, who caused the victory of Dmitrij Donskoj over the Mongols on the Snipe Field Kulikovo polje in 1380 and the regenerating Pimenskaja, an icon of the Mother of God from the 14th century that heralds the plasticity of the Renaissance and Rublev's Trinity (Fig. 109) from the iconostasis in the Troitza-Sergevich monastery in Zagorsk from *ca* 1425. The Novgorod school, the Stroganow and the Moscow icon schools remained into the 18th century.

Podlinniki, the Russian correspondence to the Greek manuals for painting, played an exceptional role in the industrial production of icons in the Post-Byzantine period, where whole Russian villages were organized in this production.

Chapter 9

Iconology – the world as icon

The Iconoclasm and the attitude of the Popes

The image controversy that raged in Byzantium in the 8th and 9th centuries caused much human suffering and great material destruction. During the Isaurian dynasty that had drawn from the aniconic conception of the Arabic storm suddenly holy images were forbidden in religion. The struggle broke out in connection with the destruction of the holy icon of Christ, a Pantocrator in semi-figure on the Chalke Bronze gate at the entrance of the sacred palace in 726 during the reign of Emperor Leon III the Isaurian (717-741). Instead of sacred images church art was substituted with naked undecorated crosses. Such a cross can be seen in the apse of Hagia Eirene church in Constantinople (Fig. 13) from the 8th century. Pope Gregory II (715-731) sent two letters to Emperor Leon III, where he pointed out that it was not the question for an emperor to judge in divine sacred matters, and even less about pictures that had apostolic tradition. Not only icons in temples and private houses were destroyed, but also statues of the Saviour that were standing at the city gates in Constantinople.

In 754 a council was convoked in Constantinople in the palace Hiereia by Leon's son the Emperor Constantine V (741-775) that condemned the icon cult in a definition, Horos. The patriarchates in the Orient as well as the Papal delegation refused to participate in this council. The Empress Irene succeeded in 787 in convoking an image-defending council in Nicea (Nicenum II) that abolished the declaration of 754 and proposed a new one. To this council delegates from all the patriarchates and legates from Pope Hadrianus I (772-795) came. The Pope sent two letters about icons, one for the Empress Irene and another for her son, the underage Constantine VI in 787. In the form of a sermon he expressed his joy over the fact that the image controversy had been settled and that the council had defined the true Orthodox belief, in particular concerning the veneration of the holy icons of Christ, the Theotokos, the apostles, prophets, martyrs and confessors. He also discussed the controversial decision of the Sixth Ecumenical Council that forbade the representation of Christ as a Lamb with reference to the passus in the Bible John 1, 20: "See the Lamb of God who takes away the sins of the world" that he juxtaposed to the holy portrait of the incarnated Word as a symbol for Christ. He ordered that all icons that had been pulled down should be replaced on their former seats in the capacity of the primate of Saint Peter that had prepared itself for the fight in defence of the images.

The acts of the council in Nicea were translated into Latin for Pope John VIII (872-882). Seventeen of the bishops who had participated in the synod hostile to the icons in 754 were present and abjured officially their mistake to condemn the images. However, the struggle flamed up again and a new Horos was formulated against the images in 815 that abolished all the icon-friendly declarations.

The definition of Nicenum II in 787 reads:

> The holy great and Ecumenical Council – convened by the grace of God and by the sanction of our pious Emperors, those lovers of Christ, Constantine and his mother Irene, for a second time in the magnificent capital of the Nicaeans of the province of the Bithynia, and in the holy church of God which is named after Wisdom – having followed the tradition of the Catholic Church, has defined the following:
>
> Christ our God, who granted to us the light of His knowledge and who delivered us from the darkness of the insanity of the idols, after He betrothed himself to His holy catholic church, which is without spot or wrinkle, commanded that she may be so preserved. He also gave assurances to his holy disciples, saying: I am with you always, to the close of the ages. He gave this commandment not only to his disciples but also to us who through them have believed in his name.
>
> However, some men, paying no regard to this gift, and encouraged by the deceitful enemy, deviated from the right thinking and, after opposing the tradition of the Catholic Church, erred in the perception of the truth. As the word of the Proverbs says, they caused the axles of their own husbandry to go astray and...they gathered bareness with their hands, for even though they are called priests – without being so – they dared to discredit the decency which dedicated items have, (a decency) proper to God. It is for them that God cries out through the words of the prophecy: Many shepherds have destroyed my vineyard and they defiled my portion. For, having followed men of impiety in their own minds, they have accused the Holy Church, which has been joined to Christ the God, and they have made no distinction between the holy and the profane, calling the icon of the Lord and those of his saints with the same name as the wooden symbols of the idols of Satan.

For this reason God the sovereign One, not bearing to see his people destroyed by such a pestilence, through his good will brought us, the leaders of the priesthood, together from all parts, through the divine zeal and inspiration of Constantine and Irene, our most faithful Emperors, so that the divine tradition of the Catholic Church may regain its authority by a common vote. Having, therefore, sought most diligently and conferred with each other, and having set as our goal the truth, we neither delete nor add anything, but preserve undiminished everything that is of the Catholic Church adhering also to the six holy Ecumenical Councils, first that which convened in the magnificent capital of the Nicaeans, and also that which convened after this in the Royal City by God... Be this as it may, and continuing along the royal pathway, following both the teaching of our holy Fathers which is inspired by God and the tradition of the Catholic Church – for we know that this tradition is of the holy Spirit dwelling in her – in absolute precision and harmony with the spirit, we declare that, next to the sign of the precious and life-giving cross, venerable and holy icons – made of colours, pebbles, or any other material that is fit – may be set in the holy churches of God, on holy utensils and vestments, on walls and boards, in houses and in streets. These may be the icons of our Lord and God the Saviour Jesus Christ, or of our pure Lady the holy Theotokos, or of honourable angels, or of any saint or holy man. For the more these are kept in view through their iconographic representations, the more those who look at them are lifted up to remember and have an earnest desire for the prototypes. Also (we declare) that one may render to them the veneration of honour: not the true worship of our faith, which is due only to the divine nature, but the same kind of veneration as is offered to the form of the precious and life-giving cross, to the holy gospels, and to the other holy dedicated items. Also (we declare) that one may honour these by bringing to them incense and light, as was the pious custom of the early (Christians); for "the honour to the icon is conveyed to the prototype" (St Basil of Caesarea, *On the Holy Spirit*, PG 32: 149 C). Thus, he who venerates the icon venerates the hypostasis of the person depicted on it. In this way the teaching of our holy Fathers – that is, the tradition of the Catholic Church, which has accepted the gospel from one end of the earth to the other – is strengthened.

In this controversy the most important theologians and brilliant thinkers in Byzantium were engaged. Because of their strong expressiveness the icons were an important element of the cult. They were conceived of as miracle-working. An Emperor, Constantine V, engaged in the struggle theoretically and wrote a treatise against the existence of the images, that is not preserved. Together with the Ecumenical Patriarch John VII Grammatikos (837-843) these two formed a front against the images. Another argument of great potentiality was that images dishonoured and profaned the holy persons and Christ could only be materialized as an image in the Eucharist. Against this the two apostles of the icon cult, John Damascenos and Theodore of Studion, answered that in the Eucharist Christ was really present and not only an image. From the conception of the Late Antique Neoplatonic doctrine of the idea about the prototype, the model, and its representation, the icon, the principal argument was developed that because Logos, the Divine Word, was incarnated in Christ and had taken material form as a human being, the matter had been divinized and therefore His holy hypostasis could be represented in the arts. The writings of the Church Father Basil the Great were referred to by both icon-friends and icon-enemies, but mostly by the former. The Ecumenical Patriarch Nicephoros I (806-815) took an active part in the defence of the holy images in the cult during the second phase of the iconoclasm.

When the struggle was finally settled in 843 after the intention in the Council of Nicea 787 had been confirmed, the image cult was again elevated to a dogma and each believer was obliged to venerate the holy images, and if not was threatened with excommunication. All the documents hostile to the icons were burnt. In the west the icon-friendly council Nicenum II was afterwards elevated to the Seventh Ecumenical Council, binding for Christianity.

An illumination in the Skylitzes matritensis from the 12th century shows how the Empress Theodora converses with the icon artist and monk Lazaros, whose hands were mutilated by her dead husband Theophilos, so as not to be able to create works of art. According to tradition it was he who created the new image of Christ Pantocrator in mosaics that was again placed on the bronze Chalke Gate outside the Sacred palace. Many gave their lives in the image struggle. The army had as a task the destruction of all sacred images and only in the utmost periphery of the Empire, on Mount Sinai and in Rome, where the Pope protected image worship, are there preserved Pre-Iconoclastic images.

Arguments and attitudes

Against the icon	**For the icon**
Pre-Iconoclastic times	
Horror imaginis, fear of pagan idols (*agalmata)*	The anthropological argument: man as God's image

Against the icon	**For the icon**
The prohibition of the Old Testament against idols (Ex 20: 3, 4)	The anagogical function of the images: to lift up the soul toward the divine
The nature of images is "spurious" (trompe l'oeil)	The communicative argument: images are the channels of divine communication. Between the image, *ektypos*, and the prototype, *typos,* there is a transcendental relation
Images are made of matter and dishonour the divine	The christological argument: Christ as God's image (*eikon tou Theou*, Philo, Col 1: 15)
The ethical image theory: the true image is the virtuous Christian	The didactic argument: images interpret the dogmas, the theoretical precepts of the faith
Iconoclastic times	
Image cult: *eidololatria,* veneration of idols	The new didactic argument: the image proclaims the doctrine of Incarnation, teaches the illiterate and stimulates the imitation of the virtues of the saints
Christ is not possible to circumscribe (*aperigraptos*)	The historical argument: images mirror historical facts
Prohibition to depict Christ. Icons of Christ are defective, they either show only His human nature or they mix or separate His two natures	The sacramental argument: images are extensions and reenactments of the Incarnation
The true image is Christ in the Eucharist	The miraculous argument: supernatural powers work through the icons, *acheiropoietoi*, which are not made by human hands
	The art shares in the validity of the Holy Scripture because the revelation has a visual aspect
	The relation between the image and the prototype does not depend on having part in each others essence but on the identity of the two hypostases
	The Eucharist is Christ Himself and not His image

The popes were asked about their opinion at an early stage and Pope Gregory II, in two letters in 726 that have been preserved, accused the Emperor Leon III the Isaurian as having, as only a prince, interfered in matters of faith in opposition to the teachings of the Church Fathers with his image offensive:

> For ten years You have ruled without mentioning the

holy images. Now You call those who venerate these images venerators of idols. Christ has abandoned You and You will end in the eternal fire. You write that nothing that has been produced as artistic handicraft might be venerated though the Holy Scripture confirms that the Ark of the Covenant and the Mercy Seat were decorated with sculptures of cherubim and seraphim and the image prohibition in Exodus was directed against the animistic idols of the Cananeans and their worship of animals. Holy images have been created since the time of the apostles to the glory of God and for liturgical use. Christ sent the impression of his sacred face, the *mandylion*, on a linen cloth to King Abgar of Edessa. In the painting sacred events in Christ's Life and the fight of the martyrs are depicted. When we enter into the basilica of San Pietro in Rome we meditate over the holy representations of Jesus Christ our Saviour, for whose sake we shed tears and ask him to save us, of the holy Mother of God whom we ask to intercede for us in front of God, of the holy Stefanus the first martyr who shed his blood for Christ's sake, whom we ask to intercede for us and in the same way with the holy images of the martyrs. Turn away Your evil thoughts and liberate Your mind from this scandalum that You enforce on the whole world. You are a destroyer and a persecutor of holy images, an heretic. You have nothing to do with the dogmas of the church, it is the matter of the bishops. Stop persecuting, write to all the parts of the world that the images shall be replaced on their holy seats. You have undressed the churches and the liturgical vestments their holy icons. You have not preserved the definitions of the Church Fathers. What belongs to our Christian church are artifacts of precious stones, wood, marble, ceramics and limestone, true images of the historical and miracle-working relations of holy authors about Christ's suffering and about his holy Mother of God, about the saints, the apostles and their actions, which are edifying and elevate the soul to God. O emperor, listen to our humility, stop persecuting the holy church! It is the task of the bishops to formulate the dogmas and not the emperor, as we are led by the Holy Spirit. The ecclesiastical institutions differ from the secular. Concerning civil and military matters You have power but You do not rule over the spiritual dogmatic order. Through Thy trespasses You have lost the Holy Spirit. You persecute us tyrannically and inhumanly. Repent and do penance and write to all regions where this scandal rages!

The papal letters in favour of the sacred images are preserved in Latin and Greek among the documents of the councils.

Chapter 10

Byzantium and the periphery

Post-Byzantine art – Abstract art and the 20th century

Byzantine art spread outside the borders of the Empire through artists of Greek origin who were sent out. Therefore to authentic Byzantine art also belongs the tradition that was brought by Greek masters to Russia, the Balkans, Italy and Sicily. Coptic and Ethiopian art also belongs to this sphere. Characteristic for these heterogeneous traditions are their root in Greek Hellenistic art, whose aesthetics and doctrine of proportions entered a fruitful synthesis with Oriental elements and was placed in the service of the Christian ideology. Late Antique Imperial iconography was administered and transformed by the Christian empire. The emperor and Christ Pantocrator formed the top of the secular and cosmic hierarchy. An effort to monumentalize, to stylize the forms towards two dimensionality, extravagant splendour and a highly developed technique were some characteristics. In order to create an abstract emotional expression plastic spatial forms were avoided. Byzantine art was, like Egyptian art, one of the most consequent expressions of a visual theology in the history of art, which intended to represent a transformed cosmos.

To draw strictly geographical and time boundaries for the Post-Byzantine tradition is difficult. For practical reasons the fall of Constantinople is used as a terminus post quem for the continuous development. After this political conditions drastically changed in the area of the Empire, that had shrunk to Greece and parts of Asia Minor. The catastrophe led to a revitalization of other centres through the emigration of Constantinopolitan elite artists who influenced development not only in Italy, but also on Mount Athos and in the Greek archipelago.

Post-Byzantine art can be defined as the art that during the centuries after the fall of the Empire consciously succeeded the Byzantine artistic tradition and took models from the Paleologian period, i.e. the art of the 14th and 15th centuries. As the imperial court, the court manufacturers and the court workshops had disappeared as commissioners and art producers, the Orthodox church remained as the proper administrator of the Byzantine artistic heritage. In certain countries, for instance Serbia, the tradition lived on in concurrence with a western Catholic influence, that influenced art in the direction of Renaissance, Baroque and Rococo, against which the church tried to defend itself. In other countries, for instance in Russia, the development went in a completely opposite direction. The tsardom was introduced in the 14th century and this power factor was strengthened during the following centuries, with adjacent favourable conditions and an unbroken continuity for the Russian Byzantine tradition. Only during the ecclesiastical schism in the 17th century did something like a critical circumstance occur. In the Balkans the Turkish government extended and limited the possibilities for a free ecclesiastical cultivation of the arts, a situation that, however, improved during the 17th century.

Post-Byzantine art that no longer included imperial monumental programs, with the exception of Russia, was concentrated on ecclesiastical art. Provincial churches were completely covered on the interior with frescoes according to a definite program and the development of the iconostasis into a completely covering wall changed the status and importance of the icons. A need for mass production of icons arose. Double-sided icons of procession became common, feast day cycles and monthly icons were painted with a splendid richness of details. Aside from the professional painting of icons, that reached an unprecedented development particularly in Russia, popular amateur painting made its entrance into art history. Profane art was pushed into the background in favour of the creation of ecclesiastical textiles and liturgical artefacts. The demand of the church to dominance over artistic production remained. The artists who preferably should belong to the spiritual stand had to prepare with fasting, Eucharist and prayers. Colours and binding means should be mixed into blessed water and the work be inaugurated by a priest. This was the prerequisite for a holy image that served liturgical purposes, either situated in the church or in the "beautiful corner", *krazhny ugulok*, at home.

Valuable collections of Post-Byzantine art are preserved in the Benaki and the Byzantine Museum in Athens. Art from this period was displayed in an exhibition in Athens in 1965/1966. There are also collections in the Vestiary of the Kremlin in Moscow, where the ecclesiastical textiles have a prominent place beside the imperial insignia. In the Vatican Museum in Rome, on Mount Athos, in the Museum of the Serbian Orthodox church in Belgrade, in the Museum of the Finnish Orthodox church in Kuopio, and in the German icon museum Rechlinghausen there are rich collections. The exposed and deposed icon collection in the National Museum in Stockholm is seconded by a Post-Byzantine icon collection in the Ny Carlsberg Glyptotek in Copenhagen.

Greece

Important artistic centres in Greece, on Mount Athos, on Cyprus and on Crete and in Mistra continued to produce in the Byzantine tradition. On Mount Athos it is possible to speak of a Renaissance during the 16th century for fresco painting. Several monastery buildings were decorated by Cretan and Serbian masters, the Lavra monastery, Koutlomousiou, Dionysiou, Dochariou, the Pantocrator monastery, Stavronikita and Xenophontos.

In Crete worked masters who had emigrated from Constantinople, like Alexios Apokavkos and Nicolaos Philanthropinos. The frescoes of the Cretan masters on Mount Athos in the Meteora monastery from the middle of the 16th century show the same austere and sober style with the emphasized volume that ruled in the icon painting. Some masters consciously returned to the artistic tradition of the 14th and 15th century, for instance Michael Damascinos who used transparent colours and a free brush stroke. Icons with one figure from the 16th century emphasize monumentality. The icon painter Euphrosynos from 1542 and the master of the 17th century Emmanuel Tzane emphasized volume and the geometrical light accents.

In the west the Cretan tradition is known through El Greco. Xenos Dighenis in Mistra and John of Patmos also found their models in the Paleologian tradition. During the 1550s there arose a Greek artistic centre in Venice, that continued this tradition with rich details in the landscape, picturesque motifs, soft modelling and restrained gestures. The icons of the 15th century are calmer and more symmetrical. Discrete genre scenes in the spirit of the Renaissance slip in. The manger is depicted in perspective and in *chiaroscuro*, rich obscure light. In the same way as the *maniera bizantina* became a dominating element in the Italian Dugento and Trecento painting, Post-Byzantine art was influenced by the Late Gothic and the Renaissance.

Bulgaria, Serbia, Romania

Not until the 17th century was a Bulgarian icon tradition developed. The Turks forbade the building of churches during the 16th century. The Athonite monk Pimen worked during the first half of the 17th century. In the monasteries in Etropole, Trnovo, Sofia, Neseber and Vraca important painting centres were installed. The icons were decorated with rich ornaments, the nimbus became punched and the frames were carved. The icons signed by Jerej Gergin, the Zograph, i.e. the icon painter, Nedelko, Zograph Stamen, the priest monk Vasilije and the Pop Petar originate from the 17th century and Nicola, the teacher Kosta and Con, the Zograph Panajot and Thoma Visanov from the 18th century. The masters used manuals, *hermeneia*, in order strictly to stick to the authentic tradition. This did not however prevent details of Baroque and Rococo character emerging.

In the 18th century a popular naive type of painting developed with realistic elements and strong colours. The genre composition of the popular saints George and Demetrios dominated. On the icons of the iconostasis silver and gold fittings tended to become completely covering. After the 18th century the use of double-sided processional icons was prohibited by the Turks. In these areas Post-Byzantine art played an important part in the strategy for the survival of Orthodoxy.

In Serbia Byzantine art continued to develop until the 17th century in an unbroken tradition. The Serbian patriarchate was reinstalled in 1557 and became an important artistic centre. In the interior of the Balkans the faithfulness to the Orthodox tradition was stronger. The most important art appeared in the frontier areas, where the nobility had taken their refuge after the political collapse during the Turkocratia. In Herzegovina and Montenegro the Byzantine style dominated, in the remaining parts a mixed style ruled with Italian elements. Icon painting experienced a renaissance because of the high iconostasis with two floors, decorated at the top with the Theotokos and the apostle John. Also the church walls were decorated with icons that sometimes were exposed in their own "proskynetaria", small altars in front of which proskynesis, falling down on the face, was practised. The importance of the icons of procession, feast day and calendar icons also increased here.

A conservative aesthetical tendency dominated. Orientalizing ornaments and stylization after Russian models counteracted the western influences of naturalism, plasticity and spatial illusion. Also here models were sought in the painting of the Byzantine 14th century. In Serbia a narrative tendency was cultivated that found its expression in the life cycle of the saints.

The master Longin was a painter and scribe at the patriarchate in Pec. He decorated the monastery in Decani with frescoes. The fresco and icon painter George Mitrofanovic was educated in the Chilandar monastery on Mount Athos, where a group of Serbian painters worked. The frescoes in the refectory of Chilandar belong to the most important works of the early 17th century. Pop Danilo from Chilandar and zograph Radul worked at the patriarchate in Pec, Avsalom Vijicic in the monastery in Moraca. Jovan from Chilandar belonged to the last generation of Serbian masters. The monastic art of the Montegrine monks continued to the end of the 17th century when the Christian offensive against the Turks failed and the material base for artistic production disappeared. Icon painting decayed to hard painted full decoration.

The tendency to decorate the interior of the church with whole covering fresco cycles was strengthened in the

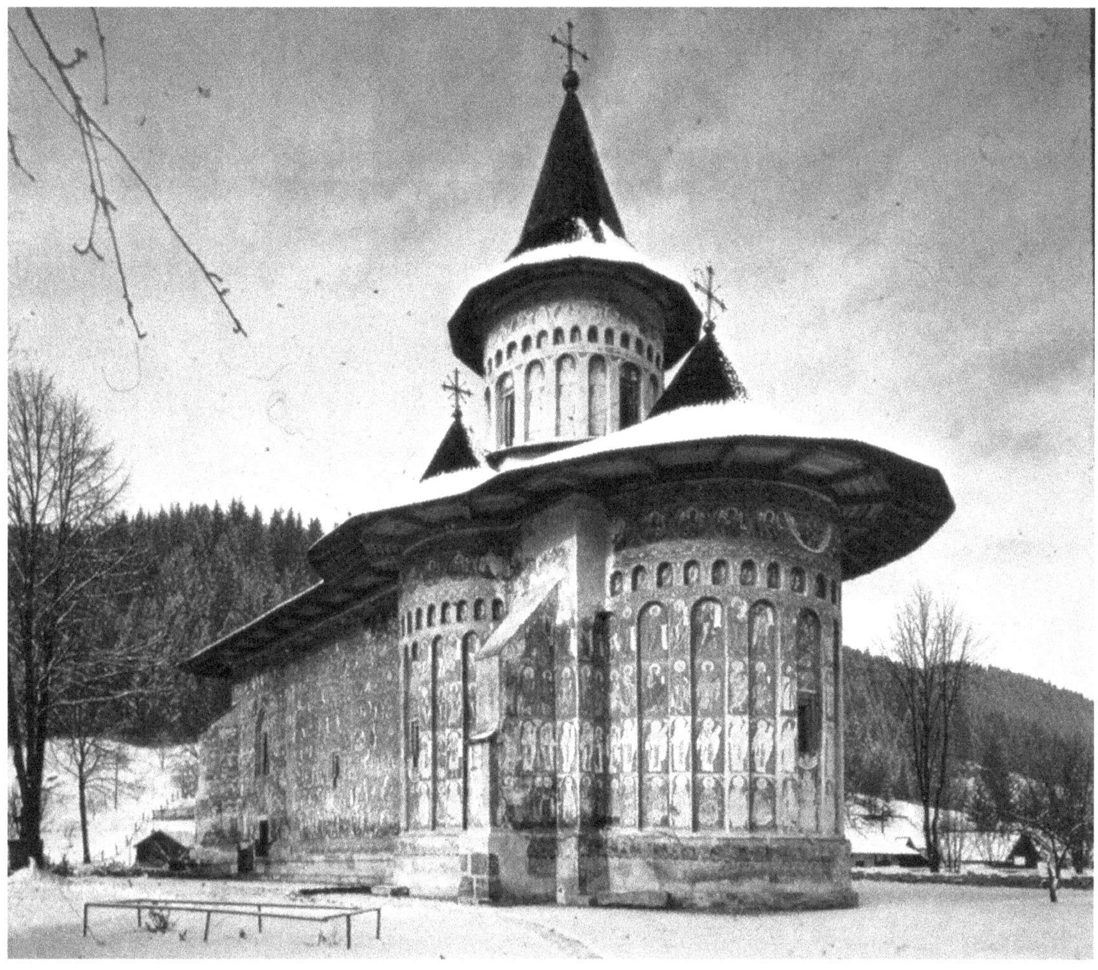

Figure 110. Voronetz, Roumania, 1488-1547

Post-Byzantine period. Most consequently this was shown in Romania, where Moldavian art reached its perfection during the reign of Prince Petru Rares in the middle of the 16th century. The completely decorated monastery churches in the interior and the exterior of the province Bukovina: Voronetz (Fig. 110), Humor, Moldovitza, Sucevitza and Arbore concluded in a crescendo, the grand finale of Byzantine art. The Acathistos hymn with all its iconographical elements and the representation of the historical topos the Siege of Constantinople stimulated the fight against the oppression of the Turks.

Russia

For Russian Byzantine art the year 1453 is no meaningful terminus. Often it is hard even for experts to determine if an icon is made in the 16th century or earlier. As a result of the fall of Constantinople Moscow proclaimed itself in the 16th century as the "Third Rome", but it was not the question of a *translatio imperii*, a transference of the Roman state as had been the case with the New Rome, Constantinople. The Moscovite state experienced prosperity during the early tsardom and imitated consciously Byzantine ceremonies and imperial insignia. In order to emphasize the dominance of Moscow spiritually and princely, some important church buildings were elevated in the Kremlin during the 15th and 16th century. From Italy Aristotele Fioravanti was called and he applied the principles of Alberti in the elevation of the well proportioned Uspenskij cathedral, the Dormition of Our Lady (Fig. 111). The interior is decorated with whole covering frescoes and the iconostasis reaches from the floor to the roof, adorned with icons of the most important masters of Russia.

The 16th century introduced a mixed style of Novgorodian and Moscovite elements. From this century on strict school identifications become impossible. The great monumental form of the Novgorodian style with emphasized verticalism and harmony was replaced by the rhythmical movement of the Moscow style, that was inspired by the style of the Paleologians. In Rublev's tradition the figures became elongated, the head and the extremities diminutive, the face traits softer and milder. Local schools inspired from Novgorod were developed in Rostov, Jaroslavl and Smolensk.

In order to draw a line of demarcation it is possible to state that the frescoes of master Dionysij in the church of the monastery of Saint Therapon north-east of Novgorod, Ferapontov monastir, was the beginning of Post-Byzantine

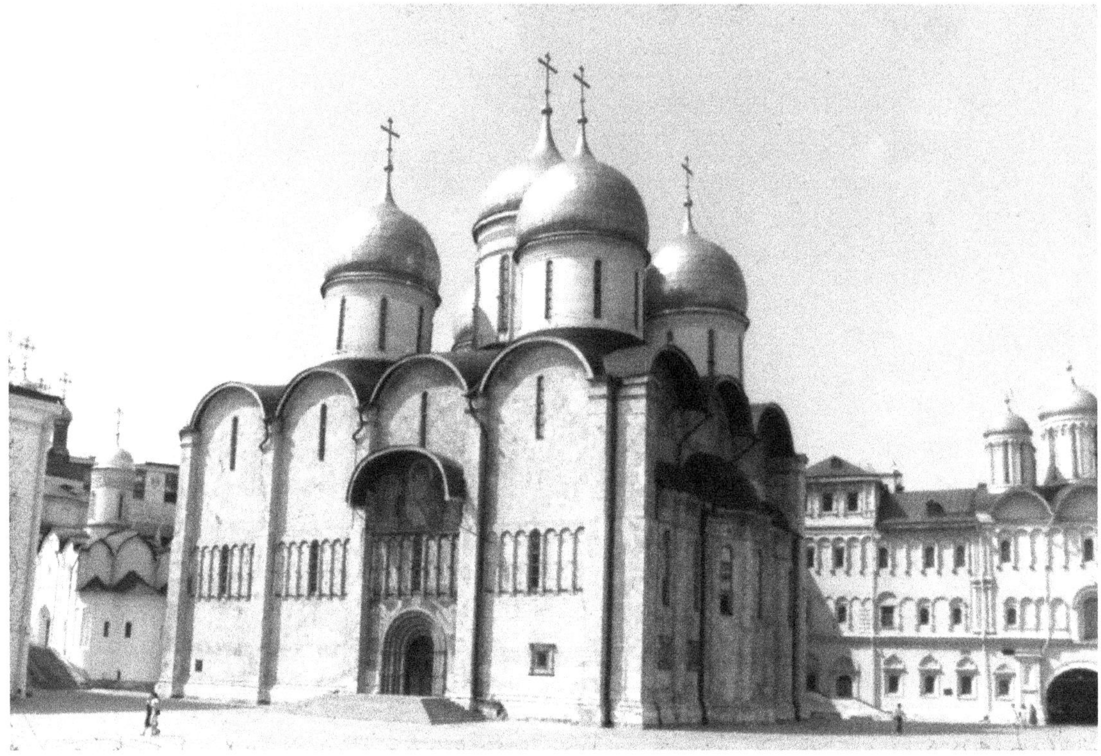

Figure 111. The Uspenskij cathedral, The Kremlin, Moscow, 1475-1479

art in 1500. In Vologda a particular imperial painting school was developed.

During the 16th century wooden churches were replaced in north and east Russia with stone churches. This meant a steadily increasing need for fresco painting, that was inspired by Paleologian art. Icon painting also increased in importance. A school associated with the magnate family Stroganov, that gave artistic commissions on behalf of the church, united the Novgorodian and Moscovite tradition with western elements. The interest in the details, the narrative tendency and the shimmering splendour of the colour is reminiscent of works of jewellery. This school flourished from 1580 to 1620. Masters known by name are Fjodor Savin, Stefan Arefjev, Nikofor Savin and Prokopij Tjirin.

During the 17th and 18th century court painting in Moscow was associated with the installed weapon arsenal Orushejnaja palata. There designers and painters worked who were appointed by the state. Simeon Ushakov, who was influenced by western illusionism, contributed to a dissolution of the tradition of icon painting in the last third of the 17th century. Also in Jaroslavl and Kostroma masters worked in this mixed style. Western artists were called to Orushejnaja palata and by way of engravings and woodcuts with illustrating iconographical descriptions, so-called *podlinniki*, western influence was spread.

The reaction came at the so-called Stroglav meeting, "The Council of the Hundred Chapters" in Moscow in 1551. It was decided that the artistic models must be Byzantine masters and the art of Rublev. Western motifs were condemned, in particular the custom of depicting God the Father in human shape. During the ecclesiastical schism in 1654 the Old believers, the *raskol′niki*, were detached from the church, who in particular cared for the icons.

The number of icon painters was enormous during the 17th and 18th centuries. Each town had between 30 and 40 officially appointed icon painters. In the agrarian villages in the government of Vladimir icons and images of saints were produced collectively in a large home industry, a type of production system with itinerant sellers and dealers. Most famous was the village Palech with its *kustari*, professional icon painters working at home. The result became a pastiche type of icon painting in the spirit of the Stroganov school difficult to date.

Other centres for the icon painting were Schuja, Kostroma and Fedoskino. About such a workshop for icon painting in the Vladimir government Maxim Gorkij wrote a famous relation. In the Finnish and Russian Carelia miracle-working Post-Byzantine icons are preserved from the Novgordian and the Moscovite tradition. Most important is the Mother of God with the Christ child in a tondo from Kalevitsa, a Znamenie, the Madonna of the Sign, surrounded by gold and pearls, now preserved in New Valamo in Finland.

The manuals for painting

An important part in the Post Byzantine tradition was played by the manuals for painting that were composed and translated. In 1599 in Russia the Typikon was completed, a manual for painting that was written by an itinerant Greek painter called Nectarios. The content indicates how frescoes and icons were painted in the Balkans during the late 16th century. From 1674 there is a Book about the art of painting by the priest Daniel, a Chilandar monk on Mount Athos who in 1667 decorated the Saint Nicholas church in the monastery. In Greece a manual on painting was composed in the 18th century by the Athos monk Dionysios of Furna and in that spirit all the Orthodox church paintings are executed today all over the world.

As long as the Orthodox church exists holy images will be painted in Post-Byzantine tradition. Two complete iconostases from the monastery workshops on Mount Athos adorn the Greek-Orthodox metropolitan church in Stockholm and the chapel in Uppsala. They are made with such skilful imitation of the Byzantine tradition that it would be unfair to dismiss them as pastiches.

Abstract art and the 20th century

In contrast to the antique artistic tradition that was plastic and naturalistic, already in Late Antiquity Byzantine art was distanced from natural representation. The visual revolution, that was carried through on the Constantinian arch around 330 AD (Fig. 2) in Rome and in the Late Antique imperial portraits, in particular the magnificent transcendental hieratic portrait masks of Constantine the Great (Fig. 1), where the visual gaze found its congenial expression and the supermundane elevation and intangibility of the emperor was represented in schematic iconographical forms, continued throughout a history of more than a thousand years in Byzantium. The asceticism that did not turn away from splendour tended to two dimensionality.

The formalized abstraction that Byzantine art elevated to a canonical norm in its liturgical and ceremonial images and that took its point of departure in Late Antique optics, can in its last consequence be considered an important factor in the development of French and Russian expressionism and suprematism of the 20th century. When abstract art at the beginning of the 20th century became a generally accepted idiom it is not astonishing that painters like Kandinsky and Malevich played a decisive part beside Matisse. All of them had been cultivated in the Byzantine tradition that had maintained itself throughout the centuries in icon painting. The renunciation of the third dimension found its modern successors. A detail from Garda church, the fish net in the fishing scene on the Sea of Tiberias (Fig. 112) where Christ comes walking on the water, shows a play with forms and ornaments that we recognize in the art of Paul Klee and Jean Miro. If the Apollinian and the Dionysian tendencies are all the time opposed to one another in artistic history the fear of the third dimension was an important incitement for the understanding of an art that unjustly has been condemned as degenerate. The contempt of Vasari for the "maniera greca" that he criticized for having lost the antique norm of beauty has contributed to the lack of understanding of the

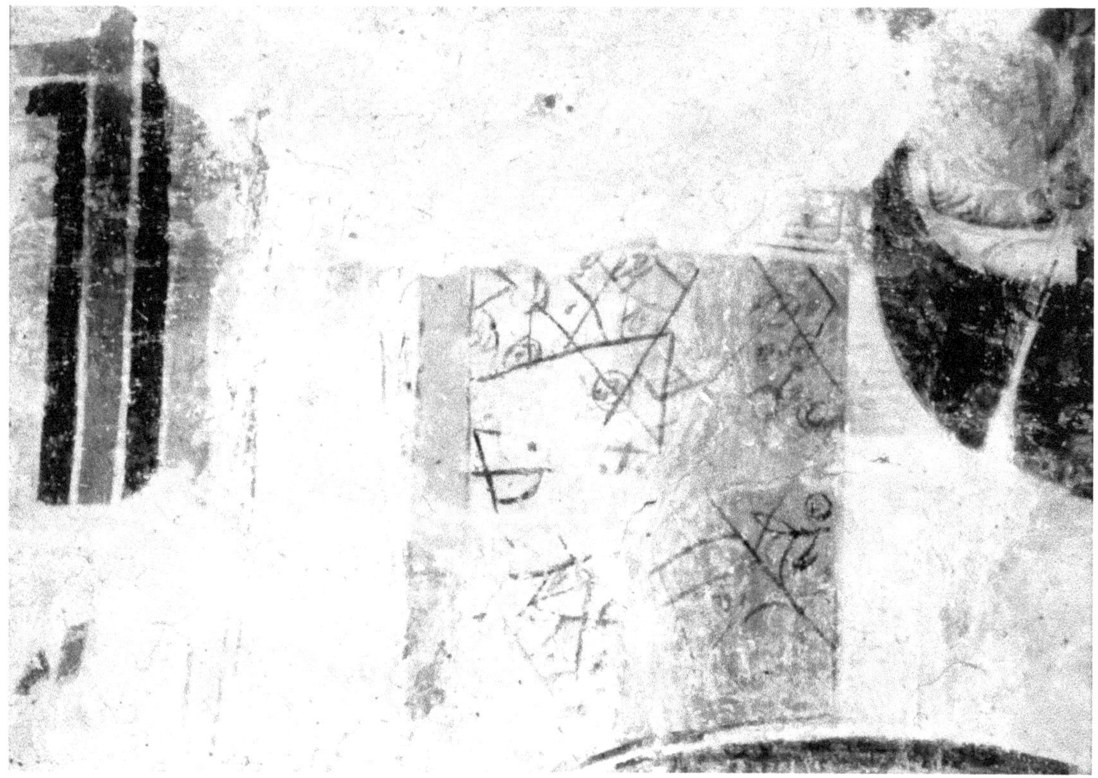

FIGURE 112. THE FISHNET IN THE SCENE CHRIST WALKING ON THE SEA OF TIBERIAS, GARDA CHURCH, FRESCO PAINTING, GOTLAND, THIRD QUARTER OF THE 12TH CENTURY

variation and manysidedness that is contained in this artistic tradition. In Kandinsky's esoteric treatise *Über das Geistige in der Kunst* the thoughts return that were expressed after iconoclasm in the restored spirit of the icon cult. It builds further on the image theoreticians from the time of the image struggle. The art is considered as a transcendental medium that represents spiritual realities in an expressive and sometimes semiotic way.

We finish with an idea from the treatise by Kandinsky. He considered spiritual life as a pyramid. On the top the arts and sciences are situated, to which belong music and literature, that are the most blessed but also have the greatest responsibility. The spiritual triangle moves slowly forwards and upwards. Nowadays one of the lower levels has accepted a materialistic credo, but the uppermost levels are still conscious about their divine vocation. The paintings of Matisse have an inner picturesque quality. In his paintings he tries to represent the divine. In order to attain this he only uses objects and the means that only belong to the painting, colours and form. The modern painting strives toward an abstract inner nature that is not naturalistic. The material is emphasized so that its spirituality might be explored. The art depends on an *inner necessity* that originates from three mystical sources. It is created by three mystical necessities. The inner necessity is a concept that Kandinsky has borrowed from the Hesychasts in the 14th century, who with the inner necessity meant the ability to do the good and follow the law and abstain from sin which is characteristic for the great mystics:

1. Every creative artist expresses what is characteristic for himself (the element of personality)
2. Every artist is a child of his own time and expresses what is typical for his own time (the element of style, the inner essences of which are combined with the language of the time and the ethnicity of the artist).
3. Every artist who serves the arts expresses what is characteristic for art in general (the pure eternally artistic element that leavens each individual artist, that can be noticed in all works of artists of any nation or era as a fundamental element in the art that is independent of time or space).

All means are permitted and ethical if they are ruled by the inner necessity. All means that do not originate from this inner necessity are repudiable. In his discourse about the colours Kandinsky characterizes the six primary colours and black and white from the point of view of the contrasts warmth and cold, their horizontal movements, where yellow approaches the beholder and blue flees away, gold expands and is excentric and blue contracts and is concentric, light and darkness, movement of resistance and rest, where the white makes eternal resistance (birth) and the black lacks resistance (death).

Blue is the typical celestial colour that creates calm. Red is warm and boundless, a living, burning quality that moves within itself, a kind of masculine maturity. It is remarkable that the combination of red and blue as contrasting colours that reinforce each other was popular among the primitive, the older German and the Italian masters. Often is seen in religious paintings and painted sculpture the Mother of God depicted in red costume with a blue cloak thrown over herself. It is as if the artist wanted to represent how celestial grace streams over the earthly human being and therefore covers the human with the divine. From the description of the concept harmony it is logical to draw the conclusion that also nowadays the inner necessity demands a boundless great arsenal of expressive possibilities.

Painting is art and art in general is not only a goalless creation of objects that loose themselves in an empty space but a mighty creative ability with a purpose that must serve the development and refinement of the human soul – the movement of the triangle. Painting is a language that speaks to the soul in its own unique way about objects, that for the soul are their daily bread, and that can only be delivered in the form of art. The artist must have a message, because his primary task is not only to master the form but to adapt the form to the content. The artist is no Sunday child. He has no right to live without responsibility. He has a difficult task to fulfil, that often becomes a cross to carry. He must be conscious that every action, thought and feeling constitutes the subtle, intangible and at the same time firm material, of which his work has been produced and that he therefore cannot be free in life, only in the arts.

Many paintings, wood cuts, miniatures and similar artistic works from the earlier periods of the art are examples of complex rhythmic compositions with a strong emphasis of a symphonic principle. You only need to think of the old German masters, or the Persians, the Japanese, the Russian icons and in particular the popular Russian graphics. In almost all these works the symphonic composition is closely connected to the melodic. That means that if the objective element is removed in order to reveal the nature of the composition itself a composition appears that is based on feelings of rest, calm repetition and a richer balanced distribution of the parts.

Finally Kandinsky remarked that according to his opinion we are approaching a time when a conscious rational system of composition will become possible, when the artists in the painting will be proud of being able to explain their works in constructivist terms (in contrast to the Impressionists who were proud of not being able to explain anything at all). In front of us there lies an era of purposeful creation, and this spirituality in the painting stands in direct organic relation to the creation of the new spiritual sphere that has already started. Because the spirituality of the arts is the soul in the future great era of spirituality.

******

Byzantium like Egypt considered art as a reservoir for divine presence. The image had the status of a sacrament. This conception of the arts and their formation was misunderstood by the Renaissance theoreticians in their newly won enthusiasm for antiquity. In our time in particular the icon arouses great interest in the west and it has become a fashion to paint icons. The Byzantine image conception was so philosophically determined and profound that the cosmos itself was considered as a holy icon.

Bibliography

Abel, Ulf and Vera Moore, *Icons*, Stockholm 2002

Amiranashvili, Shalva, *Medieval Georgian Enamels of Russia*, New York 1963

Bank, Alica, *L'art byzantin dans les musées de l'Union Soviétique*, Leningrad 1977

Belting, Hans, Cyril Mango and Doula Mouriki, *The Mosaics and frescoes of Saint Mary Pammakaristos (Fethiye Camii) at Istanbul*, Washington DC 1978

Brenk, Beat, *Die frühchristlichen Mosaiken in Santa Maria Maggiore zu Rom,* Wiesbaden 1975

Bysans och Norden, Acta universitatis Upsaliensis, series Figura, nova series 23, red Elisabeth Piltz 1988

Byzantine Court Culture from 829 to 1204, red Henry Maguire, Washington DC 1997

Byzanz, senantik og byzantinsk kunst i nordiske samlinger, Glyptoteket, Copenhagen red Jens Fleischer, Öystein Hjort 1996

Cormack, Robin, *Writing in Gold*, London 1985, idem: *The Byzantine Eye,* London 1989

Cutler, Anthony, *Transfigurations*, University Park, Pennsylvania 1975; idem: *The Aristocratic Psalters in Byzantium*, Paris 1984, *Late Antique and Byzantine Ivory Carving*, London 1998

Deichmann, Friedrich Wilhelm, *Ravenna,* Wiesbaden 1969-1976

Demus, Otto, *The Mosaics of Norman Sicily*, London 1949, idem: *The Church of San Marco in Venice*, Washington DC 1960

der Nersessian, Sirarpie, *Aght'amar, Church of the Holy Cross,* Cambridge 1965; eadem: *Miniature Painting in the Armenian Kingdom of Cilicia from the twelfth to the fourteenth century*, Washington DC 1993

Ebersolt, Jean, *Les églises de Constantinople*, Paris 1913, idem: *Sanctuaires de Byzance*, Paris 1921

Faenzen, H., W. Ivanov *et al*, *Altrussische Baukunst*, Berlin 1972

Grabar, André, *Martyrium*, London 1972; idem: *L'âge d'or de Justinien*, Paris 1966, *L'art de la fin de l'antiquité et du moyen âge*, Paris 1968, *L'iconoclasme byzantin*, Paris 1984

Grabar, André and M. Manoussacas, *L'illustration de Skylitzès de Madrid*, Venise 1979

Ikoner, Malmö museer, 1988

Kandinsky, Complete Writings on Art, I, II, ed Kenneth Lindsay, Peter Vergo, London 1982

Kiilerich, Bente and Hjalmar Torp, *Bilder og billedbruk i Byzants,* Oslo 1998

Ladner, Gerhart B., *The Concept of the Image in the Greek Fathers and the Byzantine Iconoclast Controversy,* Dumbarton Oaks Papers 7, 1-34

Lagerlöf, Erland, *Gotland och Bysans*, Uddevalla 1999

La peinture du moyen âge en Yougoslavie I-IV, ed Gabriel Millet, A Frolow, Tania Velmans, Paris 1954-1969

Lazarev, V.N., *Storia della pittura bizantina*, Turin 1967

Malmqvist, Tatiana, *Byzantine 12th century frescoes in Kastoria*, Figura 18, 1979

Mango, Cyril, *Architettura bizantina*, Milano 1974; idem: *The art of the Byzantine empire (312-1453)*, New Jersey 1972, *Byzantium – the empire of New Rome*, London 1980, *Byzantium and its Image*, London 1993

Milburn, Robert, *Early Christian Art and Architecture*, London 1988

Millet, Gabriel, *Monuments de l'Athos*, Paris 1927, idem: *Monuments byzantins de Mistra*, Paris 1910

Millingen, Alexander von, *Byzantine Churches in Constantinople*, London 1912

Mouriki, Doula, *The Mosaics of Nea Moni on Chios*, Athens 1982

Nordhagen, Per Jonas, *The frescoes of John VII in Santa Maria Antiqua in Rome*, Rome 1968

Nordström, Carl Otto, *Ravennastudien*, Stockholm 1953

Papageorghiou, Athanasios, *Ikonen aus Zypern*, Genf 1960

Patterson Sevchenko, Nancy, *Illustrated Manuscripts of the Metaphrastian Menologion*, Chicago 1990

Petterson, Lars, *Holzbaukunst auf der Halbinsel Zoonez'e im Russischen Karelen*, Helsingfors 1950

Piltz, Elisabeth, *Det levande Bysans*, Stockholm 1997, eadem: *Byzantium in the mirror – the message of Skylitzes matritensis and Hagia Sophia in Constantinople*, Oxford 2005

Rappoport, Pavel A, *Building the Churches of Kievan Russia*, London 1995

Rice, Tamara Talbot, *Ancient Arts of Central Asia*, London 1965

Rodley, Lyn, *Byzantine Art and Architecture*, Cambridge New York 1993

Sahas, Daniel, *Icon and Logos, Sources in Eighth century Iconoclasm*, Toronto 1985

Spatharakis, Ioannes, *The Pictorial Cycles of the Acathistos Hymn for the Virgin*, Leiden 2005; idem: *Dated Byzantine Wallpaintings of Crete*, Leiden 2001

Speck, Paul, *Understanding Byzantium*, London 2001

Tikkanen, J.J., *Die Genesismosaiken in Venedig und die Cottonbibel*, Helsinki 1889

Underwood, Paul A., *The Karije Djami* I-IV, New York 1966

Velmans, Tania, *La peinture murale byzantine à la fin du moyen âge*, Paris 1977

Westholm, Alfred, *Cornelius Loos: teckningar från en expedition till Främre Orienten*, Stockholm 1985

Weitzmann, Kurt, *Die byzantinische Buchmalerei des 9. und 10. Jahrhundert*, Vienna 1996; idem *et al*: *Frühe Ikonen*, Vienna 1965

www.ingramcontent.com/pod-product-compliance
Lightning Source LLC
LaVergne TN
LVHW070533110826
845147LV00017BA/979

* 9 7 8 1 4 0 7 3 0 1 0 4 4 *